The International Political Economy of China's Exchange Rate Policy Making

Zhaohui Wang

The International Political Economy of China's Exchange Rate Policy Making

Springer

Zhaohui Wang
School of International Relations and Center
for Southeast Asian Studies
Xiamen University
Xiamen, Fujian, China

ISBN 978-981-33-4577-5   ISBN 978-981-33-4578-2 (eBook)
https://doi.org/10.1007/978-981-33-4578-2

This Springer imprint is published by the registered company Springer Nature Singapore Pte Ltd.
The registered company address is: 152 Beach Road, #21-01/04 Gateway East, Singapore 189721, Singapore

Acknowledgements

I am very grateful to Shaun Breslin for providing his inspiration, encouragement and advice on this project. During my time at Warwick, he has been very generous with his time and energy, and his many comments and suggestions help me to refine and improve this work considerably. Words cannot fully express my gratitude to him. I would also like to thank all my teachers, mentors and supervisors along my academic journey, from Renmin University of China, London School of Economics to University of Warwick. Particularly, I would like to express my gratitude to three other supervisors, to whom I owe much for my intellectual development in various stages of my study and research: Bao Jianyun, Thomas Sattler and André Broome.

I gratefully acknowledge the funding sources that make this book possible. I have been funded by the Warwick-China Scholarship Council Joint Ph.D. Scholarship for my Ph.D. study and research. My fieldwork in China has been supported by the Short-Term Ph.D. Fieldwork Grant by the French Centre for Research on Contemporary China. I am also supported by the Fundamental Research Funds for the Central Universities at Xiamen University. Furthermore, I owe a great debt to my interviewees in China who are the major sources of information in the book, but they are kept anonymous for confidentiality reasons.

I cannot be more grateful to my parents for all their cultivation in my past lifetime. I would not have travelled this far without their understanding and support. I express my sincere gratitude to Zuo Yunyi, my beloved life companion. She offers me the most important love, encouragement and confidence that drive any progress I make in my work. I will never be able to adequately repay my parents and wife for their enduring loving support.

Finally, I thank Taylor & Francis Group for granting permission to reproduce materials that previously appeared in the following two articles: "China's exchange rate policy making: International pressures meet domestic politics," *Asian Studies Review*, 2017, 41(1), 20–39 (https://doi.org/10.1080/10357823.2016.1264925) and

"The resumption of China's exchange rate reform and the internationalization of RMB between 2010 and 2013," *Journal of* Contemporary China, 2017, 26(108): 852–869 (https://doi.org/10.1080/10670564.2017.1337308).

November 2020 Zhaohui Wang

Contents

Abbreviations

BEER	Behavioural equilibrium exchange rate
CCCT	China Chamber of Commerce for Import and Export of Textile and Apparel
CCP	Chinese Communist Party
CLGFE	Central Leading Group for Finance and Economy
CNTAC	China National Textile & Apparel Council
CPE	Comparative Political Economy
CPPCC	Chinese People's Political Consultative Conference
EU	European Union
FCCIE	Fujian Chamber of Commerce for Import and Export
FEER	Fundamental equilibrium exchange rate
FTIA	Fujian Textile Industry Association
FX	Foreign exchange
GDP	Gross domestic product
IMF	International Monetary Fund
IPE	International Political Economy
IR	International Relations
MFA	Ministry of Foreign Affairs
MOF	Ministry of Finance
MOFCOM	Ministry of Commerce
MPD	Monetary Policy Department
NDRC	National Development and Reform Commission
NPC	National People's Congress
PBOC	People's Bank of China
PPP	Purchasing power parity
PRC	People's Republic of China
PRD	Policy Research Department
PSC	Politburo Standing Committee
QE	Quantitative easing
RMB	Renminbi, "people's currency"

RQFII	Renminbi Qualified Foreign Institutional Investor
SAFE	State Administration of Foreign Exchange
SDR	Special Drawing Right (IMF)
SOE	State-owned enterprise
US	United States
WTO	World Trade Organisation

Chapter 1
China's Exchange Rate Policy Making: An Introduction

> *"Addressing imbalances in the global economy is a shared responsibility among the major economic regions of the world. ... Treasury is actively engaged with several economies to promote the adoption of flexible, marketbased exchange [rate] policies and to help facilitate broader adjustment. Most notable among these is China."*
> – John W. Snow, the 73rd United States Secretary of the Treasury (2003–2006).
> *"Reform of the renminbi's exchange rate is an issue of China's own sovereignty."*
> – Wen Jiabao, Premier of the State Council of the People's Republic of China (2003–2013).

1.1 Research Background

China is emerging as a great power, at least in terms of economic power—indeed, some might say that it is already risen.[1] China's economy has experienced fast Gross Domestic Product (GDP) growth since Deng Xiaoping's "reform and opening-up" policy in the late 1970s. China has become one of the most important global manufacturing centers since the 1990s. As the world's second largest economy, China's GDP share of global total has continued to grow in the last few decades, rising from 5.48 to 19.25% in the period from 1994 to 2019 (see Fig. 1.1).[2]

The rise of China's economy has had considerable impacts on the global economy in the twenty-first century. The world economy has been riven by increasingly large imbalances in the new millennium,[3] as China's trade surplus with the rest of the world, especially with the United States (US), increased dramatically after China became a member of the World Trade Organization (WTO) in 2001 (see Fig. 1.2).

---

[1] Shambaugh (2013).

[2] International Monetary Fund, *IMF World Economic Outlook*, October 2019, https://www.imf.org/en/publications/weo.

[3] Cowling et al. (2011).

Z. Wang, *The International Political Economy of China's Exchange Rate Policy Making*, https://doi.org/10.1007/978-981-33-4578-2_1

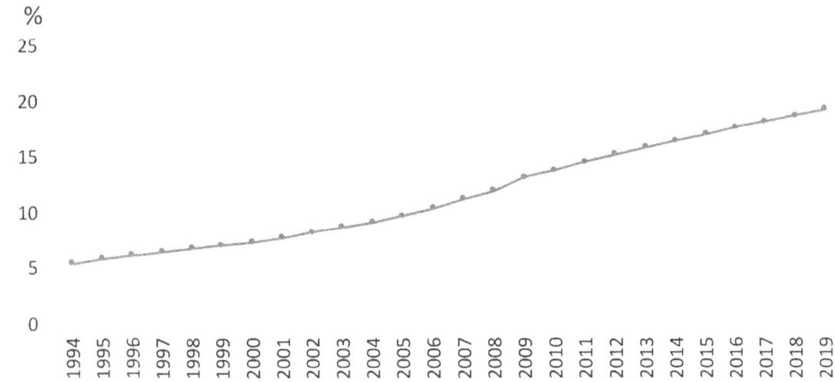

Fig. 1.1 China's GDP (based on PPP) share of world total from 1994 to 2019. *Source* International Monetary Fund (IMF), World Economic Outlook Database

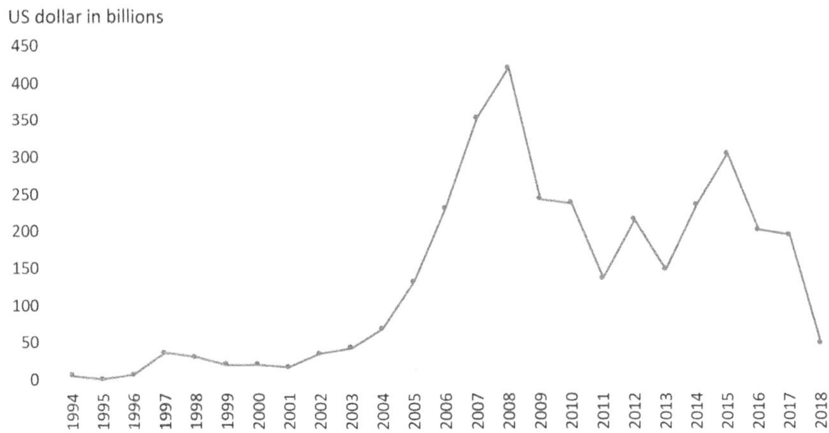

Fig. 1.2 China's current account balance, from 1994 to 2018. *Source* IMF, Balance of Payments Statistics

Arguably, the global imbalance was considered as one of the main causes of the 2008 global financial crisis.[4]

Under the circumstance, there is a growing body of literature that studies the causes of global imbalance, and particularly the US-China imbalance. One part of the literature emphasizes that the US-China imbalance originates from Chinese export-led growth and American overconsumption as well as the "Chimerica" cooperation to enable China's trade surpluses to be recycled into the US credit system to sustain

[4]See, for example, Obstfeld and Rogoff (2009), Borio and Disyatat (2011), Bernanke (2009), Krugman (2009), Wan (2014).

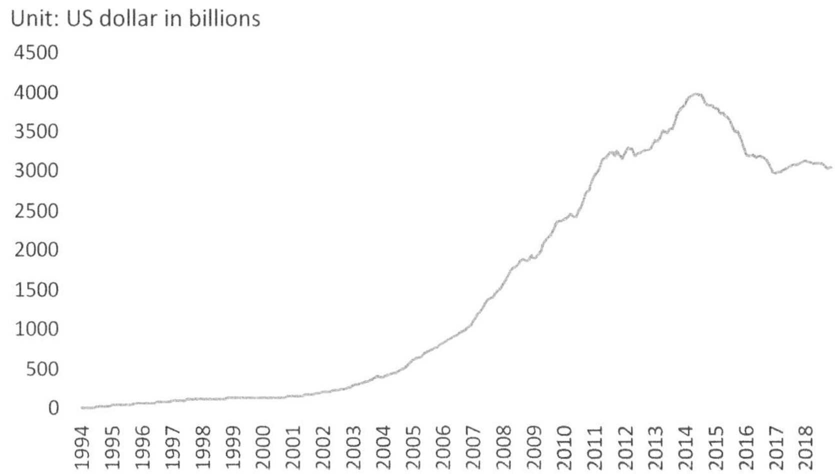

Fig. 1.3 China's foreign reserves, from 1994 to 2018. *Source* CEIC China Premium Database

domestic US consumption.[5] Specifically, the causal mechanism of the US-China imbalance is that the exchange rate and other economic policies followed by Asian countries, especially China, generated large current account surpluses. This helped boost credit expansion and risk-taking in the core capitalist countries with persistent trade deficits, especially the US. This was done by reducing world interest rates and/or simply allowing the US to borrow cheaply abroad, which was conducive to asset bubbles and, ultimately, financial instability.[6]

The other part of the literature is more narrowly focused on China and attributes the global imbalance to China's competitive trade and currency policy. China has run persistent current account surpluses in part because the Chinese government has maintained the RMB (or renminbi, often called the yuan, the official currency of the People's Republic of China) at competitive (many analysts argue, undervalued) exchange rates against the US dollar. Furthermore, People's Bank of China (PBOC, China's central bank) has engaged in massive sterilized intervention, by selling the RMB and buying the dollar, in the foreign exchange market. The corresponding result is the dramatic expansion of China's foreign reserves (see Fig. 1.3), with an around 18-fold increase in the first decade of the twenty-first century.

The large amounts of China's current account surpluses and foreign reserves imply that the RMB exchange rate is away from the equilibrium level. The RMB exchange rate, therefore, has been under increasing scrutiny in the new millennium, not only in academia but also in policy circles. Large amounts of Economics studies have applied different approaches and estimation models to measure whether the

[5]For more in-depth theoretical and empirical analysis of the Sino-American imbalance, please see Wang (2017), Lee (2014), Gamble (2009), Hung (2008, 2011), Ferguson and Moritz (2007).

[6]Wang (2017).

RMB is undervalued, and if so, by how much. However, economists have produced controversial and inconclusive results on the RMB equilibrium exchange rate. The lack of consensus among economists is largely attributed to the influence of such factors as different methodologies used, economic models applied, and explanatory variables included in different studies.

Moreover, the competing results of economics studies have contributed to the vexed international debates and bargaining between the Western and Chinese politicians. The two quotations in the epigraph demonstrate that the Western and Chinese leaders hold different views on the RMB exchange rate. On the one hand, John W. Snow, US Secretary of the Treasury, regarded China's rigid exchange rate regime as the cause of global imbalances and stressed that China should share the responsibility for addressing the global imbalances.[7] On the other hand, Wen Jiabao, China's premier of the State Council, defended exchange rate policy as an issue of sovereignty and emphasized that China possessed the right to choose the exchange rate regime that was best suited to China's economic development.[8] Furthermore, as Kroeber suggests, Western officials simply view exchange rate as a price while Chinese leaders regard the exchange rate, or price and market mechanism in more general, as a component in the toolbox of statecraft.[9]

With China's increasing integration into the world economy and China's growing impact on the global political economy, China's currency practice has been the central and contentious issue in the 2000s. Therefore, this book is dedicated to the study of China's exchange rate policy making. It is an important field as exchange rate is a major economic variable that regulates trade and capital flows across countries in an increasingly deregulated global economy. As Walter notes, "the level and the stability of the exchange rate can have significant consequences on the material well-being of individuals and firms, especially when they live or operate in countries with a high level of economic and financial integration into the world economy, or when these actors are strongly involved in international trade or finance."[10] More importantly, as mentioned before, China's exchange rate value and regime, because of the country's enormous trade and capital flows, has had considerable impacts on the global economy and has caught the attention of global commodity and financial markets and policymakers. Therefore, it is important to understand the nature and mechanism of China's exchange rate policy making.

Figure 1.4 delineates the RMB exchange rate against the US dollar from 1994 to 2018. After China unified the dual exchange rates in 1994, China adopted a de facto fixed exchange rate regime, which pegged the RMB to the US dollar after 1995. The dollar-pegged exchange rate regime lasted for ten years from 1995 to 2005. After that, China began to appreciate the RMB in a graduate manner. The RMB exchange rate continuously appreciated against the US dollar for three years from July 2005 to

[7] Snow (2005).

[8] Wen Jiabao, "Exchange rate reform is China's sovereignty and not subject to external pressure", *Xinhua*, 16 May 2005; also see Dickie (2005).

[9] Kroeber (2011).

[10] Walter (2014, p. 169).

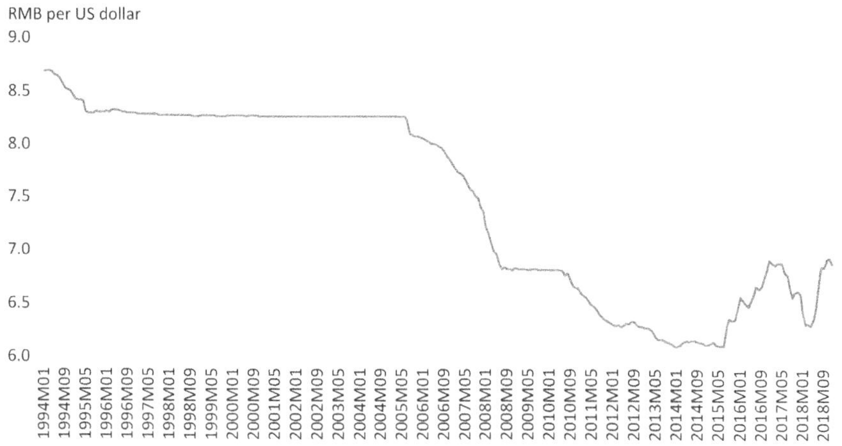

Fig. 1.4 RMB exchange rate against the US dollar, from 1994 to 2018. *Source* IMF, International Financial Statistics

July 2008. After July 2008, China returned to the dollar-pegged exchange rate regime for two years. China continued to gradually appreciate the RMB from June 2010 to 2013. The RMB exchange rate against the US dollar experienced more two-way fluctuations after 2013. In 2015, China's central bank further reformed the RMB exchange rate formation mechanism and released the RMB exchange rate index, which marked the end of RMB's crawling peg to the US dollar and the beginning of managing the RMB with reference to a basket of currencies. After 2015, the market-oriented fluctuations of RMB exchange rates against the US dollar have been more evident, which is in accordance with the overall process of China's market economic reform.

In short, China's exchange rate policy from 1994 to 2018 can generally be summarized as two phases of dollar-pegged exchange rate regime (from 1995 to July 2005 and from July 2008 to June 2010), three turning points (July 2005, July 2008, and June 2010), two phases of gradual appreciation (from July 2005 to July 2008 and from June 2010 to 2012) and the phase of two-way fluctuations (from 2014 to 2018).

The time frame of this research is mainly from 2002 to 2013. There is no denying that China's non-devaluation policy during the 1997–1998 Asian Financial Crisis and the further reform of exchange rate regime in 2015 are of great importance, but this book is particularly focused on China's exchange rate policy making in the Hu-Wen era, mainly for the reason that it is during this period that China's imbalance with the rest of the world deteriorates and there are heated international debates over the RMB exchange rate policy. Moreover, there is another important reason to choose the staring year of 2002. Japan was the first country to criticize China's currency undervaluation in 2002, and the US became the most critical actor to pressure China on the RMB exchange rate policy from 2003 onward. Considering the emergence of international pressure and the transition of China's leadership, 2002 is suitable to be the starting year to examine how the external and internal factors influenced China's exchange rate policy making.

This book explores the following research questions: What factors determined China's exchange rate policy making from 2002 to 2013? In particular, what accounted for the two phases of dollar-pegged exchange rate regime? What were the key causes of the three turning points of exchange rate policy change? How to explain the gradual, rather than one-off, pattern in the two phases of RMB appreciation? Additionally, why did some policy preferences prevail in policy making at the expense of others during different periods of time?

This book therefore seeks to enhance our understanding of China's exchange rate policy making in the twenty-first century. The author proposes an International Political Economy (IPE) approach to bridge the international politics and domestic politics to explain China's exchange rate policy making. It is argued that Chinese leaders locate at the juncture of the international system and the state-society when making international economic policy. China's central decision makers strive to reconcile international pressures, domestic ministerial interests and domestic interest groups when making RMB exchange rate policies. More specifically, the international influences played an agenda-setting role in both the 2005 and the 2010 RMB exchange rate reforms. However, the international influences were strongly mitigated by China's domestic politics. On the one hand, China's ministerial politics, in which the Ministry of Commerce (MOFCOM) was more politically powerful than the PBOC, determined the gradual nature of exchange rate reform from 2005 to 2007. On the other hand, China's interest group politics provided the most important sources for China's exchange rate policy from 2008 to 2010. To address the above questions and support the main arguments, this chapter begins by examining the existing literature on RMB exchange rate policy and the nature of China's politics. The next section depicts the state of the art in research on the RMB exchange rate and China's exchange rate policy making.

1.2 State of the Field

As mentioned before, there have been large amounts of Economics studies on the RMB exchange rate. However, it is difficult for economists to arrive at any firm and robust conclusion about the equilibrium RMB exchange rate and the precise level of RMB exchange rate misalignment. The author finds that the existing Economics studies have yielded a very wide range of estimates. Moreover, the major shortcoming of the Economics studies on the RMB exchange rate is that economists generally assume a pure economic world in which only the price and market mechanism take effect, but neglect the political factors such as the state, institutions and political leaders. The inconclusive Economics studies on the RMB exchange rate are unsatisfactory, for both researchers and policymakers. Therefore, there have been numerous attempts by scholars of political economy to interpret the nature, or explain the mechanism, of exchange rate politics and, more specifically, China's exchange rate policy making behavior.

On the one hand, the Comparative Political Economy (CPE) literature has provided more nuanced explanations by examining the domestic interests and institutions that influences exchange rate policy making. However, most of the existing CPE studies are western-centric and have their limitations when applied to explain China's case. The assumptions of the exchange rate politics models in liberal market economies with democratic politics do not hold in China, as China's institutions, characterized by one-party rule and party-state system, are fundamentally different from Western liberal democracies.

Moreover, limited work is dedicated to figuring out the political structure of China's exchange rate policy making, the interests and positions of policy elites and economic ministries and examining how the preferences of key institutional actors are aggregated. The black box of China's exchange rate policy making, filled with the interplay of China's domestic political powers and societal interests, remains unopened. Therefore, there is a need for a more "indigenous" investigation into China's political structure and process of exchange rate policy making. Lastly, the CPE literature focuses on the domestic factors but ignores the international dimension, which undeniably affects exchange rate policy of an open economy, especially a large open economy like China, in the era of globalization.

On the other hand, the IPE literature, particularly the international-domestic interactions approach, should have bridged the international politics and domestic politics to offer better explanations of China's exchange rate policy making. However, to the best of the author's knowledge, limited studies of this kind have been done in the existing literature of China's exchange rate policy. As the Chinese leaders locate at the juncture of the international system and the state-society when making international economic policy, one cannot fully understand China's exchange rate policy making without reference to interactions between international and domestic levels.

Therefore, the literature review, the second chapter of this book, will identify the limitations in the existing Economics studies on the RMB exchange rate and the research gap of the CPE and IPE approaches to China's exchange rate policy making. "The persistence of the Communist Party in China is one of the most striking feathers of the Chinese economic reform."[11] Before proceeding to develop a theoretical framework for China's exchange rate policy making, the author will engage in a brief discussion about the nature of China's politics in the Hu-Wen era, which is the important institutional foundation of China's economic policy making.

[11]Coase and Wang (2012, p. 174).

1.3 The Nature of China's Politics

The Hu-Wen era (2002–2012) was the most important period of time in which the RMB exchange rate reform took place. Hu Jintao succeeded Jiang Zemin as the General Secretary of the Chinese Communist Party (CCP) at the first Plenary Session of the 16th CCP Central Committee in November 2002. The number of Politburo Standing Committee (PSC) membership increased from seven in the era of Jiang to nine in the era of Hu. Hu Jintao was "elected" as the President of the People's Republic of China (PRC) and Wen Jiabao was appointed as the Premier of the State Council at the 1st Plenary Session of the 10th National People's Congress (NPC) in March 2003. There were both continuities and changes between the era of Jiang and that of Hu-Wen. Before we proceed to China's exchange rate policy making in the twenty-first century, it is essential to examine Jiang's legacy, and then to discuss the nature of China's politics in the Hu-Wen era.

1.3.1 Jiang Zemin's Legacy

Jiang Zemin's most important economic legacy was to ensure the continuous reform and opening-up after Deng Xiaoping's southern tour in 1992. Jiang was consistently dedicated to reforming the central planning system and creating a competitive market within China. At the 14th CCP National Congress in October 1992, Jiang delivered a report entitled "Accelerating the pace of reform and opening-up and the modernization construction to win the great victory of socialism with Chinese characteristics".[12] It was the first time that the Chinese leadership declared that the target of China's economic reform was to establish a socialist market economy. At the third Plenary Session of the 14th CCP Central Committee in November 1993, the CCP passed the "Decision of the CCP Central Committee on some issues concerning the improvement of the socialist market economy", which allowed the market to play a fundamental role in resource allocation under the macroeconomic management.[13] The mid-1990s witnessed a series of economic reforms, including reforms of enterprise system, tax sharing system, financial system, foreign trade system and foreign exchange management system. In particular, Jiang Zemin and Zhu Rongji pushed forward a large-scale privatization to reorganize the state-owned enterprises in 1997 and 1998. China experienced a dramatic transition from central planning to market economy and the nature of China's economy changed accordingly in the 1990s. As Coase and Wang noted,

---

[12]Jiang Zemin, "Historic junction: Establishing the socialist market economy", CCP News, 11 October 2007, https://cpc.people.com.cn/GB/64162/134580/137248/index.html.

[13]Tianxing Li, "30 most influential events in the 30 years of China's reform and opening-up", *China Economic Weekly*, 7 January 2008, https://finance.people.com.cn/GB/72020/74689/113951/6741527.html.

> The role of the Chinese state in the economy has become progressively less significant, no matter what measurement is used. Before the economic reforms, the Chinese people had little economic freedom and the state controlled every aspect of the economy, from production, to retail, and even consumption. Today [2012], private entrepreneurship is the primary driving force of the Chinese economy. The size of the state sector in the economy has fallen significantly relative to the non-state sector.[14]

Jiang's report at the 15th CCP National Congress in September 1997 responded to the changing nature of China's economy. Jiang declared that China's basic economic system for the primary stage of socialism was to maintain public ownership as the main form and to allow the development of multiple forms of ownership.[15] Furthermore, the second Plenary Session of NPC passed the PRC Constitutional Amendment in March 1999, which explicitly stated that the non-public sector was an important component of China's socialist market economy.[16] Last but not least, Jiang's commitment to reform and opening-up finally helped China to join the WTO in 2001. Premier Zhu Rongji was also the key supporter for China's access to the WTO.

Accordingly, Jiang's most important political legacy was probably his political thought of "Three Represents", which was closely related to the changing nature of China's economy. Jiang put forward the concept of "Three Represents" when he visited Guangdong province in early 2000. More specifically, the "Three Represents" required the CCP to "always represent the development trend of China's advanced productive forces, the orientation of China's advanced culture, and the fundamental interests of the overwhelming majority of the Chinese people".[17] Jiang's political thought of "Three Represents" was widely interpreted, both at home and abroad, as an official justification to expand the party membership to include elites of all social circles, which marked the CCP's transition from a proletarian revolutionary Party towards an elite governing Party. According to Brown, Jiang's "Three Represent" was "one such theoretical contribution, leading to the admission that entrepreneurs were also productive elements in society" and also "a partial admission that the social makeup of China was becoming more complex".[18] Miller also remarked that "Jiang Zemin's 'three represents' thus reflected the Party leadership's decision to pursue a strategy of political co-option with regard to the entrepreneurial, managerial, technical, and professional elites who were emerging in Chinese society as a consequence of the economic reforms."[19] In a nutshell, Jiang's political thought of "Three Represents" forms the theoretical basis of China's elite-coalition governance in the twenty-first century.

---

[14]Coase and Wang (2012, p. 175).

[15]Jiang Zemin, "Jiang Zemin's Report at the 15th CCP National Congress", CCP National Congress Database, 12 September 1997, https://cpc.people.com.cn/GB/64162/64168/64568/65445/4526285.html.

[16]National People's Congress of the People's Republic of China, "PRC Constitutional Amendment (1999)", 15 March 1999, https://www.npc.gov.cn/wxzl/wxzl/2000-12/10/content_7075.htm.

[17]Jiang Zemin, "Jiang Zemin put forward the important thought of 'Three Represents' Theory in 2000", *Xinhua*, 7 April 2000.

[18]Brown (2009, p. 107).

[19]Miller (2011, p. 570).

In addition to the changing nature of China's economy, China's entry into the WTO also brought about important political implications. WTO is certainly one of the key institutions to promote the Western norms of neoliberal global trade. Although there is a heated debate over the relationship between the liberal international order and the rise of China in the twenty-first century,[20] two implications of China's entry into WTO after the 15-year-long negotiations should be clear. First, the Chinese leadership recognized the key principles and values of WTO agreements. As Brown notes, "politically, the final acceptance into the WTO fold marked a moment in which China signaled a full commitment to accepting international norms, working within them, and attempting to regularize at least some of its economy with the rules established largely in the West, in North American and Europe."[21] Second, the increasing scale of China's engagement with the world economy in the twenty-first century meant that international interests were much more entangled in China's domestic politics. Special attention should be paid to the more international-domestic interactions in China's economic policy making.

1.3.2 China's Politics in the Hu-Wen Era

China's politics was more characterized by collective leadership in the Hu-Wen era than ever before. "After the passing of strongmen like Mao Zedong and Deng Xiaoping, the young generation of leaders usually does not have a strong base of legitimacy to enable individual leaders to stand above different bureaucracies and departments."[22] Hu and Wen were also widely considered to be relatively lacking in political power than Jiang Zemin and Zhu Rongji.[23] Therefore, Hu did not enjoy as much political capital as his predecessors and "seemed purposefully and consistently advertised simply as primus inter pares".[24] Brown, in his biography *Hu Jintao: China's Silent Ruler*, argues that Hu presented "a non-ego style of leadership" and "Hu's reasons for keeping a very low profile had very good intentions".[25] This part will further argue that the fundamental reason for Hu's leadership style was rooted in China's changing political-socioeconomic landscapes.

With the continuous reform and opening-up in the era of Jiang, China's economy was much more complex and China had an increasingly pluralist society in the twenty-first century. Many different interests, including international and domestic, should be taken into account when making economic policies. There was correspondingly greater pluralization and institutionalization of economic policy making

[20] See, for example, Ikenberry (2008), Breslin (2010), Hung (2012), Breslin (2013).

[21] Brown (2013, p. 53).

[22] Zheng and Chen (2015b, p. 67).

[23] See, for example, Zheng (2005), Miller (2008).

[24] Miller (2011, p. 534).

[25] Brown (2012, p. xxv).

under Hu and Wen.[26] "The complexity of market and political administration leads to a more sophisticated approach to economic policy formulation and implementation, requiring more professionalism in economic policymaking."[27] Inputs into policy deliberations mainly come from government agencies. Therefore, bureaucratic politics plays an important role in China's economic policy making. The policy outcomes cannot be well understood without "looking at the interactions of officials in different, and often competing, government agencies who are mostly motivated by their organization's interests".[28]

With an increasingly complex array of interests, Hu and Wen could only exercise effective governance by maintaining a politics of consensus at the top. Chinese politics in the Hu-Wen era was best characterized by "consensus-building collective leadership".[29] More specifically, Miller suggests that "leadership conflict and factional competition continued in the Hu era, but they now appeared circumscribed by still informal but increasingly binding norms and by pressures for a politics of consensus."[30] Brown also sheds light on Hu's special efforts to maintain the consensus-building collective leadership:

> Hu spoke, as always, as part of a collective leadership, a man who delivered consensus. He never placed himself in the position of supreme leader, avoiding the accusations of arrogance and hubris that had been levelled at the more extroverted, publicity-fond Jiang Zemin.[31]

After Hu's retirement, Brown also looks back at the Hu-Wen era and describes them as "great consensus builder" and "faithful implementer":

> Mr Hu was the great consensus builder, almost pathologically tedious in his public statements, but someone amorphous enough in their public persona to never side too obviously with any group in the party against another so that it risked causing schism. Mr Wen performed the function of faithful implementer, the reassuringly human face of the modern Chinese elite, holding the banner of reform up towards the end in ways which granted hope, even though they lacked practical details.[32]

Furthermore, it is instructive to note that the extent of pluralism in China's politics was not fixed and institutionalised in the Hu-Wen era; instead, it can be argued that the extent of pluralism was largely managed by the top leaders. As mentioned, the space for pluralism in terms of economic policy making that required technical expertise and professionalism was extended in the Hu-Wen administration, depending on the changing nature of China's economy and society and the top leaders' perspective of the nature of the problems to be solved. The relative rise of PBOC in China's bureaucracy politics was a prime example. The institutional rise of PBOC was largely

---

[26] See, for example, Zheng (2005), Mertha (2009), Tsang (2009), Miller (2009), Yi (2011), Han (2013).

[27] Yi (2011, p. 164).

[28] Joseph (2014, p. 19).

[29] Miller (2009, p. 61).

[30] Miller (2011, p. 534).

[31] Brown (2012, p. 200).

[32] Brown (2013).

attributed to its "specialized resources and capacities—information, monetary expertise, and a range of policy instruments—that have substantially boosted its role as an inflation-fight central bank".[33] By contrast, the space for pluralism in terms of "high-politics issues" such as sovereignty and human rights was heavily constrained. As Brown comments on Hu's hard line on Tibet, Xinjiang and Taiwan, "the bottom line was that going soft on these would have been political suicide."[34] Therefore, "it would be wrong to see Hu as a man without power constrained in a system where he has been swamped by the interests and influence of other powerful figures around him."[35] Hu's managed pluralism showed he was still the most important figure in China's politics and Hu-Wen's consensus-building collective leadership was adapted to China's changing political-socioeconomic landscapes after Jiang.

So far, this part of the chapter has outlined the general leadership style under the Hu-Wen era, but it has not examined Hu and Wen's specific policies in practice. Hu and Wen faced challenges in governing a society that was not only much more complex but also increasingly unequal after they took office. China's Gini Coefficient was above 0.4, the international alert line of Gini coefficient in the 2000s.[36] After the leadership transition in 2002, Hu and Wen explicitly showed their shifted priority to sustainable development and social development. Liew and Wu recognize that "there is without doubt a fundamental shift in emphasis between the Jiang Zemin-Zhu Rongji and the Hu Jintao-Wen Jiabao leadership. While the former leadership was deeply concerned with engaging the global economy, the latter is more concerned with poverty and income inequality, especially in the countryside and western China."[37] For instance, the first two public visits by Hu Jintao as general secretary were not to the modern and prosperous cities of Shanghai or Shenzhen but rather to Xibaipo (a village in Hebei) and Inner Mongolia. Particularly, Hu Jintao put forward the "scientific development outlook" in the Third Plenary Session of the 16th CCP Central Committee in 2003, which aimed to address the problems including the widening gap between urban and rural development, the uneven development among China's regions, the pursuit of economic growth at the sacrifice of environmental sustainability, and the imbalance between export-driven growth and domestic consumption.[38]

Nevertheless, it is important to note that rhetoric is not always equal to practice in China's politics. Exchange rate reform may be one of the most useful lenses to examine the extent to which Hu's proposal of scientific development outlook and Wen's economic restructuring and rebalancing were translated into concrete measures. In order to maintain an undervalued RMB exchange rate, China had to

---

[33]Bell and Feng (2013, p. 5).

[34]Brown (2012, p. 202).

[35]Brown (2012, p. xxv).

[36]Naughton (2007, p. 217); also see, Feng Liu, "China's Gini coefficient close to 0.47", *People's Daily*, 12 October 2005, https://politics.people.com.cn/GB/30178/3759688.html.

[37]Liew and Wu (2007, p. 206).

[38]Hu Jintao, "Third Plenary Session of the 16th CCP Central Committee articulated scientific development outlook", *Xinhua*, 4 August 2012.

sacrifice the welfare of the majority of ordinary Chinese and "provided extensive subsidies to global consumers and foreign direct investors, notably from the US and its allies".[39] Effective exchange rate reform could have contributed to economic rebalancing by making exports more expensive and imports cheaper, thereby alleviating the export surge and stimulating the domestic consumption.[40] The book will empirically examine China's exchange rate reforms in depth and the last chapter will draw a conclusion on the relationship between China's politics and China's exchange rate reforms in the Hu-Wen era.

1.4 Theoretical Framework and Empirical Findings in Brief

The author will first develop a theoretical framework for China's exchange rate policy making based on revision and synthesis of the existing CPE and IPE approaches. The author extends Putnam's two-level game and develops a three-level framework of China's exchange rate policy making. In the three-level game framework, China's central decision makers strive to reconcile international pressures, domestic ministerial interests and domestic interest groups when making exchange rate policy.

More specifically, the level I game examines the international influences on China's exchange rate policy making. The US government (Congress, Treasury and president) and the IMF are the main actors in the international system that exert external pressure on China's exchange rate policy. They generally urge China to appreciate the RMB at a fast pace and to move as soon as possible to greater flexibility.

The level II game involves two most important ministries with regard to exchange rate policy making within China's central government—the PBOC and the MOFCOM. They have clear but competing preferences over the level of the RMB exchange rate and the stability of the currency. The PBOC favors relatively appreciated RMB to curb imported inflation and more flexibility of the RMB exchange rate to acquire more monetary policy autonomy, while the MOFCOM has a vested interest in a depreciated and fixed RMB exchange rate to promote the competitiveness of China's export sectors. The relative power and bargaining game between the PBOC and the MOFCOM are expected to exert significant influences on the RMB exchange rate policy making.

The level III game refers to the interactions between Chinese central government and the local actors, including local governments, industry associations and private enterprises. Industry associations and private firms could communicate their preferences to local governments or bureaucracies such as the local branches of MOFCOM to impose influences on exchange rate policy. Lower-level officials may speak on behalf of these interest groups for the reason that their political careers mostly depend

[39]Di (2013, p. 124).

[40]Lardy (2012).

on the success of the local economy, to which the local industries make a considerable contribution. The policy makers in the central government cannot neglect the interests of local export enterprises and the voices of local governments in the coastal regions, given the importance of exports to China's economy.

The framework brings up such a question: why it is a three-level game and not a two-level one? A two-level game conceptualizes the policy making process as negotiations between the international and the domestic.[41] A three-level game further distinguishes the domestic games, assuming that the difference between the two domestic games is so great that it is better conceived of as two separate negotiations, rather than two parts of the same domestic game. The author understands that this assumption is analytically plausible, but cannot be taken for granted. The explanatory power of the adapted three-level game framework will be empirically applied through an examination of China's exchange rate policy making between 2002 and 2013.

In a nutshell, the three-level game of China's exchange rate policy making examines the Chinese leadership's negotiations with the international bargainers (mainly the US government and the IMF) at the international level (level I), negotiations between the central government's ministries (PBOC and MOFCOM) at the central governmental level (level II) and negotiations with the domestic interest groups and local governments at the local level (level III). The applicability of the three-level game framework will be examined in the following empirical studies. The time frame of research (2002–2013) is divided into four periods: first from 2002 to July 2005, second from July 2005 to July 2008, third from July 2008 to June 2010 and finally from June 2010 to 2013.

1.4.1 Origins of the 2005 Exchange Rate Reform, from 2002 to July 2005

China's exchange rate policy was not a key issue in the international society before 2002, though China had pegged the RMB to the US dollar after 1995. However, the year of 2003 witnessed the sudden emergence of bills and resolutions (ten in total) in the US Congress targeting China's currency manipulation and undervaluation. On the one hand, China's trade surplus rose rapidly after 2001. On the other hand, a large number of manufacturing jobs began to be lost in the US. The two phenomena were considered to be related, and China's exchange rate policy became subject to sustained American pressure.

The Congress's concern imposed unprecedented pressure on the US administration to engage with the Chinese authorities to address the RMB exchange rate issue. An analysis of the Treasury's Reports to Congress on International Economic and Exchange Rate Policies demonstrated that China's exchange rate policy became Treasury's main concern after late 2003. The Reports reiterated that China's fixed exchange rate policy was no longer appropriate and proposed a more

[41] Putnam (1988).

flexible exchange rate based on market mechanisms.[42] Instead of labelling China as a currency manipulator, the Treasury officials actively engaged with the Chinese leadership to hasten and facilitate the move to a flexible market-based exchange rate regime. The Treasury also worked with China to identify and overcome the impediments to greater exchange rate flexibility. With regard to the US president, a similar trend could be identified that President Bush stressed the desirability of flexible exchange rates but avoided the direct accusation of Beijing's currency manipulation. The IMF was even more cautious and prudent. In the 2004 Article IV Consultation Report, the IMF staff held the view that it was difficult to find persuasive evidence that the RMB was substantially undervalued, though they also proposed greater exchange rate flexibility for China.[43]

In terms of China's domestic politics, the PBOC was the key ministry leading the change for RMB exchange rate reform. Zhou Xiaochuan, then Governor of PBOC, made consistent efforts to advocate that exchange rate flexibility would provide the Chinese authorities with additional tools to control excessive monetary supply and inflationary pressure. However, PBOC's promotion of RMB exchange rate reform encountered strong opposition from the MOFCOM. MOFCOM's officials argued that the stability of RMB exchange rate was crucial for China's export and manufacturing industries and that dramatic changes would give rise to the bankruptcy of many export enterprises. The consequent economic slowdown could further undermine social stability. Particularly, after Bo Xilai succeeded Lyu Fuyuan as the Minister of Commerce in late February 2004, the MOFCOM under Bo made a loud voice to underline the importance of exchange rate stability and took a firm stand against the exchange rate reform. Therefore, the exchange rate reform was delayed in 2004.

With no clear progress by the end of 2004, the Congress set off another wave of targeting China's exchange rate policy in the first half of 2005. There were in total twelve bills concerning China's currency in 2005, eleven of which were introduced before 21 July 2005. It was a significant escalation of the currency disputes between Washington and Beijing as three bills claimed to include a 27.5% duty penalty imposed on all China's products exported to the US if China did not revalue its currency. The Bush administration became increasingly critical of China's delayed move, which could be seen from the blunter words of Treasury Secretary's statements and Treasury's Reports. The IMF also adopted an increasingly tough stance toward China's currency. In a nutshell, the re-emergence of external pressure on RMB undervaluation in the first half of 2005 brought China's exchange rate policy to a focal

[42] U.S. Department of the Treasury, "Report to Congress on International Economic and Exchange Rate Policies", April 2004, https://www.treasury.gov/resource-center/international/exchange-rate-policies/Documents/Treasury_ReportToCongressOnInternationalEconomicAndExchangeRatePolicies-2003H2_2004%20Apr%2015.pdf, pp. 10–11; U.S. Department of the Treasury, "Report to Congress on International Economic and Exchange Rate Policies", December 2004, https://www.treasury.gov/resource-center/international/exchange-rate-policies/Documents/Treasury_ReportToCongressOnInternationalEconomicAndExchangeRatePolicies-2004H1_2004%20Dec%203.pdf, pp. 9–11.

[43] International Monetary Fund, "People's Republic of China: 2004 Article IV Consultation Report", 5 November 2004, https://www.imf.org/external/pubs/cat/longres.aspx?sk=17828.0.

point within the international community. China's leaders were under so immense pressure from both the US government and the IMF that the old exchange rate regime was seemingly unsustainable.

The Chinese top leaders sat at the juncture of international and domestic politics of the RMB exchange rate reform. Internationally, the increasingly intense criticism and pressure rendered the RMB exchange rate an unavoidable issue. Domestically, the PBOC advocated a more flexible exchange rate for more monetary autonomy, while the MOFCOM, with more political clout, maintained that exchange rate stability was crucial for China's growth and employment. Under the circumstance, the Chinese leadership swung back and forth, striving to reconcile the interests of all parties, in formulating the exchange rate reform policy. Change eventually came on 21 July 2005. The PBOC announced that China would implement a managed floating exchange rate regime based on market demand and supply with reference to a basket of currencies. Furthermore, the RMB exchange rate against the dollar was revalued from 8.28 to 8.11, with a 2.1% appreciation. The daily trading price of the dollar against the RMB in the inter-bank foreign exchange market will be allowed to float within a band of $\pm$ 0.3% around the central parity published by the PBOC.[44]

This policy outcome was interpreted as a compromise between international and domestic bargainers. The international pressure did play an agenda-setting role, which means that it made China's leaders unable to avoid the RMB exchange rate issue. The growing external pressure on the RMB exchange rate issue forced the Chinese leadership to put exchange rate reform on the to-do list in 2005. The two key ministries with influence in China's bureaucratic politics were divided internally concerning the possibility of exchange rate policy change. However, the MOFCOM was more influential over the central government's decision-making than the PBOC. As a result, PBOC's wish for exchange rate reform was granted, but the MOFCOM won key ground as well. The initial RMB appreciation was limited to 2.1% against the dollar and the pace of subsequent RMB appreciation was to be relatively stable and slow.

1.4.2 Gradual Development of Exchange Rate Reform, from July 2005 to 2007

After China announced the exchange rate reform on 21 July 2005, Congress's pressure on China's currency waned gradually. There were two bills after PBOC's announcement of exchange rate reform in July 2005 and only one bill in 2006 targeting the RMB issue. However, the Treasury kept a close eye on the subsequent development of China's exchange rate reform. The Treasury's Reports recognized that China's new exchange rate mechanism remained a tightly managed currency peg against the dollar, as the initial adjustment was small, the subsequent movements of

[44]People's Bank of China (2005).

the RMB were limited and the currency basket seemed not to play a significant role.[45] The US administration closely monitored the progress made on China's exchange rate regime and continued the intensive engagement with China in 2006. With regard to the IMF, a trend can be identified whereby less pressure was placed on China's exchange rate policy in 2006. In one word, though the Treasury was not satisfied with the pace of China's exchange rate reform and maintained the engagements with the Chinese leadership, international pressure from the Congress and the IMF on the RMB exchange rate generally decreased from July 2005 to 2016. The pathway of China's post-2005 exchange rate reform was largely determined by China's domestic politics.

The Chinese leadership took a very cautious approach toward the exchange rate reform. Both the PBOC and the MOFCOM closely monitored the impact of exchange rate reform on export enterprises in the second half of 2005. As the initial revaluation was limited and the subsequent appreciation was gradual, China's exports maintained the momentum after July 2005. The MOFCOM, under the leadership of Bo Xilai, continued to be a vocal opponent of fast RMB appreciation. The MOFCOM was particularly concerned with the several export industries such as textile and apparel industries that were sensitive to RMB appreciation. Bo particularly stressed that "RMB appreciation has substantially lowered the profit of export-oriented enterprises, especially labor-intensive ones, whose profit was already very low."[46] Faced with the strong and consistent resistance from the MOFCOM, the total RMB appreciation was still small and the exchange rate flexibility was also limited after July 2005. The RMB appreciated 3.2% in total, from 8.07 to 7.81, against the dollar in 2006. Except for the initial 2.1 revaluation, the RMB appreciated 3.7% in total against the dollar from July 2005 to the end of 2006.

As mentioned, the PBOC was politically weaker and less influential in China's top leadership compared with the MOFCOM. The limited nature of the RMB exchange rate reform produced little change in the economic fundamentals that had induced the PBOC to favor additional flexibility in the first place. The preservation of a gradually and continuously appreciated RMB exchange rate ultimately eroded PBOC's monetary policy autonomy, in circumstances whereby China ran persistent current account surpluses. The PBOC faced increasing policy dilemma in simultaneously maintaining the gradually appreciated RMB exchange rates and controlling the domestic money supply.

With the gradual appreciation and limited flexibility of RMB exchange rate, China's current account surplus continued to grow rapidly in 2006. The Congress set off another wave of targeting China's exchange rate policy in the first half of 2007, which was somewhat similar to the 2005 case. There were five bills in 2007, all of which were introduced in the first half of the year. With growing pressure from the

---

[45] U.S. Department of the Treasury, "Report to Congress on International Economic and Exchange Rate Policies", November 2005, https://www.treasury.gov/resource-center/international/exchange-rate-policies/Documents/112005_report.pdf.

[please delete this line]

[46] *People's Daily*, "How will RMB exchange rate reform affect trade?", 2 June 2006, https://en.people.cn/200606/02/eng20060602_270674.html.

Congress, Treasury's stance on China's exchange rate policy became tougher, which could be seen from the blunter language of the Treasury's Reports. With regard to the IMF, one could identify the same trend of more severe pressure. It became clear that the IMF was under growing American pressure to declare the RMB "fundamentally misaligned", which worsened China's relationship with the IMF substantially in 2007.[47] Finally, Beijing took the unusual step of voting against the adoption of the 2007 Decision on Bilateral Surveillance and withdrew from the bilateral surveillance process during 2007–08.

Domestically, the priorities of MOFCOM shifted significantly in 2007. The MOFCOM used to be a vocal opponent of RMB appreciation. However, the MOFCOM softened its resistance to RMB appreciation in 2007, as its main task changed from maintaining export growth to reducing excessive trade surplus. Chinese exporters faced unprecedented trade frictions in 2006, which put enormous pressure on the MOFCOM to settle those trade disputes and preserve the interests of export industries. MOFCOM's shifted priority on balance of international payments provided political space for PBOC's advocate of exchange rate reform. The PBOC faced increasing and enormous inflationary pressure in 2007, and all the major monetary tools, including open market operations, required reserve ratio, and interest rate, were used to fight inflation. Senior officials of the PBOC actively proposed that RMB appreciation would help to reduce both domestic inflation and current account surplus.

On 18 May 2007, the Chinese leadership took the first major step to make the RMB a more flexible currency by loosening its daily trading limits. The PBOC announced that "as of 21 May 2007, the RMB-dollar trading band in the inter-bank spot foreign exchange market will be expanded from 0.3 to 0.5%, namely, the daily RMB-dollar trading band may be floated within the 0.5% range of the middle price of the dollar against the RMB."[48] Furthermore, the severe situation of inflationary cycle and PBOC's firm suggestion produced a clear shift in exchange rate strategy in the late 2007. China's top leadership accepted PBOC's basic argument to regard inflation as the most severe problem to tackle and to use currency appreciation as a tool to fight inflation. The RMB began to appreciate in a faster pace in late 2007. The RMB appreciated 6.9% against the dollar from 7.807 to 7.305 in the year of 2007; it appreciated 2.8% against the dollar from 7.511 to 7.305 in the fourth quarter, account for 40% of the total appreciation in 2007. The widened RMB-dollar trading band allowed more exchange rate flexibility and the rate of RMB appreciation sped up considerably in the fourth quarter of 2007.

[47]See, for example, Walter (2014, p. 136), Foot and Andrew (2011, pp. 113–116).

[48]People's Bank of China (2007).

1.4.3 Acceleration and Stagnation of Exchange Rate Reform, from 2008 to July 2010

The accelerated RMB appreciation continued in the first half of 2008. The substantial and faster RMB appreciation happened in the period from October 2007 to July 2008, when the Chinese leadership concentrated their attention and spared no effort to fight inflation. More specifically, the RMB appreciated 9.8%, from 7.51 to 6.84, against the dollar in the ten months, which was even larger than the previous total RMB appreciation (8.0%, from 8.11 to 7.51) for more than two years.

In the period from July 2005 to 2007, there was little pressure from export interest groups in China's exchange rate policy making. The main reason was that China's exports still grew fast and there was no sharp decline in exports as opponents of RMB exchange rate reform had feared. However, exporters became strongly opposed to the RMB appreciation in early 2008, as the pace of appreciation had accelerated. Chinese exporters grew hostile to exchange rate appreciation in 2008. Since the MOFCOM gave priority to trade surplus reduction and its stance towards RMB appreciation had changed in 2007, the only alternative for the exporters at this juncture was to mobilize resources to lobby against the rapid RMB appreciation and seek policy adjustment.

Based on questionnaire surveys and semi-structured interviews, the author took an in-depth case study on the Fujian province and illustrated the three main methods of export lobbying: guanxi-based lobbying through local governments, guanxi-based lobbying through local offices of central governmental agencies, and lobbying through trade associations. Before we proceed to the empirical findings, it is necessary for us to make a clear definition of "guanxi" herein, which has diverse meanings in the context of China's politics and society. A considerable amount of literature has been published to identify the broad meanings of guanxi and to emphasize the important roles of guanxi in China's political, economic and social fields. For instance, Yang understands guanxi in her comprehensive study on everyday social relationships in contemporary China in the following way:

> The word guanxi (pronounced guan-shee) means literally 'a relationship' between objects, forces, or persons. When it is used to refer to relationships between people, not only can it be applied to husband-wife, kinship and friendship relations, it can also have the sense of 'social connections,' dyadic relationships that are based implicitly (rather than explicitly) on mutual interest and benefit. Once guanxi is established between two people, each can ask a favor of the other with the expectation that the debt incurred will be repaid sometime in the future.[49]

Moreover, Guo defines the broad meanings of guanxi from four dimensions: "instrumental, etiquette, moral and emotional".[50] More specifically,

> The instrumental dimension primarily involves self-interested motivation: the desire for repayment of favours and for achieving personal advantage. The etiquette dimension involves the use of social rituals to establish and maintain harmonious human relations with one's

[49] Yang (1994, pp. 1–2).

[50] Guo (2001, p. 72).

> acquaintances, coworkers, colleagues, superiors or subordinates. The moral dimension is established and maintained by following a traditional system of ethics that morally obligates oneself to those within one's guanxi network. The emotional dimension is evident when friendship plays a central role in regulating interpersonal relationships.[51]

Since guanxi is seemingly ubiquitous in China's society, guanxi has played important roles in China's political economy. As to the role of guanxi in China's politics, Dittmer argues that guanxi is "the central term in our conceptualization of informal politics"[52]; Guo argues that "the volatility of Chinese politics encouraged the political elite to rely on personal relationships to get things done and promoted a culture of mutual dependence and moral obligation among the elite and between the elite and their subordinate."[53] On the other hand, there is a growing body of evidence to suggest guanxi's important role in China's socio-economic environment. To name a few, Xin and Pearce view guanxi as "substitutes for formal institutional support", in the context of China's underdeveloped legal framework.[54] Deng and Kennedy conducted surveys to investigate companies' lobbying strategies and how they engage with officials in the policy process. Their results show that.

> Companies do engage in trust-building, for example, by hosting banquets, and almost 70 per cent of respondents agree with the statement that 'guanxi is the key to influencing public policy'. On the other hand, 80 per cent of companies agree that 'good guanxi with local government is more important than with the central government'.[55]

Therefore, it can be seen that guanxi has broad meanings in the Chinese society and important roles in China's political economy. This book takes the instrumental dimension of guanxi and more narrowly defines guanxi as interpersonal connections and relationships, which aims to secure favours in personal or business relations. It is proper to refer to Kennedy's description of guanxi to elaborate the author's definition here:

> Officials provide entrepreneurs access to scarce goods, credit, government and overseas markets, and protection from onerous regulations. Entrepreneurs, in return, provide officials with payoffs and gifts, employment, and business partnerships.[56]

In this sense, guanxi-based lobbying refers to companies' strategies and tactics that entrepreneurs make use of their connections and relationships with officials if they seek to influence public policy. There is a case for arguing that guanxi is not something specific or unique to China. Informal relationships are important in any political, economic or cultural setting, and can play a role in exerting influence that is not possible through formal institutions and structures. Nevertheless, it is clear from my research in Fujian that the local actors actually involved in the process of

---

[51] Ibid, p. 72.

[52] Dittmer (1995, p. 10).

[53] Guo (2001, p. 70).

[54] Xin and Pearce (1996).

[55] Deng and Kennedy (2010, p. 110).

[56] Kennedy (2009, p. 10).

trying to influence policy think that guanxi is both distinctive and important; hence we focus on its role and significance in this piece of research.

The case study of Fujian province has three main findings that shed light on the three main methods of export lobbying. First, exporters made use of their guanxi and focused their lobbying efforts on the local governments where they were concentrated. Firms discussed their problems with municipal government officials and pressed them to persuade Beijing to stop appreciating the currency. Second, exporters could make use of their guanxi to discuss their difficulties with the local officials of central government agencies, particular the MOFCOM, and pressed them to influence central government's exchange rate policy. The local officials of MOFCOM serve as middlemen to pass along the concerns of China's export enterprises to the MOFCOM and further to the State Council. Third, trade associations for labor-intensive enterprises began to lobby for slower RMB appreciation and repeal of cuts to export rebates in early 2008. They asserted that if the central government did not intervene, large amounts of labor-intensive enterprises would go bankrupt, thousands of workers would be laid off, and social stability would therefore be threatened.

The central argument is that the exporters' lobbying imposed enormous pressure on the central government's exchange rate policy making in 2008. Faced with pressure from businesses, China's central government faced considerable pressure to raise export rebate rates and maintain the stability of the RMB exchange rate. As a result, the top leadership held several internal meetings to discuss the issues and decided to tour the key manufacturing centers in the coastal provinces. The top leadership conducted intensive research and investigation in early July 2008. Then Chinese leaders were convinced that China's export situation was severe and prompt counter-measures should be taken. They finally decided to roll out rescue policies in late July. The market-oriented RMB exchange rate reform beginning from 21 July 2005 was halted in the second half of 2008, and China returned to the de-facto dollar-pegged exchange rate regime in the turbulent times of the global financial crisis.

1.4.4 Resumption of Exchange Rate Reform, from July 2010 to 2013

While Congress's influence on the RMB issue generally diminished over time after the global financial crisis, international criticism and pressure from the US administration and the IMF still played an important role of agenda-setting in China's exchange rate policy making in 2010. Particularly, the RMB issue intensified in early 2010. The US administration became increasingly critical of China's currency undervaluation and took action to demand Beijing to make policy changes. President Obama and Treasury Secretary Geithner made use of both bilateral and multilateral channels to press China on the RMB issue. Similar to the case in 2005, international criticism and pressure from the US administration and the IMF on the RMB undervaluation gained momentum in the first half of 2010, which rendered China's leaders impossible to avoid the RMB exchange rate issue.

The Chinese leadership stood firm against the external pressure as they did in 2005. Chinese leaders did not wish to show any sign of weakness under international pressure. They consistently opposed the international criticism that the RMB was substantially undervalued and stated that wrongful accusations and pressure would not help solve the RMB issue. More importantly, there was much less internal controversy within Chinese central government with regard to the exchange rate policy in 2010. Both the PBOC and the MOFCOM held the position that a stable exchange rate was necessary in turbulent times and that the RMB exchange rate alone was not responsible for the trade imbalance. On the one hand, the PBOC reiterated the necessity of exchange rate stability in 2010, which was different from the active advocate of exchange rate reform in 2005. On the other hand, the MOFCOM withdrew its opposition to exchange rate reform and stressed the proper pace of proceeding, which was also different from the powerful resistance in 2005. With less internal controversy within the central government (between PBOC and MOFCOM), Chinese leaders were more consistent in the exchange rate policy in 2010. They did not swing back and forth and make the exchange rate reform unexpected. Instead, the Chinese leaders, including the heads of MOFCOM and PBOC, agreed on the general direction of market-oriented exchange reform in 2010. They also signaled the readiness to resume the exchange rate reform on various occasions in the first half of 2010.

However, it remained questionable why the domestic politics of exchange rate policy making in 2010 was different from that in 2005. The book further explores the origins and developments of China's RMB internationalization strategy. Starting from mid-2009, China promoted RMB internationalization as an effort to diversify the international monetary system, thereby reducing the reliance on the US dollar. It is argued that, with the development of RMB internationalization and increasing openness of capital account, a flexible exchange rate was the feasible choice to preserve the independence and effectiveness of China's monetary policy, which produced the Chinese leadership's consensus on the second round of RMB exchange rate reform. As the stability and predictability of RMB exchange rate was one of the most important attributes in improving the confidence and promoting the international use of RMB, it determined the pathway of gradual and steady appreciation in the second round of RMB exchange rate reform.

Therefore, change eventually came on 19 June 2010. Approved by the State Council, the PBOC announced a further reform of the RMB exchange rate regime based on the measures taken in 2005.[57] Continued emphasis was placed on reflecting market supply and demand with reference to a basket of currencies and the exchange rate floating bands remained the same as previously announced in the inter-bank foreign exchange market. The RMB exchange rate appreciated gradually and steadily against the dollar after PBOC's announcement. The second round of exchange rate

---

[57] People's Bank of China (2010).

reform policy could be interpreted as a hybrid outcome of both the external influences from the Western countries and the internal needs of RMB internationalization. On the one hand, international criticism and pressure from the US administration and the IMF still played an important role of agenda-setting in China's exchange rate policy making in 2010. On the other hand, Chinese central government reached the consensus that a more flexible exchange rate was necessary for further internationalizing its currency.

1.5 Methods

This book mainly employs four qualitative research methods: documentary analysis, case study, interviews and questionnaire surveys. The empirical studies use extensive documentary analysis of secondary data to examine the level I and level II games of China's exchange rate policy making. A typical case study has been conducted in Fujian province to explore the interest group politics (level III game) of China's exchange rate policy making. The author also collects primary data through interviews and questionnaires to complement the documentary analysis.

1.5.1 Documentary Analysis

In the study of China's exchange rate policy making, it is essential to conduct empirical research based on documentary analysis. The basis of primary sources derives from: (1) publicly available official documents (i.e. official reports, publications, statements, speeches from related organizations/ministries/agencies) and (2) relevant information in various published forms (i.e. official declarations and press statements as well as media reports and commentaries via newspapers and magazines).

Documentary sources offer a prime opportunity for political scientists to develop novel accounts and interpretations of significant events and policies. As Burnham, Lutz, Grant and Layton-Henry note:

> Documents, of course, do not speak for themselves but only acquire significant meaning when situated within a context set by vigorous analytical and methodological assumptions. To enable other scholars to judge the worth of research produced from documentary sources it is therefore necessary to state the working assumptions that have guided the selection of the material. This is particularly important given the range and diversity of documentary sources now available to the researcher.[58]

In the following I will specify the selection of documents to examine the level I and level II games of China's exchange rate policy making. First, the level I game examines the international influences from the US government and the IMF on China's exchange rate policy making. The bills and resolutions of the US Congress are

[58]Burnham et al. (2008, p. 212).

available to the public since January 1995 through THOMAS Library of Congress and Congress.gov.[59] Congress.gov is the official website for US federal legislative information and THOMAS Library of Congress is the database of Congress.gov. THOMAS Library of Congress offers search engines that facilitate researchers to get access to all the RMB-related bills and resolutions. Moreover, the US Department of the Treasury has published the semiannual Report to Congress on International Economic and Exchange Rate Policies since 1989. The Reports review the macroeconomic and exchange rate policies of the world's major economies. More importantly, the Reports consider whether the major US trading partners manipulate the exchange rate between their currency and the US dollar. All the Reports are available through the Treasury Resource Center.[60] Additionally, the US presidents' speeches and remarks are available through the official website of the White House.[61] The White House website also publishes statements and press releases of the US administration, including the President, the Treasury secretary and other senior government officials.[62] With regard to the IMF, it publishes the Article IV Staff Reports on People's Republic of China that include IMF's position on China's exchange rate policy every year.[63] The IMF also publishes a large number of working papers, press briefing transcripts, and conference transcripts, which are also available through the website of PRC and the IMF.[64]

Second, the level II game involves the two most important ministries (PBOC and MOFCOM) within China's central government. The stances of PBOC and MOFCOM towards the RMB exchange rate policy can be examined by the statements and speeches of PBOC's and MOFCOM's senior officials, including PBOC's Governors and Deputy Governors as well as the MOFCOM's Ministers and Vice Ministers. The official websites of PBOC and MOFCOM provide search engines that help researchers to get access to those data.[65] Furthermore, the PBOC has published Monetary Policy Implementation Reports every quarter since 2001, which provides

---

[59]THOMAS Library of Congress, https://thomas.loc.gov/home/bills_res.html; Congress.gov, https://www.congress.gov.

[60]U.S. Department of the Treasury, "Report to the Congress on International Economic and Exchange Rate Policies", https://www.treasury.gov/resource-center/international/exchange-rate-policies/Pages/index.aspx.

[61]The White House, "Speeches and Remarks", https://www.whitehouse.gov/briefing-room/speeches-and-remarks.

[62]The White House, "Statements and Releases", https://www.whitehouse.gov/briefing-room/statements-and-releases.

[63]International Monetary Fund, "People's Republic of China: Article IV Consultation Reports", https://www.imf.org/external/country/chn/index.htm?type=56.

[64]People's Republic of China and the IMF, https://www.imf.org/external/country/CHN/index.htm?type=9998#56.

[65]People's Bank of China, available from https://www.pbc.gov.cn; Ministry of Commerce of the People's Republic of China, available from https://www.mofcom.gov.cn.

crucial empirical sources to analyze PBOC's positions and operations of monetary and exchange rate policies.[66]

Third, the author mainly consults sources from the Xinhua News Agency and the People's Daily, the two most important CCP mouthpieces, for official statements, briefs for important Party meetings[67] and top leadership speeches, which shed light on the top leaders' deliberations and decisions of exchange rate policy making. In addition to consulting the scholarly works written in English, the author takes advantage of materials in Chinese. The Chinese journal database, China National Knowledge Infrastructure,[68] has been used intensively throughout the research process, providing a rich resource base beyond a sole reliance on English language literature.

1.5.2 Case Study Supplemented by Questionnaires and Interviews

The level III game involves the interest group politics of China's exchange rate policy making. Access to credible sources often makes things particularly difficult for researchers in the study of China's interest groups. Lobbying is normally not reported in Chinese newspapers and periodicals. Meanwhile, there are very limited records or documents on business lobbying in the Chinese statistical system and other government statistics. Therefore, the author has to conduct a case study supplemented by interviews and questionnaire surveys to fill the data gap.

According to Gerring, a case study is best defined as "an intensive study of a single unit for the purpose of understanding a larger class of (similar) units."[69] The strength of case study is that "it allows the researcher to use a variety of sources, a variety of types of data and a variety of research methods as part of the investigation."[70] Furthermore, "the typical case study focuses on a case that exemplifies a stable, cross-case relationship."[71] Given the size and diversity of China, it is hardly possible to find a single provincial case study that is representative of the country as a whole; no such "typical" province exists. Fujian is chosen as the case study focus for this book as it is representative not of China as a whole, but of those coastal provinces that have been most significant in driving the growth of Chinese exports in the post-Mao era. Indeed, as Fujian's economic growth has been overwhelmingly dependent on

---

[66] People's Bank of China, "Monetary Policy Implementation Reports", available from https://www.pbc.gov.cn/zhengcehuobisi/125207/125227/125957/index.html.

[67] Two Party conferences, the CCP Central Committee Conference and the Central Economic Work Conference, are of crucial importance. See CCP Central Committee Conference, available from https://www.xinhuanet.com/politics/zzjhy and People's Central Economic Work Conference, available from https://finance.people.com.cn/GB/jinji/222/2322/index.html.

[68] China National Knowledge Infrastructure (CNKI), available from https://www.cnki.net.

[69] Gerring (2004, p. 342).

[70] Denscombe (2003, p. 31).

[71] Seawright and Gerring (2008, p. 299).

exports, it has thus also become heavily sensitive to exchange rate changes in the twenty-first century. This was particularly the case when exporters in Fujian were affected by the accelerated RMB appreciation in 2008.

The author distributed 98 questionnaires to export entrepreneurs in the Fujian province and 63 valid responses were collected for analysis. The questionnaires mainly collected the following information: (1) whether the business was affected by RMB exchange rate fluctuations, (2) in which years the enterprise was significantly affected by RMB exchange rate fluctuations, (3) what measures were taken in times of volatile RMB exchange rate fluctuations, and most importantly, (4) how difficult and effective did exporters find it to communicate with local governments and industry associations in times of volatile RMB exchange rate fluctuations. The questionnaires provided a quick and affordable means for the author to obtain the general information and opinions of the local exporters in the Fujian province.

The researcher also conducted 22 semi-structured interviews with export entrepreneurs, association representatives and local government officials at different levels. The interviews aimed to further explore the interactions between exporters, industry associations and local government officials when the business of export enterprises was negatively impacted by RMB appreciation. Interviews typically lasted 1–2 h and many sources were interviewed multiple times. In order to protect the anonymity of sources, most of the interviews are cited in the footnotes as "interviews with dates".

Overall, the typical case study with questionnaires and interviews sheds light on how interest group lobbying influenced China's exchange rate policy making in 2008. The questionnaires and interviews first aimed to find out whether exporters in the Fujian province really preferred an undervalued and fixed exchange rate. Then the author sought to collect evidence of interest group lobbying. Interest groups were found to communicate their preferences to the local industry associations and government officials in difficult times of accelerated RMB appreciation. Furthermore, the interviews examined whether local politicians advocated on behalf of their constituents' preferences. Last, if the final decision taken by the top leader reflected the considerations of the government officials, industry associations and export enterprises at the local level, it could be argued that the empirical research provided support for the level III game in 2008.

It is worth noting that questionnaires and interviews supplement each other in the study. There are two obvious advantages of questionnaires. First, the information can be collected in a short period of time and in a relatively cost-effective way. Second, the results of the questionnaires can be quickly and easily quantified for analysis. However, questionnaires have some limitations, as they mainly ask closed questions. "The disadvantage of closed questions is that participants are forced to choose one of the predetermined answers rather than create their own answer. This may result in their not being able to convey their true feelings."[72] Interviews to a large extent fill in the gap by gathering more in-depth insights on the opinions, attitudes and actions of the respondents. In a nutshell, the methodological triangulation of questionnaires

[72]Burnham et al. (2008, p. 119).

and interviews in the case study gives this research a firm grounding in advancing our understanding on the inner mechanisms of the interest group politics of China's exchange rate policy making.

1.5.3 Elite/Expert Interviewing

The author has applied elite and expert interviews as a complementary research method to documentary analysis. Decision making in China's high-level politics remains an enigma to outsiders because of its opaqueness and complexity. Interviews with well-informed individuals on their knowledge and opinions on this area thus provide unique and vital resources that at least compensate the lack of open information.

However, access was the main challenge for elite and expert interviews in Beijing. It was rather difficult to get access to the key decision-makers of China's exchange rate policy or even the heads of the government departments (PBOC Governor and MOFCOM Minister). Instead, the author found it feasible to get access to some (former) members of the Monetary Policy Department (MPD), especially those who are distinguished professors at China's universities and research councils (such as Peking University, Renmin University of China, and Chinese Academy of Social Sciences). The MPD is PBOC's consultative body for the making of monetary policy and exchange rate policy. Similarly, the author interviewed some (former) officials of Comprehensive Department and Policy Research Department under the MOFCOM. It was also useful to interview Chinese officials at the National Development and Reform Commission (NDRC) and the Ministry of Foreign Affairs (MFA).

The elite and expert interviews provide unique and first-hand empirical evidence of how the political bargaining in the top-level policy consultation and decision process influenced the trajectory of China's exchange rate reform. As Burnham, Lutz, Grant and Layton-Henry note:

> Elite interviewers must be prepared to explore the world of the respondent sympathetically without being captured by it. They must have a research design that is flexible and open to new ideas and interpretations, while still being informed by an overarching theoretical framework and a central research question.[73]

During the author's fieldwork research in Beijing, a total of 13 face-to-face elite/expert interviews were conducted. Most of the elite interviews lasted around one hour and some expert interviews were longer. A semi-structured and open-ended question format (see Appendix) was used for all the interviews. Similarly, in order to protect the anonymity of sources, the details of all respondents are kept confidential and they are cited in the footnotes as "interviews with dates".

To summarize, elite and expert interviews (semi-structured and open-ended format) have been employed in this research as supplementary albeit important

[73]Burnham et al. (2008, p. 247).

sources of information in order to compensate the limitations of documentary analysis. The elite and expert interviews remain to be one of the best ways to obtain information about the decision-makers and the decision-making process.

1.6 Contributions and Outline of the Book

Thus far, this introductory chapter has presented the research background, research questions, state of the field, theoretical framework, empirical findings, and research methods. This book aims to provide three main contributions.

First and foremost, it provides original and systematic research on China's exchange rate policy making in the new millennium to the academic literature. Though there is a heated debate over the RMB exchange rate policy in the twenty-first century, little systematic work has been done to explain China's exchange rate policy making. The most important contribution of this research is to provide substantial empirical evidence based on documentary analysis and primary data from interviews and questionnaire surveys. Careful analysis of official documents as well as media reports and commentaries are supplemented by elite and expert interviews to obtain information about the decision-makers and provide insight into the decision-making process of China's exchange rate policy. Moreover, the methodological triangulation of questionnaires and interviews in the case study gives this research a firm grounding in advancing our understanding on the inner mechanisms of the interest group politics of China's exchange rate policy making. Therefore, the empirical study provides a richer portrait of the dynamics and complexity of China's exchange rate policy making.

Second, the book makes a modest theoretical contribution to the existing body of CPE and IPE literature by developing the three-level game framework to explain China's exchange rate policy making. As one of the pioneers in IPE, Strange promotes the development of the IPE discipline to overcome the "mutual neglect between International Economics and International Relations".[74] The book provides a good example to support the IPE approach that bridges the international politics and domestic politics to explain economic policy making. It is argued that the Chinese leaders sit at the juncture of the international system and the state-society when making exchange rate policy. China's central decision makers strive to reconcile international pressures, domestic ministerial interests and domestic interest groups when making RMB exchange rate policies.

Third, and related to the previous two contributions, the book also builds bridges between researchers and policymakers. Stone notes that "there is a lack of dialogue between researchers and policy-makers and that inadequate or insufficient use is made of research findings."[75] The author overcomes the problem by linking the research to a theoretical framework that guides the entire empirical investigation. On the one

[74] Strange (1970).

[75] Stone (2002, p. 288).

hand, the insights of perceptions, experiences, attitudes and actions gained from the elite and expert interviews are conducive to verifying the theoretical framework. On the other hand, the theoretical framework would help the practical policymakers, in both Western countries and China, understand the mechanism of China's exchange rate policy making. Overall, the book is a timely and rigorous study of the role that international and domestic politics play in forging China's exchange rate policy making, which promotes mutual understanding of both researchers and policymakers.

In order to achieve those contributions, the book consists of eight chapters, including this introduction and a conclusion. The introduction establishes the background for this research and formulates the research questions. The research is dedicated to explaining China's exchange rate policy making from 2002 to 2013. It then briefly reviews the state of the field and identifies the gaps in the existing literature that this research is going to fill. Based on the development of a synthesized theoretical framework, it elaborates the empirical findings and the research methods applied in this research. The rest of this book is structured as follows.

The next chapter (Chap. 2) first examines the existing Economics studies on the RMB exchange rate as well as the CPE and IPE studies on exchange rate politics. It shows that the existing Economics studies on the RMB exchange rate are inconclusive, and that the existing CPE and IPE theoretical approaches have limitations when applied to China's case. It also develops a theoretical framework of China's exchange rate policy making, based on revision and synthesis of the existing IPE approaches to exchange rate politics. Specifically, the three-level game framework examines the Chinese leadership's negotiations with the international bargainers at the international level (level I), negotiations between central government's ministries at the central governmental level (level II) and negotiations with the domestic interest groups and local governments at the local level (level III). The framework speculates that the Chinese top leadership strives to reconcile international pressures, domestic ministerial interests and domestic interest groups when making exchange rate policy.

The following five chapters (Chaps. 3–7) are in-depth empirical studies that serve to validate the applicability of the three-level game framework to China's case. The empirical studies have five major findings. First, the level I game played an agenda-setting role in China's exchange rate policy making before the 2005 exchange rate reform. Second, the level II game determined the limited scope of the initial reform and the subsequent gradual RMB appreciation. Third, the level III game provided the most important sources for China's exchange rate policy returning to the de facto dollar-pegged exchange rate regime during the global financial crisis. Fourth, the level I game once again played an agenda-setting role in the 2010 exchange rate reform, but the level II game was important as well, in which the Chinese leadership reached the consensus to allow the RMB to appreciate against the dollar in a gradual and steady manner to improve the confidence and promote the international use of RMB.

The concluding chapter summarizes the theoretical framework and the empirical findings of the book. It further relates China's exchange rate reforms to the wider context of China's politics. The empirical studies of China's exchange rate reform have suggested that the Hu-Wen administration's governance was characterized by consensus-building collective leadership and they placed priority on economic growth and social stability. The conclusion also delineates the implications of this study for future research.

Chapter 2
Literature Review and Theoretical Framework

This chapter examines the existing Economics studies on the RMB exchange rate and the CPE and IPE studies on exchange rate politics. There exist three techniques to measure the RMB equilibrium exchange rate in the Economics studies, but they have produced inconclusive results of RMB exchange rate. The chapter argues that the Economics analysis are inherently problematic as the economists neglect the important political factors such as state, institutions and political leaders. Since upward or downward shifts in a country's exchange rate and choices of exchange rate regime create both domestic and international winners and losers, the study of the RMB exchange rate policy calls for interdisciplinary approaches that combine studies of Economics, Politics and International Relations (IR). The chapter thus turns to the existing CPE and IPE literature. It critically examines the four theoretical approaches to politics of exchange rate and identifies the respective limitations of the existing studies on China's exchange rate politics.

This chapter further develops a theoretical framework of China's exchange rate policy making based on revision and synthesis of the existing CPE and IPE approaches to fill the research gap. It will first argue that two-level game framework would be suitable to explain exchange rate policy making. Then more specific and context-derived elements, such as external and domestic actors with different preferences and interests as well as China's political and socio-economic structures, will be added into the analytical framework. It sheds light on the interactive dynamics of international politics and domestic politics in the formulation of China's exchange rate policy. Finally, the chapter extends Putnam's two-level game to a three-level game and develops a theoretical framework of China's exchange rate policy making. The three-level game framework examines the Chinese leadership's negotiations with the international bargainers at the international level (level I), negotiations between central government's ministries at the central governmental level (level II) and negotiations with the domestic interest groups and local governments at the local level (level III). It argues that the Chinese top leadership strives to reconcile international

Z. Wang, *The International Political Economy of China's Exchange Rate Policy Making*, https://doi.org/10.1007/978-981-33-4578-2_2

pressures, domestic ministerial interests and domestic interest groups when making exchange rate policy decisions.

2.1 Inconclusive Economics Studies on the RMB Exchange Rate

Economists have sought to measure whether the RMB is undervalued, and if so, by how much. With the RMB exchange rate being a contentious issue in the twenty-first century, large numbers of Economics studies on the RMB exchange rate have been done, which makes a complete delineation of the existing literature elusive. Nevertheless, despite the difficulties, it remains possible to identify that economists have developed their estimation models mainly based on three techniques to measure the RMB equilibrium exchange rate: Purchasing Power Parity approach, Fundamental Equilibrium Exchange Rate approach, and Behavior Equilibrium Exchange Rate approach.

2.1.1 The Purchasing Power Parity Approach

The first one of these techniques is to identify the exchange rate that would lead to purchasing power parity (PPP), which means that exchange rate should move to the rate that would equalize the prices of an identical basket of goods and services in any two countries. The Big Mac index invented by *The Economist* follows this idea, even though the price index used to establish PPP contains only one good – the burger.[1] More rigorous studies of PPP approach on exchange rate are based on the Balassa-Samuelson hypothesis. The Balassa-Samuelson effect describes the phenomenon that the tradable sectors' productivity increase will raise the wage rates in both the tradable and non-tradable sectors, which further increase the price of non-tradable goods and services and result in the appreciation of the real exchange rate.[2]

Since China's economy has grown rapidly in the recent decades, it is especially relevant to determine whether the Balassa-Samuelson effect is valid for China's case and to further estimate the RMB exchange rate misalignment. However, there exist competing results with regard to the validity of the Balassa-Samuelson hypothesis in China's case. To name but a few, Coudert and Couharde evidence a lack of Balassa effect in China. They find a large gap between the prediction made with a Balassa-Samuelson model and the actual behavior of the RMB exchange rate, so they turn to use other method (see FEER approach below) to calculate the RMB equilibrium

[1]*The Economist*, "The Big Mac index", 7 January 2016, retrieved from https://www.economist.com/content/big-mac-index.

[2]Balassa (1964), Samuelson (1964).

exchange rate.[3] Cheung, Chin and Fujii find that there is little statistically significant evidence to suggest that the RMB is undervalued when sampling uncertainty and serial correlation are accounted for.[4] Ju, Lin and Liu demonstrate that China does not follow the prediction of the Balassa-Samuelson effect. Their model suggests that the existence of excess labor supply depresses the wage rise, and the increases in the wage rates and prices of non-tradable goods and services are very small in China.[5] Conversely, Yan and Kakkar construct sectoral total factor productivities for the tradable and non-tradable sectors from 1980 to 2003, and confirm the validity of the Balassa-Samuelson effect in determining the long-run movements of the RMB real exchange rate against the US dollar.[6] Moreover, they find that although the RMB has been undervalued against the dollar in the recent years, the misalignment is relatively small and statistically insignificant.[7]

We can see from the literature that economists are difficult to reach firm conclusions concerning the validity of the Balassa-Samuelson effect in China and the level of the RMB exchange rate misalignment using the PPP approach. Therefore, many other economists turn to the concept of equilibrium exchange rate to study the RMB exchange rate.

2.1.2 The Fundamental Equilibrium Exchange Rate Approach

In contrast to the PPP approach, the second technique is the Fundamental Equilibrium Exchange Rate approach. The concept of fundamental equilibrium exchange rate (FEER) is "based on the notion of macroeconomic balance, which has both an internal and external dimension".[8] More specifically, FEER facilitates the economy to operate at full employment and low inflation (internal balance) and a sustainable current account position (external balance).

For instance, Goldstein adopts the macroeconomic balance approach, which "views the equilibrium exchange rate as the rate that produces equilibrium in the country's balance of payments".[9] He finds that the RMB was "significantly undervalued on the order of 15–25%" and criticizes that China manipulated its currency

[3] Coudert and Couharde (2005, 2007).

[4] Cheung et al. (2005, 2007, 2009, 2010).

[5] Ju et al. (2011); also, see Lin (2007) .

[6] Yan and Kakkar (2010).

[7] Ibid.

[8] Clark and MacDonald (1998, p. 5).

[9] Goldstein (2004, p. 4).

against the IMF's rule of game.[10] The subsequent estimated undervaluation by Goldstein and Lardy in 2006 was 20–40%, which was larger than that in 2004.[11] Goldstein and Lardy go further in 2007, to propose a 35–60% real appreciation of the RMB exchange rate to eliminate China's current account surplus.[12] Anderson follows Goldstein's approach to find that RMB undervaluation was about 15–20% and the adjustment would require a revaluation of 18–25%.[13] Coudert and Couharde use the FEER method to calculate the real effective exchange rate consistent with sustainable current accounts and find that the RMB real exchange rate was highly undervalued (10–33%) between 2002 and 2005 in effective terms and even more (35%) against the US dollar.[14]

It can be seen that estimations using the FEER approach have produced more consistent results than those using the PPP approach. However, it is not surprising that economists using the FEER approach generally reach the conclusion of RMB undervaluation, for the reason that the FEER approach is based on ideal macroeconomic balance while China's external imbalance has generally deteriorated in the new millennium. Both China's trade surplus and foreign reserves have soared at accelerating rates before the outbreak of the 2008 global financial crisis. Therefore, the FEER approach has been criticized as being self-explanatory, and the corresponding results are quite predictable. Furthermore, the FEER approach seems to be problematic when applied to the US dollar exchange rate, as the US had run persistently current account deficits in the last few decades. Therefore, some other economists make use of the Behavioral Equilibrium Exchange Rate approach to measure the RMB misalignment.

2.1.3 The Behavioral Equilibrium Exchange Rate Approach

To eliminate the problem that theFEER approach is too self-explanatory, other economists tend to estimate the RMB equilibrium exchange rate by using the Behavioral Equilibrium Exchange Rate approach, which does not rely on any theory of exchange rate determination.[15] The behavioral equilibrium exchange rate (BEER) examines "the deviation between the actual exchange rate and the value given by the estimated equilibrium relationship",[16] and the analysis "typically examines the

[10]Ibid, p. 2.

[11]Goldstein and Lardy (2006).

[12]Goldstein and Lardy (2007).

[13]Anderson (2005).

[14]Coudert and Couharde (2005, 2007).

[15]Korhonen and Ritola (2009).

[16]Clark and MacDonald (1998).

departure of the country's observed real effective exchange rate at the latest date available from the equation-predicted BEER to determine whether the country is under- or overvalued".[17]

To cite but a few, Funke and Rahn find that after an overvaluation up to mid-1996, the RMB has been constantly undervalued against the US dollar. The peak undervaluation exceeded 15%, and at the end of the observed period the RMB was undervalued by 11% against the US dollar.[18] MacDonald and Dias select the sample period from 1988 Q1 to 2006 Q1 and find that the RMB was undervalued on an order of 27.3–46.6%.[19] Chen uses time series data from 1994 Q1 to 2006 Q2 and finds that the RMB real exchange rate was undervalued during most of the sample period, but this misalignment tended to become smaller and smaller.[20] Wang, Hui and Soofi find that the RMB fluctuated around its long-run equilibrium rate within a narrow band, which implies that the currency was consistently undervalued.[21] Chen, Deng and Kemme select the sample period from 1997 to 2007Q3 and find that the RMB fluctuated moderately around its long run equilibrium value with undervaluation up to 4% and overvaluation up to 6% at various points.[22] Cui examines the period of 1997 to 2012 and finds the significant undervaluation of the RMB by up to 20% and the trend of the RMB approaching to its equilibrium exchange rate since 2007 except for the period of crisis.[23] We can see that the results of the existing literature vary so widely that it is difficult for the BEER approach, rather like the PPP approach, to reach any firm conclusion about the precise level of RMB exchange rate misalignment.

2.2 Summary and Discussions

As we can see from above, the three major techniques and a large variety of estimation models have been applied to answer whether and the extent to which the RMB is undervalued in the existing Economics studies. With regard to the first question, a fair degree of agreed answer is "yes" though a small number of studies disagree, whereas as to the second question, no consensus has been reached because the existing Economics studies have yielded a very wide range of estimates. Table 2.1 shows some selected economics studies on the RMB exchange rate.

The existing approaches to the RMB exchange rate within the literature of Economics studies are not without merit, especially insofar as they draw attention to the causes of the global economic imbalance and to the possible methods to address it. However, their explanatory utility nonetheless remains circumscribed owing to

---

[17] Cline and Williamson (2007, p. 6).

[18] Funke and Rahn (2005).

[19] MacDonald and Dias (2007).

[20] Chen (2007).

[21] Wang et al. (2007).

[22] Chen et al. (2008).

[23] Cui (2013).

Table 2.1 Selected economics studies on the RMB exchange rate

Author	Year	Approach	Results
Coudert et al.	2005, 2007	PPP	A lack of the Balassa-Samuelson effect
Cheung et al.	2005, 2007, 2009, 2010	PPP	Little statistically significant evidence to support the RMB undervaluation
Yan et al.	2011	PPP	Confirmation of the Balassa-Samuelson effect, significant overvaluation during 1984–87, significant undervaluation during 1989–91 and no indication of a statistically significant misalignment in the most recent years
Ju et al.	2011	PPP	A lack of the Balassa-Samuelson effect
Goldstein	2004	FEER	Significantly undervalued on an order of 15–25%
Anderson	2005	FEER	RMB undervaluation was about 15–20% and the adjustment would require a revaluation of 18–25%
Goldstein et al.	2006	FEER	Significantly undervalued on an order of 20–40%
Goldstein et al.	2007	FEER	A 35–60% real appreciation of the renminbi is required to eliminate China's current account surplus
Coudert et al.	2005, 2007	FEER	Highly undervalued (10–33%) between 2002 and 2005 in effective terms and even more (35%) against the US dollar
Funke et al.	2005	BEER	The RMB was overvalued until the mid-1996, followed by undervaluation which peaked at 15%, and the RMB was undervalued by 11% at 2002
MacDonald et al.	2007	BEER	The RMB was undervalued on an order of 27.3–46.6%
Chen	2007	BEER	The RMB were undervalued during most part of sample period from 1994 Q1 to 2006 Q2, but the misalignment had a trend to become smaller and smaller

(continued)

Table 2.1 (continued)

Author	Year	Approach	Results
Wang et al.	2007	BEER	The RMB fluctuated around its equilibrium rate within a narrow band and were consistently undervalued
Chen et al.	2008	BEER	The RMB fluctuated with undervaluation up to 4% and overvaluation up to 6% from 1997 to 2007Q3
Cui	2013	BEER	Significant undervaluation of the RMB by up to 20% and the trend of the RMB approaching to its equilibrium exchange rate since 2007 except for the period of crisis

the lack of consensus among economists on the RMB equilibrium exchange rate and the estimation of misalignment. The IMF working paper by Dunaway and Li indicates that the wide variation in these estimates is attributed to "the influence of such factors as the different methodologies used, explanatory variables included, subjective judgments of the various researchers in deriving their results, and instability in underlying economic relationships, especially in a rapidly developing economy like China".[24]

However, if we think outside the box, the major shortcoming of the Economics studies on the RMB exchange rate is that economists generally assume a pure economic world in which only the price and market mechanism take effect, but neglect such political factors as state, institutions and political leaders. As the RMB exchange rate policy is known to be formulated and implemented by the Chinese central government, more in depth examination of China's domestic politics would be conducive to understanding the RMB exchange rate policy making. Moreover, the competing results of existing Economics studies have further stoked debates and bargaining in international politics as well as China's domestic politics. Without referring to international influences as well as the leaders, structures and processes of China's exchange rate policy making, it would not be possible to gain a deep and thorough understanding of the RMB exchange rate.[25]

In particular, it is worth examining the political factors that push the US government to pressure China and the factors in Chinese politics that impel Chinese leaders to resist American pressure. Compared with the Western counterparts, Chinese leaders hold a very different view on the exchange rate. The orthodox view of the Western politicians and mainstream economists is that China's external imbalance has explicated that the RMB exchange rate is far away from the equilibrium and

[24]Dunaway and Li (2005).

[25]Several scholars have expressed this similar view. See, for example, Wang (2005), Zhang and Zhang (2005), Liu (2013).

that policy changes should be made to address the RMB misalignment.[26] However, the Chinese side does not simply attribute the external imbalance to exchange rate misalignment. The Chinese leadership regards the exchange rate as one component in the toolkit of development strategy, in which the priority is not to create a market economy or to achieve market equilibrium but to make China a wealthy and powerful country.[27] The next section will turn to the CPE and IPE studies on China's exchange rate politics.

2.3 Critical Review of CPE and IPE Studies on Exchange Rate Politics

The opposite views of the Western and Chinese officials on the RMB exchange rate shed light upon the nature of the real world. In the words of Gilpin, one of the pioneers in the field of IPE:

> The parallel existence and mutual interaction of 'state' and 'market' in the modern world create 'political economy.' … In the absence of the state, the price mechanism and market forces would determine the outcome of economic activities; this would be the pure world of the economist. In the absence of the market, the state or its equivalent would allocate economic resources; this would be the pure world of political scientist. [28]

The world in reality is neither a pure world of economists nor one of political scientists. Instead, it is more proper to define it as a global political economy with "the reciprocal and dynamic interaction … of the pursuit of wealth and the pursuit of power".[29] By pursuit of wealth, Gilpin had in mind the realm of economics: the role of price and market mechanism, as the principal concerns of mainstream economists. By pursuit of power, he had in mind the realm of politics: the role of state and government intervention, as the main concerns of political scientists. The state and the market interact to influence the distribution of power and wealth in international relations. Therefore, the scholars of CPE and IPE have provided more nuanced explanations for exchange rate policy making. Four theoretical approaches could be identified within the existing CPE and IPE literature of exchange rate politics: the domestic interests approach, the domestic institutions approach, the international influences approach, and the international-domestic interactions approach. This section will offer a critical review of the existing studies of the four approaches.

---

[26] Kroeber (2011).

[27] Ibid.

[28] Gilpin (1987, p. 8).

[29] Ibid, p. 43.

2.3.1 *The Domestic Interests Approach*

The first theoretical perspective, the domestic interests approach, is by far the most common. Three models of exchange rate politics have been developed within this approach: the electoral model, the partisan model and the sectoral model.

The electoral and partisan models emphasize the interests of political leaders and parties in democratic regimes. Both models resonate with the theory of political business cycles.[30] They assume that a government's exchange rate policy reflects its desire for monetary policy autonomy in order to manage the domestic economy, either for office-seeking or because of partisan preferences. Specifically, elected politicians may be more likely to adopt flexible exchange rate regimes before universal suffrage, as they allow them to carry out expansionary macroeconomic policies to create strong economic growth and reduce unemployment.[31] By contrast, leftist parties are less inclined to maintain a fixed exchange rate, because they pursue looser macroeconomic policies and are less inflation-averse.[32]

The sectoral model takes into account the various effects that exchange rate policy has on domestic sectors and suggests that interest groups have different preferences regarding exchange rate level and flexibility. Furthermore, the sectoral model sees the relative power among the various socioeconomic interest groups as a key factor influencing exchange rate policy. On this basis, the sectoral model is also termed the interest group model. The sectoral model suggests that different domestic sectors have different preferred degrees of exchange rate flexibility and levels of exchange rate. More specifically, domestically based groups favor floating exchange rates, while internationally oriented economic groups prefer fixed rates; producers of tradable goods prefer a relatively depreciated currency, whereas producers of non-tradable goods and services as well as overseas investors prefer a relatively appreciated one.[33]

The three models of exchange rate politics within the domestic interests approach provide useful insights because each identifies plausible explanatory variables and elaborates the causal mechanisms. The domestic interests approach could be appropriate to explain exchange rate policy of liberal market economies with democratic politics, but suffers from three limitations when directly applied to other cases, such as China's.

First, there are no universal suffrage and electoral campaigns in China, which is an authoritarian state with no democracy at the top levels of politics. Second, the Chinese Communist Party (CCP) has been the single dominant ruling party in contemporary China, which is distinct from two-party or multi-party systems characterized by competition between leftist, (centrist,) and rightist parties. There is no serious prospect of the CCP democratizing China or handing power to a rival group in the foreseeable future.[34] Coase and Wang note that "with more than 80 million

[30]See, for example, Nordhaus (1975), Drazen (2001), Schamis and Way (2003).

[31]Tufte (1978).

[32]Oatley (1997, 1999).

[33]Frieden (1991, 1994).

[34]Brown (2016).

members (at the end of 2011), from every profession, including a rising percentage of private entrepreneurs and college graduates, the Party appears as strong as it has ever been."[35] In this sense, the electoral and partisan models seem not to be suitable for China's case. Third, although China uses markets extensively, how much political space is available for interest groups to lobby for their preferred policies remains unclear. For instance, Liew and Wu assert that China's civil society is still very weak and there is limited political space that allows interest groups to lobby for their preferred policy outcomes.[36] By contrast, Steinberg and Shih argue that the preferences of powerful interest groups provide the most convincing explanation for China's undervalued exchange rate.[37] The role of interest group lobbying in China's exchange rate policy making thus remains a rather moot point. Moreover, even if interest groups are really able to assert influences on the RMB exchange rate policy making, the assumption that exchange rate policy would directly reflect the preferences of the strongest (or stronger) sectors and interest groups could be simplistic. It requires more in-depth analysis of the political leaders and institutions involved in China's exchange rate policy making. Last but not least, even though China is an authoritarian state, it is worth noting that China's political apparatus is not a monolithic entity with a single set of policy objectives. Parochial interests are voiced and represented forcefully by the key institutional actors in the party-state system, such as the Ministry of Commerce (MOFCOM), whose raison d'être is to further the interests of China's export sectors. Therefore, the sectoral model could be revised and incorporated into a more specific and context-derived framework to explain China's exchange rate policy making, which will be elaborated in more detail subsequently.

2.3.2 The Domestic Institutions Approach

In contrast to the domestic interests approach, the domestic institutions approach emphasizes institutional and structural impacts upon exchange rate policy making. Institutions matter because they structure the way preferences are aggregated and decisions are made. Specifically, political institutions create rules for decision making, define priorities of agenda and advantage certain groups while disadvantaging others. A number of cross-sectional studies have generated findings on how political institutions affect the exchange rate policy.

First, the nature of government and condition of socio-political environment are found to have influences on the choice of exchange rate regime. Weak and unstable governments generally prefer a floating exchange rate regime with less pressure to defend the exchange rate value and more monetary policy autonomy to pursue other macroeconomic objectives such as low-inflation or low-unemployment; while

---

[35] Coase and Wang (2012, p. 174).

[36] Liew and Wu (2007).

[37] Steinberg and Shih (2012).

stronger governments in a stable socio-political environment are more likely to adopt fixed exchange rate regimes, since they are less concerned about the speculative attacks on currency and the potential regime collapse.[38]

Furthermore, the electoral system and legislative institutions also affect the choice of exchange rate regime. Leblang finds that "floating exchange rate regimes are more likely in democratic than in nondemocratic polities and that democratic polities with majoritarian electoral systems are more likely to fix their exchange rates than those with systems of proportional representation."[39] Moreover, Bernhard and Leblang note that in the systems where "opposition parties are excluded from the legislative policy process … politicians in the governing party(ies) have strong incentives not to risk their position in office" and prefer floating exchange rate arrangements.[40]

Though the domestic institutions approach provides generalized findings on the relationship between political institutions and exchange rate policy choice, it also has weaknesses. Similar to the domestic interests approach, the domestic institutions approach is Western-centric and not suitable for China's case. The strong–weak government and the electoral system analyses could not explain China's exchange rate policy making owing to the fact that, as discussed, China has been a political authoritarian state with no elections in the top-level politics. The legislative institutions analysis cannot explain China's case either, because of the political weakness of NPC in China. Although it claims to be the top legislative body that enjoys the highest authority *de jure*, NPC acts de facto as a symbolic rubber-stamp for the CCP. In a nutshell, China's institutions, characterized by one-party rule and party-state system,[41] are fundamentally different from Western liberal democracies. This requires a more "indigenous" investigation into China's political structure and process of exchange rate policy making.

However, limited work is dedicated to this important field. Liew and Wu made an original contribution in figuring out the political institutions and elites of China's exchange rate policy making in 2007, which is definitely useful but out of date for now. Liew traces the historical evolution of the institutional structure in China's exchange rate policy making, as well as the leadership transitions in the structure.[42] He also analyses the roles and responsibilities of the key economic ministries and their respective interests and positions they pursue on the RMB exchange rate policy.[43] The results of the analyses are applied to explain the RMB devaluation policy in 1989, the no-devaluation policy during the Asian financial crisis, and the reform of the RMB exchange rate regime after 2005.[44] Moreover, Bell and Feng examine the

---

[38] See, for example, Edwards (1996), Alesina and Wagner (2006), Carmignani et al. (2008).

[39] Leblang (1999, p. 599).

[40] Bernhard and Leblang (1999, p. 76).

[41] Zheng (1997).

[42] Liew (2004).

[43] Ibid.

[44] Liew and Wu (2007).

institutional rise of China's central bank and argue that the rising authority of PBOC explains the shift to the partial liberalization of China's exchange rate regime in 2005.[45] Steinberg argues that "the combination of a powerful manufacturing sector, state-controlled labour system, and state-controlled financial system helps explains why China has maintained an undervalued exchange rate."[46] Though the existing limited work figures out the interests and positions of policy elites and economic ministries, it has not closely examined the way in which the preferences of the key institutional actors are aggregated in the institutional structure. The black box, filled with the interplay of China's domestic political agents, remains unopened. One of the major contributions of this book will be to use process-tracing to provide in-depth analysis on how the interactions of China's key economic ministries influence the RMB exchange rate policy making.

Last but not least, both the domestic institutions approach and the domestic interests approach focus on the domestic factors but ignore the international dimension, which affects exchange rate policy of an open economy in the era of economic globalization. In the perspective of the third theoretical approach, one cannot fully understand a country's domestic political economy without reference to its structural position and international relations in the global political economy.

2.3.3 The International Influences Approach

Contrary to the previous domestic politics approaches based on unit-level or state-level perspectives, the third theoretical approach—the international influences approach—attaches importance to the role of international influences on China's exchange rate policy making. It is an IPE approach as it is concerned with the ways in which international political forces affect countries' exchange rate policy and shape their economic interactions. The international influences in the existing studies mainly refer to international criticisms of China's exchange rate practices and international pressure on China to revalue its currency.

With regard to the relationship between international pressure and China's exchange rate policy, there have been divisive debates among scholars and analysts. On one side of the spectrum is the argument that the increasing US criticisms of China's currency practices gave rise to China's exchange rate reform in 2005 and the subsequent RMB appreciation. For example, Li uses the "variable coefficient–panel data model" to find that the US played a leading role in the RMB appreciation and the Congress bills aimed at the RMB exchange rate were the direct fuse in the revaluation.[47] Chao and Tung argue that in addition to the economic and domestic factors, China's exchange rate policy was influenced by American political pressure and that this pressure led to the reform of RMB exchange rate regime and the widening of

[45] Bell and Feng (2013).

[46] Steinberg (2015, p. 117).

[47] Li (2011).

RMB exchange rate's floating band.[48] Zhu, Zhao and Wang establish the "political cycle spillover effect model" and find that the American political cycle had short-term impacts on the RMB exchange rate.[49] Their empirical evidence further suggests that the RMB appreciation rate was significantly reduced in the first year after the US presidential election, but significantly enhanced in the first year after the mid-term election.[50]

On the other side of the spectrum is the argument that external pressure is unlikely to yield any major change in China's exchange rate policy. For instance, Liu and Zhou explore the impact of political pressure from the US on the RMB exchange rate and find that the overall result was not significant.[51] Liu and Pauwels find little evidence to suggest that the external pressure had any influence on the daily changes of the CNY/USD spot exchange rate, which means the pace of the RMB appreciation was unlikely to be affected by the political pressure.[52] Hu and Liu find that external political pressure did not have a significant influence on the daily returns of CNY/USD exchange rate, but had statistically significant impacts on the conditional volatility of RMB exchange rate.[53]

In addition, some other findings show rather mixed results. Zhang investigates the impact of US political pressure from three aspects and finds that "the political pressure from Congress and the US public media alone have little impact on the RMB exchange rate in the short run, while the political pressure from American lobbyists have a positive impact on the appreciation of RMB exchange rate."[54] Xiao and Pan build a game model of the domestic and foreign interest groups to analyze the effect of external pressure on the appreciation of RMB exchange rate. They have two major findings: (1) the pressure from the US legislative bodies had significant impacts on the RMB exchange rate whereas the pressure from the US executive authority did not; (2) the external pressure could promote the RMB appreciation in the short run but not in the long run.[55]

Existing studies on the RMB exchange rate within the international influences approach are not without merit, especially insofar as they draw attention to the role of international influences in China's exchange rate policy making, their explanatory utility nonetheless remains circumscribed owing to their competing results, just like the Economics studies. More importantly, because China, unlike Japan in the 1980s, is a more independent geopolitical entity, it has more capacity to resist bowing to the international pressure on its currency. International influences do play some role in the exchange rate policy making of China as an open economy, but the exchange rate decision of China as a large economy is undeniably influenced by China's domestic

[48] Chao and Tung (2013).

[49] Zhu et al. (2015).

[50] Ibid.

[51] Liu and Zhou (2011).

[52] Liu and Pauwels (2012).

[53] Hu and Liu (2013).

[54] Zhang (2013).

[55] Xiao and Pan (2013).

political economy. Therefore, it calls for a synthesized perspective to study China's exchange rate policy making, which combines the IPE and CPE approaches. The fourth theoretical approach focused on international-domestic interactions will be discussed in detail as follows.

2.3.4 *The International-Domestic Interactions Approach*

As a synthesized perspective of the previous three theoretical approaches, the fourth approach attaches importance to the international-domestic entanglements, which is heavily indebted to the theoretical turn of IR studies in the 1990s. The IR theories in the 1970s and early 1980s gave analytical priority to systemic variables such as international system and international institutions whereas downplayed unit-level variables. To cite but a few big names, Gourevitch introduces the notion of "the second image reversed" to emphasize the international sources of domestic politics and argues that the international systems are causes instead of consequences of domestic politics.[56] Waltz, the founder of structural realist theory, analyzes how the anarchic structure of international system explains states' behaviors and interactions therein.[57] In particular, he develops his systemic theory based on the assumption that states are rational and unitary actors only with different military capabilities and he overall neglects the domestic political economy of the unit level.[58] Keohane and Nye, the founders of liberal institutionalist theory, develop the concepts of "complex interdependence" and focus on the roles that international institutions play in helping the rational self-interested states to obtain the collective benefits.[59]

With the end of the Cold War and the increasing globalization of the world economy, IR scholars paid more attention to the heterogeneity of states and examined the interactions between systemic and domestic variables. The late 1980s and 1990s saw a theoretical turn to the combination of international-domestic interaction analysis. Putnam first introduced the two-level game as a metaphor for international-domestic interactions.[60] The two-level game approach "recognizes that central decision-makers strive to reconcile domestic and international imperatives simultaneously".[61] Garrett and Lange recognize the "increasingly anachronistic" IPE-CPE divide and propose to "bridge this divide by using an open-polity model to analyse the mediating effects of domestic institutions between internationally driven changes in the preferences of actors in the private sphere and public policy outcomes".[62] Keohane and Milner edit a volume on "internationalization and domestic politics"

[56] Gourevitch (1978).

[57] Waltz (1979).

[58] Ibid.

[59] Keohane and Nye (1977), Keohane (1984).

[60] Putnam (1988).

[61] Ibid, p. 460.

[62] Garrett and Lange (1995, p. 654).

and generally propose a theoretical framework that internationalization, as the central explanatory variable, affects policy preferences of actors, their national policy and further political institutions within countries.[63] Milner also suggests that states are not unitary actors and that both international and domestic explanations are required for foreign policy making.[64]

The theory of neoclassical realism emerged in the late 1990s and became a mainstream IR theory for foreign policy analysis in the 2000s. As Rose coined the term:

> Neoclassical realism argues that the scope and ambition of a country's foreign policy is driven first and foremost by the country's relative material power. Yet it contends that the impact of power capabilities on foreign policy is indirect and complex, because systemic pressures must be translated through intervening unit-level variables such as decision-makers' perceptions and state structure.[65]

Neoclassical realism focuses on the interaction between international system and internal dynamics of states. More importantly, neoclassical realists take relative power distribution as the independent variable to explain state behavior, while at the same time, they emphasize the process whereby such intervening variables as the perceptions of decision-makers, a country's state apparatus and its relations to the society shape specific policy response to international structural pressure.[66] Neoclassical realism is one of the most widely-used explanatory theories within the international-domestic interactions approach.

Exchange rate policy, as a salient component of foreign economic policies, should have benefited from the insights of international-domestic interactions approach. However, to the author's best knowledge, limited studies of this kind have been done in the existing literature on China's exchange rate policy.[67] Perhaps the reason for this anomaly is that China's exchange rate policy is seen more as an economic policy than a foreign policy. As mentioned before, the focus of the RMB exchange rate has been to measure whether and to what extent the RMB is undervalued, but the economists have generated inconclusive results. Therefore, the research gap of China's exchange rate policy making is prominent, and political scientists are expected to fill it up. It is not uncommon to see such news as China's contest with the US on the currency

---

[63] Frieden and Rogowski (1996).

[64] Milner (1997).

[65] Rose (1998, p. 146).

[66] Ibid. Also, see Lobell et al. (2009), Kitchen (2010), Rathbun (2008), Foulon (2015).

[67] Bowles and Wang argue that three factors could explain why China has been so reluctant to significantly revalue its currency while it stood to the no-devaluation policy in the Asian financial crisis: firstly, the diminished ability of China's policy makers to use the export tax rebate policy to mitigate the effects of a revaluation; secondly, the regional context has changed as time goes by; and thirdly, in the international game of "problem assignment" China refuses to accept that the US trade deficit is its problem. Di argues that both a major shift in China's economic model away from exports and investment towards consumption in the domestic dimension and the promotion of the RMB internationalization programme in the international dimension should be taken into consideration to explain China's continuation of exchange rate system reform since 2010. See Bowles and Wang (2006), Di (2013).

issue and China's concerns with the negative effects of RMB appreciation upon its export sectors, therefore it is hard to argue against that Chinese leaders sit at the juncture of the international system and the state when making exchange rate policy. One cannot fully understand China's exchange rate policy making without reference to interactions between international and domestic levels.

2.4 Summary and Discussions

This section has provided a critical review of CPE and IPE studies on exchange rate politics. In broad terms, the existing theoretical literature on exchange rate politics can be divided into four main approaches: the domestic interests approach, the domestic institutions approach, the international influences approach and the international-domestic interactions approach. Though the domestic interests and domestic institutions approaches within the CPE literature help us to understand the various formation mechanisms of exchange rate policy, their explanatory utility remains circumscribed owing to the fact that the existing studies are Western-centric and inapplicable to China's domestic political and socio-economic structures. Special consideration should be given to China's political institutions characterized by the party-state system and the policy elites and economic ministries within the political structure. Furthermore, the international influences approach within the IPE literature suggests that the international dimension should be well incorporated into China's exchange rate policy analysis. The international-domestic interactions approach, as a synthesized perspective of the CPE and IPE approaches, should have offered more nuanced explanations of China's exchange rate policy making. Nevertheless, limited studies of this kind have been done and the research gap is expected to be filled up.

Additionally, it is worth pointing out that the delineation of the CPE and IPE literature, just like the Economics studies, on exchange rate politics is not exhaustive. For instance, Kettell establishes a theoretical framework based on the "Open Marxist approach" that views exchange rate policy making as:

> a component part of a wider governing strategy that is made by the core executive with a view to containing class struggle, to providing favourable conditions for capital accumulation, and to ensuring a sufficient degree of governing autonomy for the pursuit of high political aims.[68]

More importantly, the executive makes use of the governing strategy of "depoliticisation" to:

> ease pressure on the governing authorities by fragmenting and redirecting class dissatisfaction over economic conditions and policymaking away from the state and into less threatening channels.[69]

thereby enhancing credibility for key economic policy decisions. However, Kettell only applies his theoretical framework to Britain's exchange rate policy making in

[68] Kettell (2004, p. ix).

[69] Ibid, p. 26.

three key episodes—the return to the gold standard in 1925, membership of the European Exchange Rate Mechanism from 1990 to 1992, and the possibility of joining the Single European Currency.[70] He does not mention other country's exchange rate policy making and whether the Open Marxist approach is appropriate to explain China's case.

While the open Marxist depoliticized approach may well have salience in the contexts of other political economies, it does not seem to fit with the aims or tools of the Chinese party-state elite. The lack of independence of China's central bank should be emphasized here. As we shall see subsequently in the book, the PBOC is not a genuinely independent institution like the central banks in the US and the European countries. The PBOC is under the guidance and supervision of the State Council. While there are accounts that recognize PBOC's rising authority in China's party-state system, the fact remains that the PBOC operates under the leadership of the State Council and PBOC's policies, including exchange rate policy without doubt, ultimately serve the goals of China's macroeconomic management.[71] Therefore, the governing strategy of "depoliticisation" that emphasizes lending power to the central bank and enhancing the government's responsibility and accountability does not make real sense in China. In contrast, the Chinese leadership strives to emphasize that the macroeconomic management is under the Party's control, rather than handing power to the market. As Bell and Feng argues,

> The party elite sees the financial section as one of its central concerns in relation to political stability and economic growth and is therefore an extremely sensitive area over which the Party has traditionally been reluctant to relinquish power.[72]

As a result, the PBOC's institutional rise within China's party-state system, at best, means that the Party is trying to promote the idea of a meritocratic and skilled state bureaucracy with different skill sets in different agencies performing functional tasks. However, the book will further demonstrate that the central bank independence is not visible in China's political system, and China's exchange rate reform was a highly-politicized issue rather than a governing strategy of depoliticization. Therefore, the applicability of Kettell's Open Marxist depoliticized approach to explain China's exchange rate policy making is questionable.[73]

To summarize, the above examination has shown that the existing Economics studies on the RMB exchange rate are inconclusive and the existing CPE and IPE theoretical approaches have limitations when applied to China's case. On the one hand, the critical review of the CPE literature suggests that special consideration

---

[70]Ibid.

[71]Bell and Feng (2013). Also, see Sect. 4.3 "PBOC's increasing policy dilemma" as an example of PBOC's subordination within the hierarchy.

[72]Ibid, p. 9.

[73]There is no deny that the Open Marxist approach (or the World System perspective) could explain the US-China economic imbalance. For example, see Wang (2017), Lee (2014). However, the Open Marxist approach sees the executive as a monolithic entity with a single set of policy objectives. The book will demonstrate that it is not true for China's case. It is more useful to closely examined China's political structure and the key institutional actors in China's exchange rate policy making.

should be given to China's political institutions characterized by the party-state system and the policy elites and economic ministries within the political structure. On the other hand, the international influences approach within the IPE literature suggests that the international dimension should be well incorporated into China's exchange rate policy analysis. Therefore, one of the main contributions of this chapter is to identify the research gap in the existing studies of China's exchange rate policy making. A more illuminating analytical framework derived from revision and synthesis of the existing CPE and IPE theoretical approaches will offer better explanations of China's exchange rate policy making. The next section will develop a three-level game framework, which forms the theoretical basis for the subsequent chapters to empirically examine the international political economy of China's exchange rate policy making between 2003 and 2013.

2.5 Theoretical Framework of China's Exchange Rate Policy Making

This section develops a theoretical framework of China's exchange rate policy making based on revision and synthesis of the existing CPE and IPE approaches to exchange rate politics. It will first argue that a two-level game framework would be suitable to explain exchange rate policy making. Then more specific and endemic elements, such as external and domestic actors with different preferences and interests as well as China's political and socio-economic structures, will be added into the theoretical framework. The analysis sheds light on the interactive dynamics of international politics and domestic politics in the formulation of China's exchange rate policy. Finally, the chapter extends Putnam's two-level game to a three-level game and develops a theoretical framework of China's exchange rate policy making. The three-level game framework examines the Chinese leadership's negotiations with the international bargainers at the international level (level I), negotiations between central government's ministries at the central governmental level (level II) and negotiations with the domestic interest groups and local governments at the local level (level III). It argues that the Chinese top leadership strives to reconcile international pressures, domestic ministerial interests and domestic interest groups when making exchange rate policy.

2.5.1 Two-Level Game in Comparison to Neoclassical Realism

As mentioned in the literature review, two-level game and neoclassical realism are two important theories in the international-domestic interactions approach to exchange rate politics. In this part, I will examine these two theories in more depth

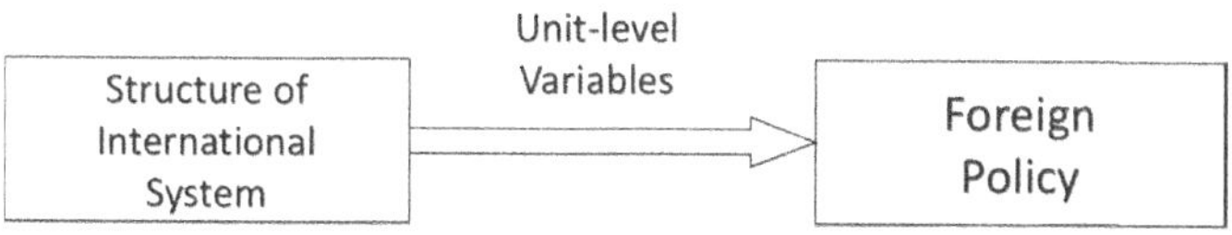

Fig. 2.1 Neoclassical realist framework for foreign policy making

and argue that two-level game is more applicable to explaining exchange rate policy making than neoclassical realism.

The most salient feature of neoclassical realism is that it gives analytical priority to the international structure, which ultimately determines the range of acceptable foreign policies. As Rose explains the basic tenet of neoclassical realism:

> the scope and ambition of a country's foreign policy is driven first and foremost by its place in the international system and specifically by its relative material power capabilities … [T]he impact of such power capabilities on foreign policy is indirect and complex, because systemic pressures must be translated through intervening variables at the unit-level.[74]

It could be seen that, according to neoclassical realists, the structure of international system determines the basic contour of a country's foreign policy and the domestic factors play a secondary role (see Fig. 2.1). This approach is plausible in traditional IR studies, where security studies dominate in foreign policy analysis and survival is seen as the primary motivation of all states in the anarchic international system, but this premise is questionable in the study of IPE issues with strong domestic implications, in part because it neglects the fact that domestic survival of politicians could be as important to decision making as the survival of the state itself—if not more so. This qualification seems to apply in the case of exchange rate policy making.

As discussed, upward or downward shifts in a country's exchange rate and choices of exchange rate regime create both domestic and international winners and losers. Since the first and foremost objective for politicians is to stay in power,[75] exchange rate policy adopted by any top leader will try to ensure that s/he will lead her/his nation at home and on the world stage. On the one hand, for most leaders making exchange rate policies, the implications for their domestic support and power base are very immediate considerations, so their exchange rate policies tend to be framed with the regime's continuity—and often their personal survival—in mind. On the other, the international forces prompting a policy revision are relatively remote. Those disadvantaged in international trade are not very likely to form a serious retaliatory coalition or launch a tightly directed currency war against an exchange rate "offender". The international institutions with responsibility in this arena, notably the IMF, seem incapable of exercising firm surveillance over the exchange rate policies

[74]Rose (1998, p. 146).

[75]Mesquita et al. (2005), also see Brown (2016).

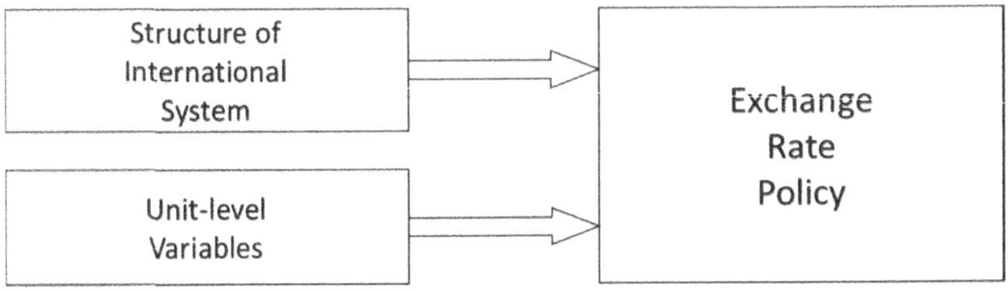

Fig. 2.2 Two-level game framework for exchange rate policy making

of its members.[76] This applies to not only small countries as price takers in the global economy but also large countries especially like China.[77]

Therefore, the claim by neoclassical realists about the fundamental influence of international structure or external factors seems exaggerated or too determining for exchange rate policy making. Compared with neoclassical realism, two-level game that presumes no analytical priority is more suitable to explain exchange rate policy making. The two-level game approach begins by assuming that the policy decision makers are typically trying to do two things, that is, they seek to manipulate international and domestic politics simultaneously. Putnam describes the two-level game in the following way:

> At the national level, domestic groups pursue their interests by pressuring the government to adopt favorable policies, and politicians seek power by constructing coalitions among those groups. At the international level, national governments seek to maximize their own ability to satisfy domestic pressures, while minimizing the adverse consequences of foreign developments. Neither of the two games can be ignored by central decision-makers, so long as their countries remain interdependent, yet sovereign.[78]

This is particularly true for China's exchange rate policy making, for two reasons. First, China is a geopolitically independent state that has a greater degree of freedom in the international system; or at the very least, more autonomy and freedom than many other state actors. Second, China's domestic considerations could at times have greater roles in directing the Chinese leadership's exchange rate policy making, especially when the international environment is relatively stable. Therefore, I suggest the position that the two-level game framework, in which "central decision-makers strive to reconcile domestic and international imperatives simultaneously",[79] could be better suited to explain exchange rate policy making. I make the following assumption in the two-level game framework for China's exchange rate policy making: in theory, though the structure of international system has an impact, the unit-level variables play important influences on policy decision as well (see Fig. 2.2). In practice,

[76] Mussa (2008).

[77] Randall (2006).

[78] Putnam (1988, p. 434).

[79] Ibid, p. 460.

this theoretical framework calls for operationalization to define the variables of international structure and domestic politics into measurable factors and invites further empirical studies to determine under what circumstances what factor(s) mattered in China's exchange rate policy making.

2.5.2 Conceptualizing the External Influences on China's Exchange Rate Policy Making

Based on the insights of the two-level game framework, this part will operationalize the variable of international structure by examining the international influences on China's exchange rate policy making and the next section will deal with the domestic variables.

Influenced by the mainstream tenets of neoliberalism, government officials of the US and other major developed economies as well as the IMF, generally ascribe the international economic imbalance to price distortion, which is the misalignment of exchange rate. Western politicians assert that large amounts of China's current account surplus and foreign reserves indicate that the RMB exchange rate is far away from its equilibrium level. Therefore, officials of Western governments have consistently pressured China to appreciate the RMB at a fast pace and to move as soon as possible to greater flexibility. It will first elaborate the reason for the US-centric approach to examine the external influences and then specifically explore the main actors in the international system that influence China's exchange rate policy making.

Though Japan was the first country to criticize China's currency undervaluation in 2002, the US was subsequently the prominent force pressuring China on its exchange rate policy. Yang, Yin and He described the background of the Chinese currency debate:

> The current bashing of China's currency has gone beyond the United States. At the early stages of the current debate, Japan's Vice Minister for Finance Haruhiko Kuroda accused China of exporting deflation to its neighbors [in 2002]. Japan's Finance Minister Masajuro Shiokawa argued that 'the fact that the (RMB's) exchange rate is extremely low vis-á-vis the U.S. dollar may be a problem' [in August 2003]. Similarly, some European Union government officials also urge China to gradually loosen the Chinese RMB's peg to the dollar.[80]

If we examine China's bilateral trade data with the US, the European Union (EU) and Japan (see Fig. 2.3), it is not difficult to understand the context. China's trade surplus with Japan rose quickly from 0.13 billion dollars in 2000 to 2.27 billion dollars in 2001, which produced Japan's criticism of China's currency undervaluation in 2002. However, the situation changed dramatically after 2002, as China ran persistent trade deficits with Japan from 2002 to 2013. In contrast, China's trade surplus with the US and the EU increased dramatically after 2003. Then America took over Japan's

[80] Yang et al. (2007, p. 127).

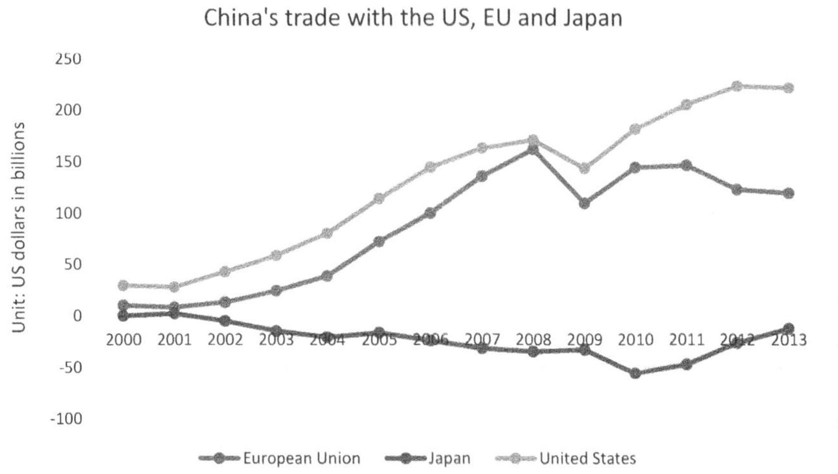

Fig. 2.3 China's trade with the US, the EU and Japan, from 2000 to 2013. *Source* IMF, Direction of Trade Statistics Database

criticism of China's currency. Though attention should also be paid to the EU's pressure on China's exchange rate policy, there are two reasons to focus on the US side. First, the US was the most important source of pressure on China's exchange rate policy, at least in the opinion of many Chinese researchers. For example, Changyong Yang from the NDRC Research Institute of Foreign Economic Relations published a research article, which claimed that "America is the main force to put pressure on the RMB exchange rate, and the Congress, government and interest groups are the troika of the pressure."[81] Second, many Chinese government officials and analysts held the opinion that the EU just followed the US, though that was not always the case as a matter of fact. For instance, Jinbin Wang, a professor of Economics from Renmin University of China, commented that:

> It was a mistake for the EU to follow the US to put pressure on the RMB, and the EU and the US should not use their economic difficulties as an excuse to demand China bear the cost of creating their domestic employment.[82]

Similarly, Wenxing Niu, a famous Chinese financial commentator, made the following remarks:

> The Europe echoed the US's criticism on China's currency, as the Europe and the US shared the common interests. Japan did not follow suit, because Japan had a large trade surplus with China, but Japan would go along with the US in other ways, such as conducting military exercise and making troubles in the Diaoyu Island.[83]

---

[81] Yang (2012).

[82] Sun (2010).

[83] Niu (2010).

Therefore, even though the EU did not necessarily follow the US in practice, it is widely perceived in China that the US was the most important source of pressure on China's exchange rate policy and Europe was very much in a secondary position. The fact that this book is rather US-centric is therefore a consequence of the way that the relative importance of different external actors has been perceived within Chinese academic and policy circles.

First, the US Congress has particular concerns with China's undervalued currency and the US trade deficit with China, which deteriorates the business and employment of the US. After 2003, both senators and representatives proposed that the US should press China to abandon the unfair exchange rate policy and to allow a substantial appreciation of the RMB, thereby generating a long list of bills and resolutions targeting on the RMB issue in the following years (see Appendix A).[84]

Second, the US Department of the Treasury submits reports to Congress on International Economic and Exchange Rate Policies on a semi-annual basis.[85] The Treasury analyses the exchange rate policies of America's major trading partners, and considers whether countries manipulate exchange rate between their currency and the US dollar for the purposes of preventing effective balance of payments adjustments or gaining unfair competitive advantage in international trade. Though the Treasury has never determined China as a currency manipulator since China joined the WTO, it expressed its concerns with the issues of China's trade imbalance and exchange rate in varying degrees during different periods of time. Furthermore, the Treasury Secretary and the US president can raise the RMB issue and impose pressure on China through bilateral and multilateral channels. For instance, the Treasury Secretary invites Chinese Finance Minister and Central Bank Governors of both countries to hold the US-China Joint Economic Committee every year, as a way to engage with China to promote the adoption of a market-based exchange rate.

Finally, the IMF, as a transnational liberal regime, undertakes the duty to "exercise firm surveillance over the exchange rate policies of members, and shall adopt specific principles for the guidance of all members with respect to those policies".[86] The IMF also holds bilateral discussions with China and issues a staff report for the Article IV Consultation usually every year.[87] Though the IMF does not severely criticize the RMB undervaluation, it has always emphasized the need to allow greater flexibility of the RMB exchange rate.[88] The IMF has also argued that the price distortion jeopardizes China's own economy by relying unduly on large scale investment in export

---

[84]For the full database of the U.S. Congress bills and resolutions, see Thomas Library of Congress, available from https://thomas.loc.gov/home/bills_res.html; Also, see Hufbauer and Brunel (2008).

[85]For the full list of Reports on International Economic and Exchange Rate Policies, see U.S. Department of the Treasury Resource Centre, available from https://www.treasury.gov/resource-center/international/exchange-rate-policies/Pages/index.aspx.

[86]IMF, Articles of Agreement of the International Monetary Fund, retrieved from https://www.imf.org/external/pubs/ft/aa/#a4s3.

[87]For the full list of the Article IV Consultation Reports between IMF and China, available from https://www.imf.org/external/np/sec/aiv/index.aspx?listby=c.

[88]See, for example, People's Republic of China: Article IV Consultation Report (2004, 2005, 2006), retrieved from https://www.imf.org/external/country/CHN/index.htm?type=9998#56.

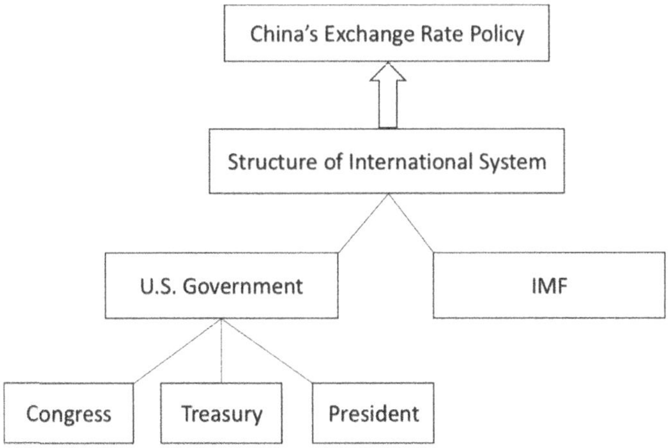

Fig. 2.4 International influences on China's exchange rate policy making

manufacturing while depressing the domestic consumer market, thereby proposing China to embrace greater exchange rate flexibility.[89]

To summarize, the US government (Congress, Treasury and the president) and the IMF are the main actors in the international system in the theoretical framework of China's exchange rate policy (see Fig. 2.4). Considering that China's economic relations with the US are vital to the Chinese economy and China's commitments to the international institutions in the new millennium, these external factors are supposed to exert influences on China's exchange rate policy making.

2.5.3 Opening the Black Box: The Domestic Sources of China's Exchange Rate Policy

Since the Western-centric CPE approaches have their limitations when directly applied to explain China's case, this part specifically examines the domestic institutions of China's exchange rate policy making and explains the key institutional actors as well as interest groups in the political and social-economic structures.

First, I will sketch the political structure of the RMB exchange rate policy making. As mentioned before, the power structure of China's politics is characterized by one-party rule and the party-state system.[90] The CCP is embedded into the leadership, the executive and other wider institutional bodies in China's political structure. According to the CCP Constitution, the Central Committee is the Party's supreme decision-making body, but in practice, the policy decisions of the Central Committee

[89]See, for example, People's Republic of China: IMF Article IV Consultation Report (2006), retrieved from https://www.imf.org/external/pubs/ft/scr/2006/cr06394.pdf.

[90]See, for example, Lieberthal and Oksenberg (1988), Hamrin (1992), Zheng (1997).

Table 2.2 The fifteenth central committee PSC

Hu Jintao	CCP general secretary, PRC president
Wen Jiabao	Statecouncil premier
Wu Bangguo	NPC chairman
Jia Qinglin	Chinese people's political consultative conference (CPPCC) chairman
Zeng Qinghong	PRC vice president
Huang Ju	State council vice premier
Wu Guanzheng	Central discipline inspection commission secretary
Li Changchun	Central commission for guiding cultural and ethical progress secretary
Luo Gan	Central political and legal affairs commission secretary

Table 2.3 The sixteenth central committee PSC

Hu Jintao	CCP general secretary, PRC president
Wen Jiabao	State council premier
Wu Bangguo	NPC chairman
Jia Qinglin	CPPCC chairman
Li Changchun	Central commission for guiding cultural and ethical progress secretary
Xi Jinping	PRC vice president
Li Keqiang	State council vice premier
He Guoqiang	Central discipline inspection commission secretary
Zhou Yongkang	Central political and legal affairs commission secretary

are determined by the Politburo, especially the Politburo Standing Committee (PSC) with a significantly smaller number of the Politburo members.[91] Therefore, the PSC acts as the de facto top leadership body, making key decisions in all major policy spheres. For example, the PSC members in the Hu-Wen era were shown as follows (Tables 2.2 and 2.3).

The PSC's decisions are heavily influenced by information and recommendations provided by a number of research and advisory bodies called Central Leading Groups.[92] The Central Leading Groups are "ad hoc supraministerial coordinating and consulting bodies formed to build consensus on issues that cut across the Party, government and military system when the existing bureaucratic structure is unable to do so."[93] The corresponding group for exchange rate policy is the Central Leading Group for Finance and Economy (CLGFE). The CLGFE, led by either the CCP General Secretary or the Premier (both of them are PSC members), is actually a joint organ of the Politburo and the State Council. The Politburo and the PSC normally

91 Liew (2004, p. 24), Liew and Wu (2007, p. 146).

92 Bell and Feng (2013, p. 49).

93 Zheng and Chen (2015b, p. 67).

rubber-stamp CFELG's decisions because the senior members of the PSC are always also leaders of the CFELG and the State Council.

During the period from 2003 to 2013, Hu Jintao left control of the economy to the premier, Wen Jiabao. Wen was both the chair of CLGFE and the premier of the State Council. The key decisions of financial and economic policies ultimately rested on the CLGFE, and Wen was the final decision maker. However, many observers and political analysts have suggested that Wen was not as dominant in the bureaucracy as his predecessor Zhu Rongji and that there was greater pluralization and institutionalization of economic policy making under Wen.[94] Both the CLGFE and the State Council meetings served as a forum for policy debates and deliberations among the top ministerial leaders. On the one hand, the State Council is the highest executive organ in China's political structure. The State Council supervises and coordinates a number of ministries and commissions.[95] On the other hand, members of CLGFE typically include heads of key ministries in the State Council, particularly PBOC, MOFCOM, NDRC, and Ministry of Finance (MOF). Therefore, the Party leaders and the top bureaucrats can express their views and preferred policies in the CLGFE and the State Council meetings. The State Council meetings are more frequent than the CLGFE meetings, and their functions of policy debates and deliberations overlap from time to time.

With regard to exchange rate policy, the final key decisions are made by Wen, and sources of policy inputs for policy deliberations and decisions are usually from PBOC, MOFCOM, NDRC and MOF. The PBOC and the MOFCOM are the two most important ministries, as they have clear but competing preferences over exchange rate level and flexibility, whereas the NDRC and the MOF do not have as clear preferences. I will elaborate the four ministries' positions on exchange rate policy in more detail as follows.

The PBOC is perceived as an advocate of RMB exchange rate reform. Though the PBOC makes monetary and exchange rate policy announcements, it is not a genuinely independent institution as the central banks in the US and the European countries are. The PBOC is under the guidance and supervision of the State Council. As the central bank, the PBOC has the main duty to maintain the steady price of the RMB. Therefore, the PBOC favors a relatively appreciated RMB to curb imported inflation and more exchange rate flexibility to acquire more monetary policy autonomy. On the other hand, the MOFCOM is an executive agency of the State Council with the main duty to foster China's international economic relations. The MOFCOM has been an opponent of RMB exchange rate reform, as it prefers a depreciated and fixed RMB exchange rate to maintain the competitiveness of export sectors.[96] Both of

[94]See, for example, Mertha (2009), Yi (2011), Han (2013).

[95]For the organizational structure of the State Council, see State Council Organization Chart for more details, available from https://english.gov.cn/state_council/2014/09/03/content_281474985533579.htm.

[96]There is no denying of a counter-argument that the MOFCOM is charged with both internal and external trade. However, the MOFCOM is much more concerned with exports, considering the importance of exports to China's economy and the importance of economic growth to CCP's legitimacy and China's socio-economic stability. There are also studies suggesting that exporters'

these two ministries have their subordinate departments that conduct research and provide inputs for exchange rate policy making, including the State Administration of Foreign Exchange (SAFE) and the MPD supervised by the PBOC as well as the Policy Research Department (PRD) and the local branches supervised by the MOFCOM.

The NDRC is one of the most influential ministries within the State Council. NDRC's primary interest in exchange rate policy is predictability of the economic environment, with a more flexible exchange rate regime potentially complicating that predictability. However, because the NDRC has such a broad mandate to coordinate economic and social development,[97] including maintaining macroeconomic stability and pushing forward strategic economic restructuring, the NDRC tends to take policy positions that are closely in line with the consensus of China's top leadership as a whole.[98] With regard to the MOF, its preference on exchange rate reform is more or less self-conflict. On the one hand, the MOF does not favor RMB undervaluation, because the rising tax rebate with the surging export places heavy burdens on it. On the other hand, as the holder of US Treasury securities, the MOF does not favor RMB appreciation that will lower the value of dollar-denominated debts. Furthermore, Liew and Wu mentioned that the MOF would like to reduce its loans to sub-national governments, but "appreciation of the renminbi will very likely lower the chances of it being successful".[99] The reason was that "renminbi appreciation lowers prices and increases real interest rates, and most of the poor countries struggling to repay MOF loans rely on agriculture, which will be affected adversely by a higher renminbi."[100]

Therefore, the PBOC and the MOFCOM have clear but competing preferences on the RMB exchange rate policy. They are the two most important ministries that provide policy inputs for CLGFE's exchange rate decision-making. It is plausible to assume that the relative power and bargaining game between the PBOC and the MOFCOM are expected to exert significant influences on the RMB exchange rate policy making. Therefore, it would be instructive to compare the political resources of these two institutional actors, such as their administrative rankings and representation in important decision-making bodies. Such comparisons might yield suggestions as to how the relative political clout of these two key ministries could influence China's exchange rate policy choice. Empirical studies will be done in the following chapters.

---

growing leverage in the central government's policy-making process secured the priority and favour given to enhancing China's export competitiveness. See, for example, Kaplan (2006), Hung (2011), Hung (2015).

[97]NDRC, Main Functions of the NDRC, retrieved from https://en.ndrc.gov.cn/mfndrc/.

[98]Each year at the National People's Congress, the NDRC presents a work report alongside the Premier's government work report. To take the year of 2005 for example, Ma Kai (the NDRC Chairman) hewed closely to the formulation that Wen Jiabao had previously institutionalized, claiming to constantly improve the RMB exchange rate formation mechanism and keep the RMB exchange rate stable at a rational and balanced level. The NDRC supported PBOC's advocate of exchange rate reform, but in the meanwhile it repeated MOFCOM's stress of stable exchange rate.

[99]Liew and Wu (2007, p. 205).

[100]Ibid.

Last but not least, though the political space for interest group lobbying in China remains controversial, as a working hypothesis it is plausible to assume that their voices would not be neglected completely in the process of exchange rate policy making. Firstly, the symbiotic relationship between state-owned enterprises (SOEs) and government could provide substantial political resources for SOEs to lobby for their favorite policies.[101] The formal channels of interest representation and informal patronage networks enable SOEs to impose direct influences upon top-level policy deliberation and decision. Secondly, industry associations and private firms, could communicate their preferences to the local governments or bureaucracies such as the local branches of MOFCOM to impose influences on exchange rate policy. Partly, the reason is that the lower-level officials may speak on behalf of these interest groups because their political careers are dependent on the success of their local economy, to which the local industries make a considerable contribution.[102] Perhaps more importantly, given the importance of exports to China's economy and the dominance of urban-industrial elites from coastal regions,[103] the interests and voices of the local enterprises in the export-oriented coastal regions could not be neglected in the process of China's exchange rate policy making. This could be particularly true when China's export sectors faced enormous difficulties in the year of 2008.[104]

To summarize, this section develops an endemic theoretical framework to open the black box of China's domestic exchange rate politics (see Fig. 2.5). China's exchange rate policy is determined by the economic policy executive (CLGFE), comprised of the heads of the Party (PSC) and the Government (State Council). Two key ministries (PBOC and MOFCOM) with competing interests in exchange rate level and flexibility play critical roles in the process of policy initiation and deliberation. Other domestic actors—including SOEs, industry associations, private firms, and some local governments—especially those in the coastal regions could also exert influences in the process of exchange rate policy making.

2.5.4 Extending the Two-Level Game: Three-Level Game of China's Exchange Rate Policy Making

[101]This is particularly true for those SOE heads who also sit in the Central Committee. Furthermore, the CCP issued a cadre exchange policy that encouraged circulation of leaders among SOEs, party organizations and government departments in 2006. See CCP Central Committee, "Party and Government Cadres Exchange Regulations", *Xinhua*, 6 August 2006, retrieved from https://news.xinhuanet.com/politics/2006-08/06/content_4926453.htm.

[102]Steinberg and Shih (2012).

[103]Hung (2011, p. 310).

[104]For instance, China's textile industry was hit hard by the RMB appreciation in early 2008; see "Textile Industry Faces Imminent Danger", retrieved from https://finance.sina.com.cn/blank/cjsd_fzy.shtml. Furthermore, the subsequent empirical study shows that the appeal of policy rescue by the textile enterprises and trade associations reached the MOFCOM and the State Council, which exerted considerable influence on the exchange rate policy making in 2008.

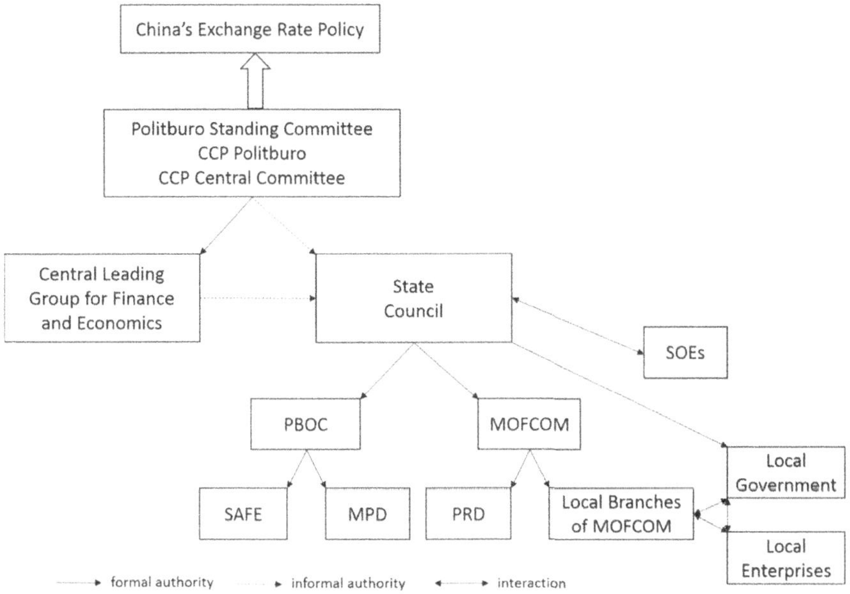

Fig. 2.5 Domestic sources of China's exchange rate policy making

Bringing together the foregoing analysis of both the external and domestic sources of China's exchange rate policy making, this section extends Putnam's two-level game and develops a three-level framework of China's exchange rate policy making. The three-level game sees China's central decision makers as the key agent (CLGFE) uniting international and domestic arenas. In the three-level game framework, China's central decision makers strive to reconcile international pressures, domestic ministerial interests and domestic interest groups when making exchange rate policy. More specifically, the three-level game (see Fig. 2.6) refers to the Chinese leadership's negotiations with the international bargainers (mainly the US government and the IMF) at the international level (level I), negotiations between central government's ministries (PBOC and MOFCOM) at the central governmental level (level II) and negotiations with the domestic interest groups and local governments at the local level (level III).

One may come up with such a question: why it is a three-level game and not a two-level one? The answer is that two-level game conceptualizes the policy making process as negotiations between the international and the domestic, whereas a three-level game further distinguishes the domestic games, assuming that the difference between the two domestic games is so great that it is better conceived of as two separate negotiations, rather than two parts of the same domestic game. This assumption is analytically plausible, but cannot be taken for granted. The explanatory power of the adapted three-level game framework will be empirically applied through an examination of China's exchange rate policy making between 2003 and 2013.

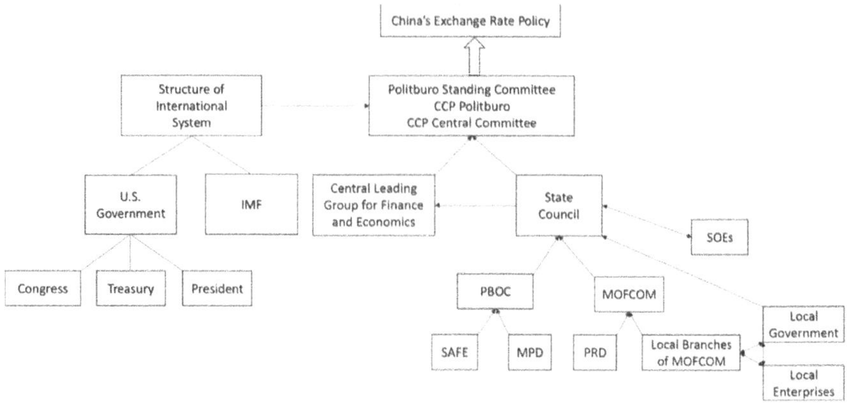

Fig. 2.6 Three-level game of China's exchange rate policy making

To summarize, Putnam's two-level game explores how policy outcomes are affected by the entanglement of domestic factors and international affairs. The above adapted three-level game framework can provide more accurate and contingent explanations for China's exchange rate policy making. It, however, limits generalizability and parsimony of the resulting explanations. It remains a problem as to whether the three-level game framework could be applied to explaining exchange rate policies of other countries. The research scope of this book is limited to China's case, and the problem of theoretical generalizability will probably be dealt with in future comparative studies. The book literally invites further revisions and explanations of the three-level game framework to explain exchange rate policy making of other countries.

2.5.5 Concluding Remarks

As China's economic influence in the world is rapidly increasing, it is essential to understand how the international system and China's domestic politics affect the RMB exchange rate policy making. Neoclassical realists are correct to emphasize that the structure of international system conditions a country's foreign policy choices, but it does not mean that domestic considerations are unimportant or secondary, especially for exchange rate policy making. Instead, the two-level game theory contends that at times domestic factors can exert a decisive influence on exchange rate policy making. The chapter argues that the two-level game theory with no analytical priority presumed is more suitable to explain exchange rate policy making.

More importantly, the chapter has further specifically examined the external factors and domestic sources of China's exchange rate policy making. It develops a three-level game framework that sheds light on the dynamism and complexity of China's exchange rate policy making. The three-level game refers to the Chinese leadership's negotiations with the international bargainers (mainly the US government and the IMF) at the international level (level I), negotiations between central government's ministries (PBOC and MOFCOM) at the central governmental level (level II) and negotiations with the domestic interest groups and local governments at the local level (level III). In a nutshell, China's top leadership strives to reconcile international bargainers, domestic ministerial interests and domestic interest groups when making the RMB exchange rate policy.

It is worth noting that the relative importance of the three level games remains a puzzle in the theoretical framework, which needs to be further examined in the empirical study. In the following chapters, the three-level game framework will be applied empirically through an examination of China's exchange rate policy making between 2003 and 2013. Chap. 3 will explore the initiation of China's exchange rate reform in 2005; Chap. 4 will analyze the subsequent development of the exchange rate reform from 2005 to 2007; Chap. 5 will mainly investigate the interest group politics of China's exchange rate policy making between 2008 and 2010; and Chap. 6 will analyze the resumption of RMB exchange rate reform after June 2010. The empirical studies will present more nuanced explanations of China's exchange rate policy making and shed light on the relative importance of the three level games.

Chapter 3
The RMB Depeg from the US Dollar, 2003–2005

Based on the three-level game framework developed in Chap. 2, this chapter will empirically examine the initiation of China's exchange rate reform in 2005. It shows how the international factors played an agenda-setting role in China's exchange rate policy making from 2003 to 2005 and explains how China's domestic politics determined the pathway of the exchange rate reform.

More specifically, the US government raised concerns with the RMB exchange rate issue after September 2003 and the international criticism and pressure gained substantial momentum in 2005. The growing external pressure on the RMB exchange rate issue forced China's leaders to put exchange rate reform on task list in 2005. The level I game played the important role of agenda-setting, but, more importantly, the level II game produced a compromise between the PBOC and the MOFCOM. Despite PBOC's active advocate for exchange rate reform, Chinese domestic opponents of exchange rate reform, primarily the more political powerful MOFCOM, limited the scope of reform, including the size of the initial appreciation and the speed of subsequent appreciation following the July 2005 announcement.

The empirical study supports the central argument that China's central decision makers were at the nexus of international and domestic politics and reconciled international pressure and domestic bargainers when making the exchange rate policy decision in 2005. The chapter will first discuss the external influences and then examine PBOC's and MOFCOM's respective positions in the exchange rate reform. The level I game and level II game will be combined to explain the Chinese leadership's decision of exchange rate reform policy in July 2005.

3.1 The Emergence of Congress Pressure in 2003

Before examining the emergence of Congress pressure on the RMB issue in 2003, this section begins by introducing some background to China's exchange rate system and international trade relations from 1994 to 2003. China abandoned the dual exchange

Z. Wang, *The International Political Economy of China's Exchange Rate Policy Making*, https://doi.org/10.1007/978-981-33-4578-2_3

rate system and unified the RMB's official and swap market rates to a single official rate in 1994. China adopted a de facto fixed exchange rate regime[1] and kept the RMB closely pegged to the dollar at the rate of 8.28 RMB per dollar from 1995. During the 1997–98 Asian Financial Crisis, China carried out the promise of non-devaluation by keeping the RMB stable and won wide praise in the international community. After that, the nominal value of the RMB vis-à-vis the dollar fluctuated in a very narrow range. China's dollar-pegged exchange rate during the late 1990s and early 2000s seemed no problem. However, the situation changed dramatically after 2002.

The year of 2003 marked a turning point in both China's position in the global trade and finance. China's trade and current account surpluses rose rapidly from 2003, as did its bilateral trade surplus with the US. China's international reserves continued to increase in the 2000s and the growth accelerated after 2003. Furthermore, it was around 2003 when a large number of manufacturing jobs began to be lost in the US and China's exchange rate policy became subject to sustained American pressure. American labor unions and manufacturers contended China's artificially cheap exports hurt US workers and businesses and waged the battle against China's exchange rate policy.[2] As a result, the fourth quarter of 2003 witnessed the sudden emergence of bills and resolutions in the US Congress targeting China's unfair trade practices associated with RMB undervaluation.

On 5 September 2003, Senator Charles Schumer introduced in the Senate the first bill to address RMB manipulation: S.1586 "To authorize appropriate action if the negotiations with the People's Republic of China regarding China's undervalued currency and currency manipulation are not successful".[3] The bill claimed that the RMB was artificially pegged at a significantly undervalued rate to the dollar, which was estimated to be between 15 and 40% or an average of 27.5%. The undervalued RMB made American products more expensive for Chinese consumers and Chinese product cheaper for American consumers, which gave rise to the US trade deficits with China. The bill further asserted that "China's undervalued currency and the United States trade deficit with the People's Republic of China is contributing to significant United States job losses and harming United States businesses."[4] Considering Chinese government's intervention in the foreign exchange market to maintain the undervalued RMB, the bill accused that China had violated the principles of WTO as a member since 2001. Based on these findings, the bill requested that the

[1]In paper China announced to adopt a managed floating exchange rate regime based on supply and demand of foreign exchange market on 1 January 1994, but in practice China tightly managed RMB's peg to the dollar. See "Evolution and China's exchange rate regime", 18 August 2005 *Xinhua*, retrieved from https://news.xinhuanet.com/banyt/2005-05/18/content_2970176.htm; Goldstein and Lardy (2009, p. 6).

[2]See, for example, Hufbauer and Wong (2004), Scott (2010, 2011, 2012).

[3]The U.S. Congress, "S.1586: To authorize appropriate action if the negotiations with the People's Republic of China regarding China's undervalued currency and currency manipulation are not successful", 5 September 2003, retrieved from https://www.congress.gov/108/bills/s1586/BILLS-108s1586is.pdf.

[4]Ibid, p. 2.

President make a certification to the Congress that China would no longer manipulate its undervalued currency to gain an unfair competitive advantage in international trade, and authorized the Secretary of the Treasury to "begin negotiations with the People's Republic of China to ensure that the People's Republic of China adopts a process that leads to a market-based system of currency valuation."[5] An identical bill H. R. 3364 was also subsequently introduced by Representative Sue Wilkins Myrick on 21 October 2003.[6]

Just three days later, on 8 September, Senator Joseph Lieberman introduced S. 1592 Fair Currency Enforcement Act of 2003 "to require negotiation and appropriate action with respect to certain countries that engage in currency manipulation".[7] The bill exemplified China, Japan, South Korea and Taiwan as currency manipulators and highlighted China's particular aggressive intervention in the foreign exchange market. The bill required the Treasury to collaborate with the IMF to determine whether any Asian country was manipulating its exchange rate to prevent effective balance of payment adjustment. Two similar bills, H. CON. RES. 285 and H. R. 3269, were introduced by Representatives Donald Manzullo and John Dingell on 17 September and 8 October respectively.[8]

On 10 September, Representative Phil English followed closely to introduce H. R. 3058 Currency Harmonization Initiative through Neutralizing Action Act of 2003 that required the Treasury to submit a report that analyzed and computed the rate of RMB's misalignment against the dollar.[9] In particular, the bill included a strict clause that the Treasury shall "impose on all products of China that enter the customs territory of United States, in addition to any duty that otherwise applies, a tariff equal to the applicable percentage of the appraised value of the product at the time of entry"

---

[5]Ibid, pp. 4–5.

[6]The U.S. Congress, "H. R. 3364: To authorize appropriate action if the negotiations with the People's Republic of China regarding China's undervalued currency and currency manipulation are not successful", 21 October 2003, retrieved from https://www.congress.gov/108/bills/hr3364/BILLS-108hr3364ih.pdf.

[7]The U.S. Congress, "S. 1592 Fair Currency Enforcement Act of 2003: To require negotiation and appropriate action with respect to certain countries that engage in currency manipulation", 8 September 2003, retrieved from https://www.gpo.gov/fdsys/pkg/BILLS-108s1592is/pdf/BILLS-108s1592is.pdf.

[8]The U.S. Congress, "H. CON. RES. 285: Expressing the concern of the Congress regarding the detrimental impact on the United States economy of the manipulation by foreign governments of their currencies", 17 September 2003, retrieved from https://www.gpo.gov/fdsys/pkg/BILLS-108hconres285ih/pdf/BILLS-108hconres285ih.pdf; The U.S. Congress, "H. R. 3269: Expressing the concern of the Congress regarding the detrimental impact on the United States economy of the manipulation by foreign governments of their currencies", 8 October 2003, retrieved from https://www.congress.gov/108/bills/hr3269/BILLS-108hr3269ih.pdf.

[9]The U.S. Congress, "H. R. 3058 Currency Harmonization Initiative through Neutralizing Action Act of 2003: To require the Secretary of the Treasury to analyze and report on the exchange rate policies of the People's Republic of China, and to require that additional tariffs be imposed on products of that country on the basis of the rate of manipulation by that country of the rate of exchange between the currency of that country and the United States dollar", 10 September 2003, retrieved from https://www.congress.gov/108/bills/hr3058/BILLS-108hr3058ih.pdf.

to offset China's currency undervaluation.[10] An identical bill S.1758 was introduced by Senator George Voinovich on 20 October 2003.

In addition to the above accusations of currency undervaluation and manipulation, three bills in 2003, S. RES. 219, H. RES. 414 and S. RES. 262, further urged the Treasury Secretary to press China to move quickly to a market-based exchange rate regime, either bilaterally or through the IMF.[11] To summarize, there were in total ten Congress bills (see Appendix A) in 2003 to target the RMB issue. The Congress concern imposed unprecedented pressure on the US administration to engage with the Chinese authorities to address the issue, which will be elaborated in more detail as follows.

3.2 The US Administration's Engagements with China, 2003–2004

Before 2003, China's exchange rate regime was not a core issue in American executives' speeches and meetings with Chinese leaders. However, growing concern from the Congress over the American manufacturing unemployment associated with undervalued RMB imposed enormous pressure on the US Administration to take action after 2003. The Treasury's Reports to Congress on International Economic and Exchange Rate Policies was a convincing illustration of the dramatic change of the US government's stances towards China's exchange rate policy. Under the Omnibus Trade and Competitiveness Act of 1988, the Treasury is required to submit Reports to Congress on International Economic and Exchange Rate Policies on a semi-annual basis.[12] The Treasury analyzes the exchange rate policies of America's major trading partners, and consider whether countries manipulate the exchange rate between their currency and the US dollar for purposes of preventing effective balance of payments adjustments or gaining unfair competitive advantage in international trade.

Before September 2003, the Treasury did not consider China's dollar-pegged exchange rate regime as a problem to the US-China bilateral trade relation. All the

---

[10]Ibid, pp. 6–7.

[11]The U.S. Congress, "S. RES. 219: To encourage the People's Republic of China to establish a market-based valuation of the yuan and to fulfill its commitments under international trade agreements", 9 September 2003, retrieved from https://www.congress.gov/108/bills/sres219/BILLS-108sres219ats.pdf; The U.S. Congress, "H. RES. 414: To encourage the People's Republic of China to fulfill its commitments under international trade agreements, support the United States manufacturing sector, and establish monetary and financial market reforms", 28 October 2003, retrieved from https://www.congress.gov/108/bills/hres414/BILLS-108hres414eh.pdf; The U.S. Congress, "S. RES. 262: To encourage the Secretary of the Treasury to initiate expedited negotiations with the People's Republic of China on establishing a market-based currency valuation and to fulfill its commitments under international trade agreements", 6 November 2003, retrieved from https://www.congress.gov/108/bills/sres262/BILLS-108sres262is.pdf.

[12]The U.S. Congress, "H.R.4848: Omnibus Trade and Competitiveness Act of 1988", 16 June 1988, retrieved from https://www.congress.gov/bill/100th-congress/house-bill/4848.

Reports in the 1990s and early 2000s briefly summarized China's economic growth, international trade, fixed exchange rate and capital controls in no more than three paragraphs. With regard to the dollar-pegged exchange rate, the Reports generally used descriptive words or statements and offered no comments. For example, the May 2003 Report described China's exchange rate regime and capital account in the following way: "China maintains a de facto currency peg to the dollar, which it has kept within a tight band since 1995. … China continues to maintain wide-ranging controls on both capital outflows and inflows."[13] The Reports neither appreciated nor depreciated China's dollar-pegged exchange rate and capital control. Therefore, the Reports rarely provided policy recommendations or imposed pressure on China's exchange rate policy. The only anomaly was probably the June 2001 Report, in which "Treasury officials urged China to move, over time, to a more flexible exchange rate regime".[14] Yet such pressure disappeared in the subsequent Reports before September 2003.

In response to the emerging Congress bills on the RMB undervaluation and manipulation in the second half of 2003, Treasury's October 2003 Report marked a difference by dedicating six paragraphs (around one A4 page) to China unprecedentedly. It was the first time that the Report made the explicit statement that the dollar-pegged exchange rate policy was "not appropriate for a major economy like China and should be changed."[15] The Report suggested that greater exchange rate flexibility would not only "allow China greater scope to maintain a low-inflation monetary policy" but also "improve the allocation of resources and the quality of financial intermediation in the Chinese economy."[16]

Since then, China's exchange rate policy has been the main concern in Treasury's Reports. The two Reports in April and December 2004 dedicated around ten paragraphs (no less than one A4 page and a half) to China. Both Reports reiterated the fact that China's fixed exchange rate policy was no longer appropriate and proposed a more flexible exchange rate based on market mechanisms, while they recognized that the exchange rate reform could not be expected to happen overnight and China

[13]U.S. Department of the Treasury, "Report to Congress on International Economic and Exchange Rate Policies", May 2003, retrieved from https://www.treasury.gov/resource-center/international/exchange-rate-policies/Documents/Treasury_ReportToCongressOnInternationalEconomicAndExchangeRatePolicies-2002H2_2003May06.pdf, pp. 4–5.

[14]U.S. Department of the Treasury, "Report to Congress on International Economic and Exchange Rate Policies", June 2001, retrieved from https://www.treasury.gov/resource-center/international/exchange-rate-policies/Documents/Treasury_ReportToCongressOnInternationalEconomicAndExchangeRatePolicies-2000H2_2001Jun22.pdf, p. 14.

[15]U.S. Department of the Treasury, "Report to Congress on International Economic and Exchange Rate Policies, October 2003", retrieved from https://www.treasury.gov/resource-center/international/exchange-rate-policies/Documents/Treasury_ReportToCongressOnInternationalEconomicAndExchangeRatePolicies-2003H1_2003Oct%2030.pdf, p. 7.

[16]Ibid, p. 7.

needed time and steps to lay the groundwork.[17] Accordingly, the Treasury's Reports did not brand China as a currency manipulator as suggested by the Congress bills. It could be seen that the rhetoric of Treasury's Reports on China's exchange rate policy was much less hostile and more advisory than that of Congress bills.

After September 2003, the Treasury actively engaged with the Chinese leadership to hasten and facilitate the move to a flexible market-based exchange rate regime. Secretary Snow travelled to China for discussions with senior Chinese officials on financial issues including exchange rate policy in September 2003. He described the US-China trade relation as win–win, which was completely different from the Congress's zero-sum game logic:

> Our trade with you makes your economy stronger. Your trade with us makes our economy stronger. As our economies are stronger, benefits are extended to the rest of our trading partners. So just as China benefits from our market, U.S. businesses and consumers should benefit from Chinas growth.[18]

Snow expressed the firm belief that exchange rate flexibility was good for both China and the US as well as the regional and global trading partners. However, Snow's pressure remained quite gentle. When explicitly asked whether the RMB was undervalued and its relationship with American manufacturing job loss, Snow avoided answering the question directly and vaguely responded that "the answer is to place your confidence in markets."[19] When asked about the timetable of China's exchange rate reform, Snow cautiously stated that the objective of China's commitment to a more flexible exchange rate was more important than the timetable:

> I don't think it's helpful for us to try to talk about a timetable. I do think it's helpful though to see that reaffirmation of the policy direction, and to see the progress that's being made in the commitment.[20]

As mentioned in the Treasury's Reports, the Treasury recognized that China took time and steps to move to a more flexible exchange rate regime. Snow acknowledged that China was taking concrete steps to modernize its financial infrastructure with the goal of achieving a flexible currency in his statement on the trade relationship between the US and China on 28 April 2004.[21] Based on this understanding, Snow

[17]U.S. Department of the Treasury, "Report to Congress on International Economic and Exchange Rate Policies", April 2004, retrieved from https://www.treasury.gov/resource-center/international/exchange-rate-policies/Documents/Treasury_ReportToCongressOnInternationalEconomicAndExchangeRatePolicies-2003H2_2004%20Apr%2015.pdf, pp. 10–11; U.S. Department of the Treasury, "Report to Congress on International Economic and Exchange Rate Policies", December 2004, retrieved from https://www.treasury.gov/resource-center/international/exchange-rate-policies/Documents/Treasury_ReportToCongressOnInternationalEconomicAndExchangeRatePolicies-2004H1_2004%20Dec%203.pdf, pp. 9–11.

[18]U.S. Department of the Treasury, "Press Roundtable Transcript with Treasury Secretary Snow in Beijing China", 3 September 2003, retrieved from https://www.treasury.gov/press-center/press-releases/Pages/js692.aspx.

[19]Ibid.

[20]Ibid.

[21]U.S. Department of the Treasury, "Statement by Treasury Secretary John W. Snow on US-China Trade Relationship", 28 April 2004, retrieved from https://www.treasury.gov/press-center/press-releases/Pages/js1483.aspx.

publicly opposed the retaliatory tariffs in the RMB-related bills introduced in the Congress. Snow maintained that "the most effective way at this time to achieve the goal of a flexible, market-based exchange rate in China is to maintain the persistent engagement we have established rather than through a trade petition. Economic isolationism does not work and it's a path we will not follow."[22]

In practice, the Treasury also worked with China to identify and overcome the impediments to greater exchange rate flexibility. The Treasury appointed a senior financial expert to serve as Secretary Snow's emissary in Beijing.[23] The role of the financial ambassador was to ensure close communications on exchange rate and other financial issues between Beijing and Washington. Moreover, the Treasury launched the technical cooperation programme and held three sessions with Chinese officials in 2004. The meetings dealt with the creation of market mechanisms necessary for a flexible exchange rate regime, including but not limited to banking supervision, development of financial instruments and foreign reserve management.[24]

With regard to the US president, one can identify a similar trend. No mention of China's exchange rate policy was made in speeches or press briefings before September 2003.[25] From September 2003 onwards, President Bush started to frequently raise the RMB issue in a similar way to Secretary Snow. He stressed the desirability of flexible exchange rates but said little to explicitly criticize Beijing's currency manipulation and unwillingness of revaluation. The consistent objective of the Bush administration was to maintain engagements with China, rather than to forcibly pressure China, to push forward exchange rate reform.

Besides the US government, the IMF could also exert influences on China's exchange rate policy, as one of IMF's duties is to "oversee the international monetary system in order to ensure its effective operation" and to "oversee the compliance of each member with its obligations".[26] In the 2004 Article IV Consultation Report, the IMF staff held the view that it was difficult to find persuasive evidence that the RMB was substantially undervalued. They emphasized that greater exchange rate flexibility would enhance China's ability to pursue an independent monetary policy and adjust to shocks. However, they also realized that Chinese authorities faced a dilemma of exchange rate reform: a small initial appreciation could exacerbate the

---

[22] Ibid.

[23] U.S. Department of the Treasury, "Secretary Snow appoints Ambassador Paul Speltz as economic and financial emissary to China", 14 April 2004, retrieved from https://www.treasury.gov/press-center/press-releases/Pages/js1325.aspx.

[24] U.S. Department of the Treasury, "Report to Congress on International Economic and Exchange Rate Policies", December 2004, https://www.treasury.gov/resource-center/international/exchange-rate-policies/Documents/Treasury_ReportToCongressOnInternationalEconomicAndExchangeRatePolicies-2004H1_2004%20Dec%203.pdf, p. 10.

[25] The White House, "Speeches and Remarks of the White House", https://www.whitehouse.gov/briefing-room/speeches-and-remarks; The White House, "Press Briefings of the White House", https://www.whitehouse.gov/briefing-room/press-briefings.

[26] IMF, "Articles of Agreement of the International Monetary Fund", retrieved from https://www.imf.org/external/pubs/ft/aa/#art4.

speculative capital inflows, while a larger initial move would probably have a negative impact on employment.[27] Therefore, the IMF's stance toward China's exchange rate remained rather cautious and prudent until 2004.

In summary, the surge of US trade deficit with China in 2003 and the rise of unemployment in the US manufacturing sector caused considerable concern in the US over the RMB exchange rate, which was considered to give an unfair trade advantage to China. From then on, Congressmen introduced bills against China's currency regime in the US Congress. They called for substantive RMB revaluation in the short run and marked-based exchange rate in the long run. Treasury Secretary Snow and US President Bush have also repeatedly raised this issue and insisted on the need to move to greater exchange rate flexibility. Even though they put sustained pressure on China, the US administration took a rather cautious and gentle stance. They emphasized the constructive and collaborative approach adopted by Chinese and American leaders. The external influences of the US government played an agenda-setting role, which rendered China's leaders unable to avoid the RMB exchange rate issue. The international attention to the RMB exchange rate issue forced the Chinese leadership to put exchange rate reform on the policy agenda. However, to explain the pathway and timing of China's exchange rate reform, one needs to further explore China's domestic politics. The next two sections will examine the two key institutional actors (PBOC and MOFCOM) in the level II game respectively.

3.3 PBOC as an Outspoken Advocate for Exchange Rate Reform

The most important institutional actor advocating the RMB exchange rate reform was the PBOC, the central bank of China. One of the central arguments of PBOC's officials was that exchange rate flexibility would provide Chinese authorities with additional tools to control excessive monetary supply and inflationary pressure.

The primary advocate for a more flexible RMB exchange rate was Zhou Xiaochuan, PBOC's governor from December 2002 to 2016. Before that, Zhou served as the vice-governor of PBOC from 1991 to 1995, the director of SAFE from 1995 to 1998, the governor of China Construction Bank from 1998 to 2000, and the chairman of China Securities Regulatory Commission from 2000 until his appointment as the governor of PBOC in 2002.[28] Zhou was widely regarded both inside and outside the Chinese bureaucracy as a financial reformer or liberal who actively advocated for reform and liberalization of China's financial system.[29] Zhou held the firm belief that China's tightly managed and closed financial system could not be sustainable

---

[27] IMF, "People's Republic of China: 2004 Article IV Consultation Report", 5 November 2004, retrieved from https://www.imf.org/external/pubs/cat/longres.aspx?sk=17828.0.

[28] People's Bank of China, "Zhou Xiaochuan", retrieved from https://www.pbc.gov.cn/hanglingdao/128697/128719/index.html.

[29] See, for example, "Zhou Xiaochuan: An economist to govern the central bank", *People's Daily*, 1 January 2008, retrieved from https://paper.people.com.cn/dd/html/2008-01/01/content_39049474.htm; Jamil Anderlini, "Zhou Xiaochuan, Beijing's central radical banker", *Financial Times*, 14

and should be gradually reformed. He was quoted within a People's Daily article discussing the advantages of a floating exchange rate system over a fixed one:

> A fixed exchange rate is like a shield in the hand when you are fighting; however you attack me, I will remain unmoved; if I fail to hold on, the impact will cause influence. A floating exchange rate is like a foam-rubber cushion, if you want to fight your way in, I will react softly, ok, you've come in, but I will not let you hit me; when you want to quit, I will give you a pinch and let you go only after you have taken a layer of your skin off.[30]

When asked how to address the issue of fixed RMB exchange rate before Snow's visit in September 2003, Zhou aptly put it: "if all countries agree that the Asian financial crisis has passed and all the problems left by the crisis have been sorted out, China would consider moving the RMB towards a free-floating currency and improve its formation mechanism of the foreign exchange rate."[31] Zhou's reply hinted that China's stance on the exchange rate was not invariable but contingent, which provided the first glimpse of an opening position.

Furthermore, in the 2004 spring meetings of the IMF and the World Bank Group, Zhou exchanged views with Snow on RMB exchange rate reform. Zhou made public remarks that "greater exchange rate flexibility of RMB exchange rate was a medium to long-term goal of the Chinese authorities."[32] In the 2004 annual meetings of the IMF and the World Bank Group, when asked what was the direction and objective of RMB exchange rate reform, Zhou stated that it was "to improve the RMB exchange rate mechanism and maintain the RMB exchange rate at a reasonable and equilibrium level."[33] When requested to further explain the policy objective, he specifically interpreted that "to improve the RMB exchange rate mechanism meant greater exchange rate flexibility and a reasonable and equilibrium level meant market-based exchange rate aiming at international balance of payment."[34] In short, the PBOC under Zhou made consistent efforts towards deepening reforms and opening up in the financial and monetary domains.

In addition to the voices of PBOC's leader, the central bank is assisted by the MPD, which serves as an advisory and deliberate body to bring in outside academic expertise and incorporate representatives of other ministries on the critical issues in China's

---

August 2015, retrieved from https://www.ft.com/cms/s/0/53ba324c-41cd-11e5-b98b-87c7270955cf.html#axzz3rkDOUOdG.

[30] "RMB exchange rate reform–decided out of China's own need", *People's Daily*, 29 July 2005, retrieved from https://en.people.cn/200507/29/eng20050729_199105.html.

[31] "Zhou Xiaochuan elaborates on three conditions for the free floating RMB exchange", *SINA Finance*, 4 September 2003, retrieved from https://finance.sina.com.cn/g/20030904/0750432690.shtml.

[32] "Zhou Xiaochuan: Greater exchange rate flexibility as medium to long-term goal of RMB exchange rate", *China News*, 25 April 2004, retrieved from https://www.chinanews.com/n/2004-04-25/26/429775.html.

[33] "Zhou Xiaochuan on financial macro-regulation and RMB exchange rate", *Xinhua*, 2 October 2004, retrieved from https://news.xinhuanet.com/stock/2004-10/02/content_2047358.htm.

[34] Ibid.

monetary policy making.[35] MPC reserves one of the thirteen seats for an academic member and Professor Yu Yongding's appointment as the financial expert of MPC is a typical example to demonstrate PBOC's reformist orientation.[36] Yu served as the Director of the Institute of World Economics and Politics at the Chinese Academy of Social Sciences. He was widely known as a consistent proponent of RMB exchange rate reform. He boldly promoted RMB appreciation and a more flexible exchange rate regime even in the year of 2003 when China faced growing international pressures for RMB revaluation. Yu was one of the few scholars who advised to eliminate RMB appreciation phobia and move to balanced economic development.[37] Yu pointed out the increasingly heavy cost of foreign exchange sterilization in order to perpetuate the fixed exchange rate and pushed for a more flexible exchange rate regime.[38]

Furthermore, at the Davos World Economic Forum in early 2005, Yu commented to reporters that the time was right for China to revalue the RMB and move to greater flexibility. However, after that the PBOC immediately announced that Yu's remarks were purely personal and academic opinions which did not represent central bank's policy, and that the current RMB exchange rate policy would remain unchanged.[39] One cannot simply assume that the PBOC did not support Yu's viewpoint. In nature, PBOC's announcement implied that, on the one hand, the Chinese authority did not intend to reveal the timetable of the exchange rate reform in order to minimize hot money inflow that would take advantage of RMB appreciation and that, on the other hand, there were still struggles in the process of China's domestic exchange rate policy making. Chinese domestic opponents of exchange rate reform, primarily the more political powerful MOFCOM, will be examined in the following section.

3.4 MOFCOM as a Powerful Opponent of Exchange Rate Reform

PBOC's promotion of RMB exchange rate reform encountered with strong opposition from the MOFCOM. The MOFCOM succeeded Ministry of Foreign Trade and Economic Cooperation and merged with the former State Economic and Trade Commission into a ministry mandated to oversee both domestic and foreign trade and investment in 2003. According to Frieden's sectoral model of exchange rate politics, non-tradable and import-competing sectors favor flexible exchange rate, whereas

[35] People's Bank of China, "PBOC Monetary Policy Department Ordinance", retrieved from https://www.pbc.gov.cn/huobizhengceersi/214481/214543/214782/2847827/index.html.

[36] People's Bank of China, "Personnel adjustment of PBOC Monetary Policy Department", 3 September 2004, retrieved from https://www.pbc.gov.cn/bangongting/135485/135491/135597/1002313/index.html.

[37] Yu (2003).

[38] Yu (2004).

[39] "Closed-door debate of G7 Meeting: Jin Renqing and Zhou XiaoChuan fight against the demonization of RMB", *SINA Finance*, 2 February 2005, retrieved from https://finance.sina.com.cn/g/20050202/14521342990.shtml.

tradable and export sectors prefer fixed exchange rate.[40] Analytically the MOFCOM incorporates a diverse and inherently contradictory set of interests in relation to the RMB exchange rate. However, practically the MOFCOM placed importance on exports and minimized the negative impact of RMB revaluation and appreciation on export enterprises, given the fact that the export sectors remained a vital engine for China's economic growth in the 2000s. Therefore, the MOFCOM took a firm stand against substantial revaluation and fast appreciation of the RMB exchange rate.

MOFCOM's officials consistently argued that the stability of RMB exchange rate was crucial for China's export and manufacturing industries and that dramatic change would lead to bankruptcy of many export enterprises and economic slowdown, which could further undermine social stability. The first Minister of Commerce is Lü Fuyuan from March 2003 to December 2004. After he took office, Lü stressed that currency policy adjustment should be based on the domestic situation of a nation,[41] which implies that China's exchange rate policy would not be subject to external pressure. At a press conference following the closing of the 5th Asia-Europe Economic Ministers' Meeting, Lü declared that China's current major task was to maintain stable economic growth and that China would maintain the value of its currency.[42] Furthermore, the MOFCOM stressed that China should learn a lesson from Japan's experience of fast yen appreciation from 1985 to 1995, which was part of the reason that Japan fell into economic recession in the following years.[43]

Due to health conditions, Lü retired early and was succeeded by Bo Xilai. Bo Xilai was named the Minister of Commerce in late February 2004 and in office from March 2004 to December 2007. As the son of Bo Yibo, one of China's revolutionary elders, Bo Xilai was often regarded as a princeling who had much more political influence in China's politics.[44] Bo's public statements on the exchange rate issue were relatively sparse in 2004, probably for the reason that the momentum for exchange rate reform did not begin to build significantly until early 2005. However, Bo Xilai was undoubtedly very influential in meetings within the State Council.[45] The MOFCOM under Bo made an extremely loud voice to maintain the stable exchange rate and limit the scope of reform in the first half of 2005, which will be elaborated in more detail subsequently.

---

[40] Frieden (1991, 1994).

[41] "Minister of Commerce Lv Fuyuan: renminbi adjusts based on own goals", *SINA Finance*, 27 July 2003, retrieved from https://finance.sina.com.cn/g/20030727/1150383441.shtml.

[42] Ministry of Commerce, "China to maintain stability of RMB yuan: Minister", 25 July 2003, retrieved from https://english.mofcom.gov.cn/aarticle/newsrelease/commonnews/200307/20030700112290.html.

[43] See, for example, Ministry of Commerce, "Observation: the experiences and lessons of the yen's appreciation for Chinese RMB", 5 August 2003, retrieved from https://sanfrancisco.mofcom.gov.cn/article/ztdy/200308/20030800114857.shtml; Ministry of Commerce, "Lessons from yen appreciation", 18 December 2003, retrieved from https://www.mofcom.gov.cn/article/s/200312/20031200161190.shtml.

[44] Ramzy (2010).

[45] "Bo Xilai appears on Asia's most influential people list", *People's Daily*, 18 December 2009, retrieved from https://en.people.cn/90001/90776/90882/6846512.html.

3.5 Re-Emergence of External Pressure on RMB Undervaluation in 2005

With Bush administration's extensive engagements with China's senior officials, the year of 2004 was a relatively calm year for Congressmen's battle with China's exchange rate. There were only two bills and resolutions (H. R. 4986 and H. CON. RES. 498) targeting China's currency in 2004 and both bills essentially did not add new point to the bills of 2003.[46] The reason behind this was probably that Chinese leaders adopted a constructive and collaborative approach to address the RMB exchange rate issue with the Bush administration in 2004.

In September 2004, the Treasury held the 16th US-China Joint Economic Committee meeting in Washington. Wen Jiabao declared that China would "further advance the reform and forge a mechanism which is more adapted to the changes in market supply and demand, with still better flexibility."[47] In the communiqué of the Joint Economic Committee meeting, China "reaffirmed its commitment to further advance reform and to push ahead firmly and steadily to a market-based flexible exchange rate."[48] Zhou Xiaochuan also referred to the movement to a flexible exchange rate as a top priority issue for China. All of these indicated that China would adopt a more flexible exchange rate regime in the near time. Based on these positive messages, Snow made the public remarks that "the progress China is making toward a more flexible, market-based exchange rate demonstrates that the Administration's engagement with China is yielding results."[49]

However, the Chinese leadership did not actually reach the internal consensus of exchange rate reform as it looked like from the outside. Though the international community widely deemed China to be prepared for the exchange rate reform in late 2004, China offered no timetable all along and hesitated to initiate any significant move. Worse still, shortly after the announcement of Joint Economic Committee

---

[46]The U.S. Congress, "H. R. 4986: To require the Secretary of the Treasury to analyze and report on the exchange rate policies of the People's Republic of China, and to require that measures consistent with the obligations of the United States under the World Trade Organization be taken to offset any disadvantage to United States producers resulting from China's exchange rate policies", 22 July 2004, retrieved from https://www.congress.gov/108/bills/hr4986/BILLS-108hr4986ih.pdf; The U.S. Congress, "H. CON. RES. 498: Urging the President to take immediate steps to establish a plan to adopt the recommendations of the United States-China Economic and Security Review Commission in its 2004 Report to the Congress in order to correct the current imbalance in the bilateral trade and economic relationship between the United States and the People's Republic of China, 23 September 2004", retrieved from https://www.gpo.gov/fdsys/pkg/BILLS-108hconres498ih/pdf/BILLS-108hconres498ih.pdf.

[47]U.S. Department of the Treasury, "Report to Congress on International Economic and Exchange Rate Policies", December 2004, retrieved from https://www.treasury.gov/resource-center/international/exchange-rate-policies/Documents/Treasury_ReportToCongressOnInternationalEconomicAndExchangeRatePolicies-2004H1_2004%20Dec%203.pdf, p. 10.

[48]Ibid.

[49]U.S. Department of the Treasury, "Treasury efforts yielding results on China currency", 9 September 2004, retrieved from https://www.treasury.gov/press-center/press-releases/Pages/js1897.aspx.

statement, Li Ruogu, a deputy governor of PBOC, claimed that "China has an 8000-year history" and "a decade is truly a short period" in the meeting of G7 finance ministers, who for the first time invited China to join.[50] Li's remarks suggested that China provided no time frame and the RMB exchange rate reform could be postponed indefinitely. The shifting position of Chinese officials gave rise to the re-emergence of Congress bills targeting the RMB issue.

The Congress set off another wave of targeting China's exchange rate policy in the first half of 2005. There were totally twelve bills concerning China's currency in 2005, eleven of which were introduced before 21 July 2005 (see Appendix A). The number of bills and resolutions targeting the RMB issue and the pressure from the Congress reached its apex. Particularly, three bills (S. 14, S. 295 and H. R. 1575) included a punitive measure that a rate of 27.5% duty would be imposed on all China's products imported directly or indirectly into the US if China did not revalue its currency.[51] As it might lead to serious trade conflicts between the US and China, this could be taken as a significant escalation of the currency dispute between Washington and Beijing. Furthermore, the bill H. R. 1498 Chinese Currency Act of 2005 was introduced on April 6 to clarify that China's currency manipulation was actionable, considering China had given no indication of any intent to correct the RMB's undervaluation in the foreseeable future.[52]

With enormous pressure from the Congress, the Bush administration also became increasingly critical of China's delayed move, which could be seen from the blunter words of Treasury Secretary's statement and Treasury's Reports. Snow warned "China's rigid currency regime has become highly distortionary" and urged China to move to a more flexible system as soon as possible.[53] The Treasury's May 2005 Report claimed that China's exchange rate policy was distortionary and detrimental to China's economy itself, its trading partners and the global economy, which means that China's exchange rate policy became the focal point of not only the US but

---

[50]"Inviting China to dinner", *The Economist*, 4 October 2004, retrieved from https://www.economist.com/node/3258391.

[51]The U.S. Congress, "S. 14 Fair Wage, Competition, and Investment Act of 2005: To provide fair wages for America's workers, to create new jobs through investment in America, to provide for fair trade and competitiveness, and for other purposes", 24 January 2005, retrieved from https://www.congress.gov/109/bills/s14/BILLS-109s14is.pdf; The U.S. Congress, "S. 295: To authorize appropriate action if the negotiations with the People's Republic of China regarding China's undervalued currency are not successful", 3 February 2005, retrieved from https://www.congress.gov/109/bills/s295/BILLS-109s295is.pdf; The U.S. Congress, "H. R. 1575: To authorize appropriate action if the negotiations with the People's Republic of China regarding China's undervalued currency are not successful", 12 April 2005, retrieved from https://www.congress.gov/109/bills/hr1575/BILLS-109hr1575ih.pdf.

[52]The U.S. Congress, "H. R. 1498 Chinese Currency Act of 2005: To clarify that exchange-rate manipulation by the People's Republic of China is actionable under the countervailing duty provisions and the product-specific safeguard mechanisms of the trade laws of the United States, and for other purposes", 6 April 2005, retrieved from https://www.congress.gov/109/bills/hr1498/BILLS-109hr1498ih.pdf.

[53]U.S. Department of the Treasury, "Statement of Secretary John W. Snow on the FOREX Report", 17 May 2005, retrieved from https://www.treasury.gov/press-center/press-releases/Pages/js2449.aspx.

also the international community. Moreover, the Treasury threatened that China would "likely meet the statute's technical requirements for designation", if it did not substantially reform its currency policy.[54] This was probably the most severe critic and warning of China's dollar-pegged exchange rate policy in the Treasury's Reports since 1994. Furthermore, from this report onwards, China's exchange rate policy was systematically analyzed at the beginning of the report as a "key finding".

Finally, like the US administration, the IMF adopted an increasingly tough stance towards China's currency practice. IMF's proposal on the RMB exchange rate reform was much more straightforward in 2005 than before. In the 2005 Article IV Consultation Report, the IMF particularly emphasized that an early move would be desirable given that China's economy was currently quite strong and further delay would entail additional costs to China's economy. In response to China's concerns about the impact on China's economy, the IMF staff changed the view of 2004 and argued in 2005 that the effects on growth and employment of an initial change in the RMB exchange rate were likely to be moderate.[55] Additionally, IMF staff and Chinese authorities shared the view that greater flexibility, not simply a revaluation, remained a key objective for the exchange rate reform.

To summarize, the re-emergence of external pressure on RMB undervaluation in the first half of 2005 brought China's exchange rate policy to a focal point of the international community. Chinese leaders were under so immense pressure from both the US and the IMF that the old exchange rate regime was seemingly unsustainable. However, to fully explain the final outcome of 2005 exchange rate reform, one needs to examine more closely how the internal political struggle influenced top leaders' decision-makings in China.

3.6 China's Internal Political Struggle Before 21 July 2005

When the momentum for exchange rate reform began to build significantly in early 2005, the MOFCOM made a loud voice for maintaining the stable exchange rate and limiting the scope of reform. Minister Bo persistently made two arguments to preserve fixed exchange rate and oppose fast appreciation.

The first argument was that exchange rate appreciation would be counterproductive to China's exports and manufacturing industries. It was reported that if theRMB were to rise by 3–5% in 2005 against the dollar, the growth rate of China's exports might drop to 10% or below; a rise of 15% or more might cause its export growth

[54]U.S. Department of the Treasury, "Report to Congress on International Economic and Exchange Rate Policies", May 2005, retrieved from https://www.treasury.gov/resource-center/international/exchange-rate-policies/Documents/Foreign%20Exchange%20Report%20May%202012.pdf.

[55]IMF, "People's Republic of China: 2005 Article IV Consultation Report", 17 November 2005, retrieved from https://www.imf.org/external/pubs/cat/longres.aspx?sk=18709.0.

to go into decline.[56] The RMB revaluation would also increase the risks of international investment in China[57] and transfer the manufacturing plants to other more competitive countries in Asia,[58] which would dampen China's economic growth.

The second argument was that the profit margins in export industries were low and any pace of annual RMB appreciation above the low single digits would push a significant share of export firms into a money-losing position, resulting in significant job losses and potential social instability. In this sense, Bo insisted that the one-off revaluation of the RMB with substantial appreciation was by no means a feasible policy option. Therefore, Bo strongly advised the central government to remain cautious about the RMB exchange rate reform.[59]

Bo's tough stance towards the RMB exchange rate issue was reflected not only in domestic policy deliberations but also in international negotiations. In the APEC Trade Ministers' Meeting in early June 2005 Bo argued that Europe and America's link between China's textile exports and RMB revaluation made the issues more complicated and controversial.[60] He also declared that China would not yield to trade protectionism from American and European counterparts.[61] Peter Mandelson, European Commissioner for Trade from 2004 to 2008, admitted that Bo was a tough negotiator with good negotiating tactics and strong personal characteristics after China and the EU reached a textile agreement on 10 June 2005, which prevented a potential textile trade war between China and the EU.[62] Furthermore, faced with growing international pressures that pushed China to revalue its currency to address the trade imbalance, the MOFCOM under Bo consistently responded that RMB appreciation would not solve the problem of the US trade deficit.[63]

---

[56] "National Bureau of Statistics official: RMB appreciation will lead to a substantial decline of export", *China News*, 11 May 2005, retrieved from https://www.chinanews.com/news/2005/2005-05-11/26/572505.shtml; Yi (2011).

[57] Ministry of Commerce, "Japanese multinational enterprises most worried that China would revalue the yuan", 28 January 2005, retrieved from https://www.mofcom.gov.cn/article/i/jyjl/j/200501/20050100340375.shtml.

[58] Ministry of Commerce, "Retail manufacturers moved to India under RMB appreciation pressure", 24 May 2005, retrieved from https://www.mofcom.gov.cn/article/i/jyjl/j/200505/20050500098484.shtml.

[59] "Bo Xilai said the government was to be cautious about the RMB exchange rate reform", *SINA Finance*, 4 May 2005, retrieved from https://finance.sina.com.cn/g/20050504/081045839.shtml.

[60] "Bo Xilai asserted the textile trade should not be linked with RMB appreciation", *SINA Finance*, 3 June 2005, retrieved from https://finance.sina.com.cn/g/20050603/08311652628.shtml.

[61] "Bo Xilai's strongly-worded statement: China will not accept the wrong logic of the Europe and America", *SINA Finance*, 3 June 2005, retrieved from https://finance.sina.com.cn/20050603/1016102971.shtml.

[62] "The EU Commissioner for Trade Peter Mandelson: Bo Xilai is a tough negotiating partner", *Xinhua*, 13 June 2005, retrieved from https://news.xinhuanet.com/fortune/2005-06/13/content_3077026.htm.

[63] Ministry of Commerce, "The US trade deficit will not decrease even if the RMB appreciates", 25 April 2005, retrieved from https://www.mofcom.gov.cn/article/i/jyjl/j/200504/20050400080169.shtml; Ministry of Commerce, "RMB appreciation will not reduce the US trade deficit", 11 May 2005, retrieved from https://www.mofcom.gov.cn/article/i/jyjl/l/200505/20050500087898.shtml.

It is also worth noting that though the MOFCOM strongly advocated for the interests of export sectors, at this stage there were few signs of direct lobbying from export enterprises.[64] The exporters were earning handsome profits from the continuous export growth thanks to the exchange rate stability during this period of time.[65] Therefore, China's internal battles over the RMB exchange rate reform were generally behind closed doors in the central government.

Chinese top leaders sat at the juncture of international and domestic politics of the RMB exchange rate reform. Internationally, the intense criticism and pressure rendered the RMB exchange rate an inevitable issue that needed action. Domestically, the PBOC advocated a more flexible exchange rate for more monetary autonomy, while the MOFCOM, with more political clout, maintained that exchange rate stability was crucial for China's growth and employment. Under these circumstances, the Chinese leadership swung back and forth, with the difficulties to reconcile the interests of all parties, in formulating the exchange rate reform policy.

First, on the one hand, Chinese leaders were committed to embracing a more market-based exchange rate regime but on the other hand they were also concerned with the possible negative effects that reform would incur. In his Report on the Work of the Government at the NPC in 2005, Wen Jiabao committed to promote the exchange rate reform, which was not in the Report of 2004, while pledged to "keep the RMB exchange rate basically stable at an adaptive and equilibrium level".[66]

Second, on the one hand China began to reform the financial institutions and prepared for greater exchange rate flexibility in 2004, but on the other hand China's senior officials, including those of PBOC, repeatedly insisted that no specific timetable or schedule would be provided with regard to the RMB exchange rate reform.[67] When asked about the reform plan and the first change of RMB exchange rate at a press conference in March 2005, Wen dodged to answer the question directly and vaguely responded that it would come from the unexpected.[68]

Last but not least, on the one hand Chinese top leaders had made public commitments to carry out exchange rate reform to ease the international tension in 2004, but on the other hand they would not like to show any sign of weakness under international pressure. Wen emphasized that China would not be subject to external

---

[64]For more details see the case study on interest group lobbying in the Fujian province in Chap. 5.

[65]Steinberg and Shih (2012).

[66]Wen (2004, 2005).

[67]See, for example, "SAFE Director Guo Shuqing: no timetable for RMB exchange rate reform", *SINA Finance*, 6 March 2005, retrieved from https://finance.sina.com.cn/g/20050306/09581406822.shtml; "Zhou Xiaochuan said China may accelerate RMB appreciation but currently offered no timetable", *SINA Finance*, 25 April 2005, retrieved from https://finance.sina.com.cn/g/20050425/081232734.shtml.

[68]"Full transcript of Premier Wen Jiabao", *Xinhua*, 14 March 2005, retrieved from https://news.xinhuanet.com/newscenter/2005-03/14/content_2696724.htm.

pressure to revalue the RMB on various occasions.[69] He even further asserted that RMB revaluation was an issue that involved China's sovereignty:

> RMB exchange rate reform is China's sovereignty. Each country has the right to choose the exchange rate regime and the reasonable level based on its own national conditions. We follow the law of market economy, but by no means yield to external pressure. Any pressure, hype, or politicization of economic issue will not help to solve the problem. We will take the initiative to promote the exchange rate reform as long as the conditions are met, even if there is no external pressure; we will not act rashly if the conditions are not met, even faced with enormous external pressure.[70]

One should not consider Chinese top leaders' wavering over exchange rate reform as betokening their strategic uncertainty or inconsistency. It, at most, reflected that Chinese top leaders faced challenges to balance the interests of both international and domestic bargainers and remained cautious about the RMB exchange rate reform. This argument could be supported by Wen's three principles of China's exchange rate reform, which later became a consensus among the Chinese leadership. As Wen noted, the RMB exchange rate reform must adhere to the three principles of own initiative, controllability and gradualism.[71] Own initiative means that the timing and substance of RMB exchange rate reform should be based on China's national conditions; controllability means that exchange rate reform should be under control to prevent financial market turmoil and economic volatility; and gradualism means that the reform must proceed step by step instead of going too fast.

3.7 Explaining the Outcome: China's Exchange Rate Reform on 21 July 2005

Change eventually came on 21 July 2005. Approved by the CLEFG and the State Council, the PBOC announced that China would implement a managed floating exchange rate regime based on market demand and supply with reference to a basket of currencies. Furthermore, the RMB exchange rate against the dollar was revalued from 8.28 to 8.11, with a 2.1% appreciation. The daily trading price of the dollar against the RMB in the inter-bank foreign exchange market will be allowed to float within a band of $\pm$ 0.3% around the central parity published by the PBOC.[72]

---

[69] "Wen Jiabao reiterated that China would not be subject to external pressure to revalue the RMB", *Xinhua*, 30 November 2004, retrieved from https://news.xinhuanet.com/fortune/2004-11/30/content_2275409.htm.

[70] "Wen Jiabao: exchange rate reform is China's sovereignty and not subject to external pressure", *Xinhua*, 17 May 2005, retrieved from https://news.xinhuanet.com/fortune/2005-05/17/content_2964746.htm.

[71] "Wen Jiabao stressed the three principles of RMB exchange rate reform", *Xinhua*, 27 June 2005, retrieved from https://news.xinhuanet.com/fortune/2005-06/27/content_3140594.htm.

[72] People's Bank of China, "Public Announcement of the People's Bank of China on Reforming the RMB Exchange Rate Regime", 21 July 2005, retrieved from https://www.pbc.gov.cn/zhengcehuobisi/125207/125217/125922/125945/2816977/index.html.

This policy outcome should be interpreted as Chinese top leaders' reconciliation between the international and domestic bargainers. The US government raised concerns with the RMB exchange rate issue after September 2003, and the international criticism and pressure gained substantial momentum in 2005. The international attention played an agenda-setting role, which means that it made China's top leaders unable to avoid the RMB exchange rate issue. The growing external pressure on the RMB exchange rate issue forced the Chinese leadership to put exchange rate reform on task list in 2005. However, to explain the pathway of China's exchange rate reform, one needs to further explore China's domestic politics.

Two key ministries with competing preferences were divided internally in the State Council. PBOC's officials were particularly interested in the exchange rate reform, which would endow them with more monetary policy autonomy. This proposal was mitigated by two obstacles. One was financial and short-term. In 2004, PBOC's consideration was mitigated by the difficulties that an appreciation and more flexibility needed to meet the prerequisites of banks' capital adequacy, disposition of non-performing loans and development of financial instruments in the interbank foreign exchange market. The other was political and long-term. The MOFCOM, with their constituencies within China's state-owned enterprises and the more politically powerful Minister Bo Xilai, was considered far more influential over the central government's decision-making than the PBOC.

Chinese domestic opponents of exchange rate reform, primarily in the MOFCOM, limited the scope of reform, including the size of the initial appreciation and the speed of subsequent appreciation following the July 2005 announcement. As a result of compromise, PBOC's wish for exchange rate flexibility was granted, but the MOFCOM won key ground as well. The initial RMB appreciation was limited to 2.1% against the dollar and the pace of subsequent appreciation was to be relatively stable and slow. In retrospect, the compromise of the 2005 RMB exchange rate reform was typical of China's consensus-oriented leadership style, which has been discussed in the part of the nature of China's politics in the Hu-Wen era in the introduction.

To summarize, this chapter has shed light on the policy process and decision of China's exchange rate reform in 2005. The empirical study supports the key argument that China's central decision makers were at the nexus of international and domestic politics and reconciled international pressure and domestic bargainers when making the exchange rate policy decisions in 2005. Specifically, international influences played an agenda-setting role in the 2005 exchange rate reform. However, the international influences were strongly mitigated by China's domestic politics. China's ministerial politics, in which the MOFCOM was more politically powerful than the PBOC, determined the limited nature of exchange rate reform. The RMB depeg from the US dollar in July 2005 was a watershed in China's exchange rate policy. The next chapter will further examine the subsequent development of the exchange rate reform from July 2005 to 2007.

Chapter 4
The Faltering RMB Exchange Rate Reform, 2005–2007

The Chap. 3 has elaborated how international factors played an agenda-setting role in China's exchange rate policy making and explained how China's domestic politics determined the timing and pathway of the exchange rate reform in July 2005. The limited scope of the initial exchange rate reform was the result of a compromise between the two key ministries (PBOC and MOFCOM), which typically reflected China's consensus-oriented leadership in the Hu-Wen era.

This chapter will further examine the subsequent development of the exchange rate reform from July 2005 to 2007. It is argued that with softened international pressure and MOFCOM's sustained resistance against RMB appreciation from July 2005 to 2006, the gradually and continuously appreciated RMB exchange rate ultimately eroded PBOC's monetary policy autonomy. However, the situation changed dramatically in 2007. Internationally, external pressure for accelerated RMB appreciation regained momentum. Domestically, the MOFCOM also shifted priority from maintaining export growth to reducing excessive trade surplus owing to the large amounts of trade frictions in 2006. Under the circumstances, the PBOC was endowed with more political space for advocating exchange rate reform. The Chinese leadership finally accepted PBOC's recommendation to regard inflation as the most severe problem to tackle and to use currency appreciation as a tool to fight inflation. The daily RMB-dollar trading band was expanded in mid-2007 and the RMB appreciated at a faster pace in the fourth quarter of 2007.

This chapter reaffirms the central argument of the previous chapter, namely that the Chinese leadership was at the nexus of international and domestic politics and reconciled international pressure and domestic bargainers when making exchange rate policy decisions. The chapter will examine the evolution of both the international pressure and the domestic bargaining game between the MOFCOM and the PBOC after the July 2005 exchange rate reform announcement. As with Chap. 3, the level I game and level II game will be combined to explain the Chinese leadership's decision in regard to exchange rate policy from 2005 to 2007.

Z. Wang, *The International Political Economy of China's Exchange Rate Policy Making*, https://doi.org/10.1007/978-981-33-4578-2_4

4.1 Softened International Pressure from July 2005 to 2006

After China announced the exchange rate reform on 21 July 2005, the Congress's pressure on China's currency waned gradually. There were two bills after the announcement in 2005 and only one bill in 2006 to target the RMB issue.

The first bill, H. R. 3283 the United States Trade Rights Enforcement Act, introduced on 28 July was a revised bill of 14 July. Similar to the previous bills in the first half of 2005, the 14 July bill condemned China's currency manipulation and urged China to move to market-based exchange rate regime. By contrast, the 28 July bill changed the rhetoric and remarked that China's transition to a more flexible exchange rate was "a welcome move" and "positive development".[1] The bill also required the Treasury to further investigate China's exchange rate mechanisms, including the basket of foreign currencies and the degree to which the RMB moved to the market-based value. The other bill (S. RES. 270) on 6 October 2005 continued to urge the IMF to investigate whether China was manipulating the exchange rate between the yuan and the dollar.[2]

The only bill related to the RMB in 2006 was the United States Fair Currency Practices Act of 2006 (S. 3992). The bill clarified the definition of exchange-rate misalignment, elaborated the way to determine whether exchange-rate misalignment was occurring and mandated the corresponding measures of Treasury and President.[3] While the 2006 bill still highlighted China's massive intervention in the foreign exchange market to keep its currency undervalued, it did not include any strict clause such as retaliatory tariffs on China's products, like those in 2005.

Even though the Congress became less concerned with China's currency after the 21 July 2005 announcement, the Treasury kept a close eye on the subsequent development of China's exchange rate reform. The November 2005 Report commended China's 21 July announcement to initiate the market-determined currency reform in the key findings, but it also pointed out that "China's actual operation of its new system was highly constricted".[4] Specifically, the Report found that the new RMB exchange rate mechanism remained a tightly managed currency peg against the dollar, as the initial adjustment was small, the subsequent movements of the RMB were limited

---

[1]The U.S. Congress, "H. R. 3283 United States Trade Rights Enforcement Act: To enhance resources to enforce United States trade rights", 28 July 2005, retrieved from http://www.gpo.gov/fdsys/pkg/BILLS-109hr3283eh/pdf/BILLS-109hr3283eh.pdf.

[2]The U.S. Congress, "S. RES. 270: Expressing the sense of the Senate that the International Monetary Fund should investigate whether China is manipulating the rate of exchange between the Chinese yuan and the United States dollar", 6 October 2005, retrieved from https://www.congress.gov/109/bills/sres270/BILLS-109sres270is.pdf.

[3]The U.S. Congress, "S. 3992 United States Fair Currency Practices Act of 2006: To amend the Exchange Rates and International Economic Policy Coordination Act of 1988 to clarify the definition of manipulation with respect to currency, and for other purposes", 28 September, retrieved from https://www.congress.gov/109/bills/s3992/BILLS-109s3992pcs.pdf.

[4]U.S. Department of the Treasury, "Report to Congress on International Economic and Exchange Rate Policies", November 2005, retrieved from https://www.treasury.gov/resource-center/international/exchange-rate-policies/Documents/112005_report.pdf, p. 2.

and the currency basket seemed not to play a significant role. The Report repeated the proposal that more exchange rate flexibility was necessary to give China a sufficiently autonomous and effective monetary policy to sustain growth and avoid inflation.

Subsequent Reports confirmed the 2005 November Report's observation that China's actual operation was not consistent with its 21 July announcement of exchange rate reform. For example, the 2006 May Report recognized that on the one hand, Chinese leaders made firm commitment and delivered clear statements to move towards a more flexible exchange rate; on the other hand, they consistently emphasized the gradual adjustments in managed RMB exchange rates. Therefore, the Treasury closely monitored the progress made on China's exchange rate regime and continued the intensive engagement with China in 2006.[5]

With regard to the IMF, one can also identify a trend whereby less pressure was placed on China's exchange rate policy in 2006. In the 2006 Article IV Consultation Report, the IMF recognized that Chinese government had undertaken several reforms to deepen the foreign exchange market though they emphasized that exchange rate reform would have to be gradual and controllable. The IMF advocated greater exchange rate flexibility and aimed to address China's concern with the potential negative impact of substantial appreciation on China's economy. On the one hand, the staff did not accept the analogy that China would embrace a lost decade like Japan in the manner that a significant RMB appreciation could push the economy into deflation and prolonged recession. On the other hand, the staff stressed that exchange rate flexibility, not just appreciation, was imperative for China's economic rebalancing. Greater flexibility of exchange rate would also contribute to the sustainability of China's growth by helping to the rebalance the economy over the medium term.

To summarize, though the Treasury was not satisfied with the pace of China's exchange rate reform and maintained the engagements with the Chinese leadership, international pressure from the Congress and the IMF on the RMB exchange rate generally decreased from July 2005 to 2016. It reinforced the argument that international factors played an agenda-setting role in China's exchange rate policy making while China's domestic politics determined the pathway of the exchange rate reform. In other words, external pressure was strongly mediated by the domestic institutions. The next two sections will respectively examine the relationships between the two key ministries (MOFCOM and PBOC) and the subsequent exchange rate reform.

---

[5]U.S. Department of the Treasury, "Statement of Treasury Secretary John W. Snow before the Senate Committee on Banking, Housing, and Urban Affairs on International Economic and Exchange Rate Policies", 18 May 2006, retrieved from https://www.treasury.gov/press-center/press-releases/Pages/js4271.aspx.

4.2 MOFCOM's Sustained Resistance Against RMB Appreciation, 2005–2006

After the initial 2.1% revaluation on 21 July 2005, the RMB appreciated 0.5%, from 8.11 to 8.07, against the dollar until the end of 2005. The 0.5% appreciation in the latter half of 2005 was definitely slow, and many observers even asserted that it was almost negligible. However, this section shows that both the PBOC and the MOFCOM kept a close eye on the impact of RMB appreciation on China's exports. This implies that the Chinese leadership took a very cautious approach toward the exchange rate reform.

The PBOC closely monitored the impact of exchange rate reform on export enterprises in the second half of 2005. The PBOC conducted monthly questionnaire surveys to investigate the impact of the 21 July revaluation and subsequent RMB appreciation. According to the 2005 Third Quarter Monetary Policy Implementation Report, the exchange loss of the sample enterprises owing to the initial 2.1% appreciation was 130 million RMB, which accounted for a modest 0.013% of the enterprises' sales revenues in the same period.[6] The negative impact of RMB appreciation on exports was also limited, with only 6.6% of the sample enterprises cutting down export production and 13.7% transferring exports to domestic sales.[7] 2005 Fourth Quarter Monetary Policy Implementation Report found that enterprises were generally adapted to the new exchange rate regime, as exports and export orders continued to grow and most enterprises used various exchange rate hedging instruments to eliminate their foreign exchange risks.[8] The report concluded that the new RMB exchange rate formation mechanism operated smoothly after 21 July, and the RMB exchange rate remained basically stable at a reasonable and adaptive level, in accordance with the State Council's deployment.

The conclusion of PBOC's report did not come as a surprise, considering the slow pace of RMB appreciation. However, PBOC's optimism about the RMB exchange rate reform was challenged by the MOFCOM. The MOFCOM took into account the comparative performances of export enterprises before and after the exchange rate reform announcement. Since the initial revaluation was modest and the subsequent appreciation was very slow, China's exports maintained the momentum in the second half of 2005. However, the Minister of Commerce Bo Xilai asserted that the RMB appreciation actually stimulated imports but restrained exports. Bo cited statistics of exports and imports to support his argument:

---

[6] People"s Bank of China, "2005 Third Quarter Monetary Policy Implementation Report", 9 November 2005, http://www.pbc.gov.cn/eportal/fileDir/history_file/files/att_11618_1.pdf, p. 12.

[7] Ibid, p. 13.

[8] People's Bank of China, "2005 Fourth Quarter Monetary Policy Implementation Report", 21 February 2006, http://www.pbc.gov.cn/eportal/fileDir/history_file/files/att_11619_1.pdf, pp. 14–16.

China's import increased by 15% in the first 7 months of 2005 while the increase surged to 20% in the following 5 months; but for export, the increase was 30% in the first 7 months whereas the increase was 24.7% in the following 5 months.[9]

More importantly, the MOFCOM was particularly concerned with the several export industries that were sensitive to RMB appreciation. The MOFCOM recognized that the RMB appreciation imposed different impacts on different enterprises. More specifically, the enterprises that procured raw materials in the domestic market and exported products to the international markets were most sensitive to currency revaluation.[10] Textile and apparel enterprises were the typical industries that encountered enormous challenges. Immediately after the announcement of exchange rate reform, there was a forecast report estimating that with every 1% of RMB appreciation, the profit of cotton textile industry would fall about 12%, wool textile industry 8%, and apparel industry about 13%.[11] At the end of 2005, statistics showed that the growth rate of textile exports had been in decline, and the MOFCOM claimed that "the continuous RMB appreciation was a real threat to exports."[12] The MOFCOM took a rather firm stance towards the negative impacts of RMB appreciation on textile industries within the Chinese bureaucracy. MOFCOM's voice did count in the Chinese leadership, and consequently the State Council instructed the Tariff Policy Department under the MOF to stop taxing on textile export to relieve the pressure of textile exporters from 1 January 2006.[13]

Furthermore, Bo continued to be a vocal opponent of fast RMB appreciation in 2006. While being interviewed by the Japanese media during the Sino-Japanese Forum on Energy-Saving Cooperation, Bo made public remarks that "RMB appreciation has substantially lowered the profit of export-oriented enterprises, especially labour-intensive ones, whose profit was already very low."[14] He took the textile industry, whose profitability was just 3%, as an example to argue that RMB appreciation had put many Chinese enterprises in a difficult position.[15] Furthermore, the MOFCOM Policy Research Department formed a research group to systematically

[9]"How will RMB exchange rate reform affect trade?", *People's Daily*, 2 June 2006, retrieved from http://en.people.cn/200606/02/eng20060602_270674.html.

[10]Ministry of Commerce, "Different impacts of RMB exchange rate change on enterprises", 2 December 2005, retrieved from http://www.mofcom.gov.cn/article/resume/n/200512/20051200939621.shtml.

[11]"Textile industry faces imminent transformation", *Xinhua*, 21 July 2005, retrieved from http://news.xinhuanet.com/fortune/2005-07/21/content_3247487.htm.

[12]Ministry of Commerce, "Unfavourable situation for textile export", 30 December 2005, retrieved from http://pep.mofcom.gov.cn/article/guonyw/bt/200512/20051201239070.shtml.

[13]Ministry of Finance, "End to tax on textile exports from next year", 14 December 2005, retrieved from http://www.mof.gov.cn/zhengwuxinxi/caijingshidian/xinhuanet/200805/t20080519_22347.html.

[14]"How will RMB exchange rate reform affect trade?", *People's Daily*, 2 June 2006, retrieved from http://en.people.cn/200606/02/eng20060602_270674.html.

[15]"Bo Xilai: RMB appreciation caused many Chinese textile enterprises to get into trouble", China Internet Information Center, 1 June 2006, retrieved from http://www.china.com.cn/chinese/news/1225973.htm.

study the impacts of RMB appreciation in 2006. Though the study report recognized the role that RMB appreciation played in external and internal rebalancing, it stressed the disastrous effects of fast and substantial appreciation on China's exports. The main finding of the study report was that 3% RMB appreciation would not seriously affect China's international trade, as long as the appreciation was kept modest and under control.[16]

Though the MOFCOM strongly advocated for the interests of export sectors, there were still few signs of direct lobbying from export enterprises after the announcement of exchange rate reform. China's overall export maintained momentum and exporters did not pay close attention to the slowly appreciating exchange rate. The domestic economy was growing quickly at the rate of 12.7% in 2006.[17] Moreover, tradable producers were making additional profits from investing in China's booming real estate and stock markets. For instance, the stock market entered a period of hypergrowth, which saw the Shanghai Stock Exchange Composite more than double in the year of 2006.

The pace of RMB appreciation was slightly faster in 2006 because there was no enormous decline in China's exports as opponents had feared since the 2005 exchange rate reform. Nevertheless, the total appreciation was still small and the exchange rate flexibility was also limited, faced with the strong and consistent resistance from MOFCOM. The RMB appreciated 3.2% in total, from 8.07 to 7.81, against the dollar in 2006. Except for the initial 2.1% revaluation, the RMB appreciated 3.7% in total against the dollar from July 2005 to the end of 2006.

4.3 PBOC's Increasing Policy Dilemma

Compared with MOFCOM, the PBOC was politically weaker and less influential in China's top leadership. This section will elaborate that the PBOC faced rising challenges from rapid expansion of domestic money supply in the process of RMB exchange rate management. The limited nature of the RMB exchange rate reform produced little change in the economic fundamentals that had induced the PBOC to favor additional flexibility in the first place. As the central bank, PBOC's major duties are formulating and implementing monetary policy to control inflation and maintaining the RMB exchange rate at stable and adaptive level.[18] However, one of the most daunting challenges confronting the PBOC in the first decade of the new millennium was the inherent contradiction within these two main duties. The

---

[16]Ministry of Commerce, "Impact of renminbi appreciation on China's international trade", 25 August 2006, retrieved from http://www.mofcom.gov.cn/article/resume/n/200608/20060802972660.shtml.

[17]The economic growth rate of 12.7% in 2006 is the second highest in the twenty-first century (14.2% in 2007 as the highest), according to the National Bureau of Statistics of the People's Republic of China.

[18]People's Bank of China, "About PBC", retrieved from http://www.pbc.gov.cn/publish/english/952/index.html.

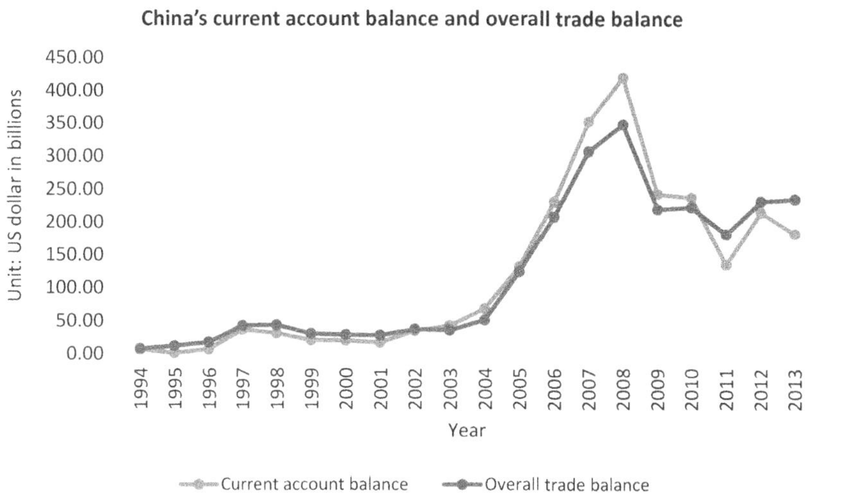

Fig. 4.1 China's current account balance and overall trade balance, from 1994 to 2013. *Source* IMF, Balance of Payments Statistics & Direction of Trade Statistics

key argument of this section is that the preservation of a gradually and continuously appreciated RMB exchange rate ultimately eroded PBOC's monetary policy autonomy, under the circumstance that China ran persistent current account surpluses.

The explanation of the causal mechanism should start from China's foreign exchange system. In November 1993, the Third Plenum of the Fourteenth CCP Central Committee approved a comprehensive reform package in which foreign exchange management reform was highlighted as a key element for the socialist market economy. After 1 January 1994, the foreign exchange retention regime was abolished and replaced by the foreign exchange surrender and purchase system.[19] Firms were required to surrender their foreign exchange earnings from current account transactions and purchase foreign exchange from a foreign exchange designated bank when a payment in foreign currency was needed. Foreign-funded enterprises were also included in the foreign exchange surrender and purchase system after 1996. Furthermore, a national inter-bank foreign exchange market was established to link all the designated banks and to terminate the foreign exchange swap business in the local and unlinked swap centers. In particular, the PBOC determined a benchmark rate that reflected the market conditions, and all designated foreign exchange banks could only buy and sell foreign exchange within a certain band above or below this benchmark rate. The new foreign exchange system enhanced the effectiveness of the central bank's market intervention and capacity of foreign exchange accumulation.

China kept running persistent current account surpluses after 1994 (see Fig. 4.1).

---

[19]Lou (1997).

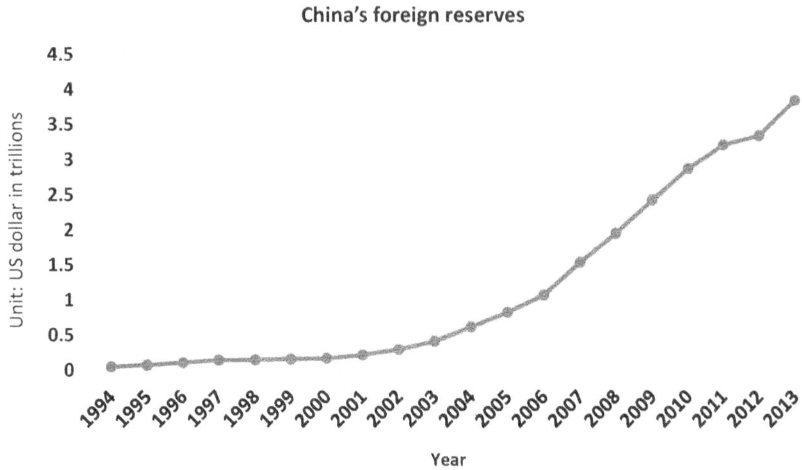

Fig. 4.2 China's foreign reserves, from 1994 to 2013. *Source* IMF, International Financial Statistics

With the foreign exchange surrender and purchase system, China accordingly accumulated foreign reserves (Fig. 4.2). Both the current account surplus and foreign reserve grew at a relatively slow speed before 2000. However, the growth accelerated dramatically in the new millennium. After China joined the WTO in 2001, China experienced a sharp increase in both current account surplus and capital inflows. To keep the RMB exchange rate fixed or gradually appreciated against the dollar, the PBOC needed to intervene massively in the foreign exchange market, selling the RMB and buying the dollar. However, in doing so, it directly increased the base money, which is called the position for forex purchase.[20] Figure 4.3 shows that the position for forex purchase continued to increase in the first decade of the twenty-first century.

According to the equation of money supply, money supply equals base money times money multiplier. The growing position for forex purchase was considered as passive money supply, as it was not under the control of the central bank but subject to the supply and demand of currencies in the foreign exchange market. To prevent the expansion of position for forex purchase from giving rise to high inflation or overheating, the PBOC must engage in sterilization operations in the domestic money market. PBOC's sterilization typically referred to two tools of monetary policy, open market operations and reserve requirement ratio. These two monetary policy tools and the corresponding money supply will be examined as follows to demonstrate that the regime of limited exchange rate flexibility and the pathway of continued gradual appreciation actually implies a cost in terms of loss of control over domestic monetary policy. The PBOC faced increasing dilemma to simultaneously

[20]People's Bank of China, "Financial term: position for forex purchase", 16 September 2013, retrieved from http://wuhan.pbc.gov.cn/wuhan/123527/614607/index.html.

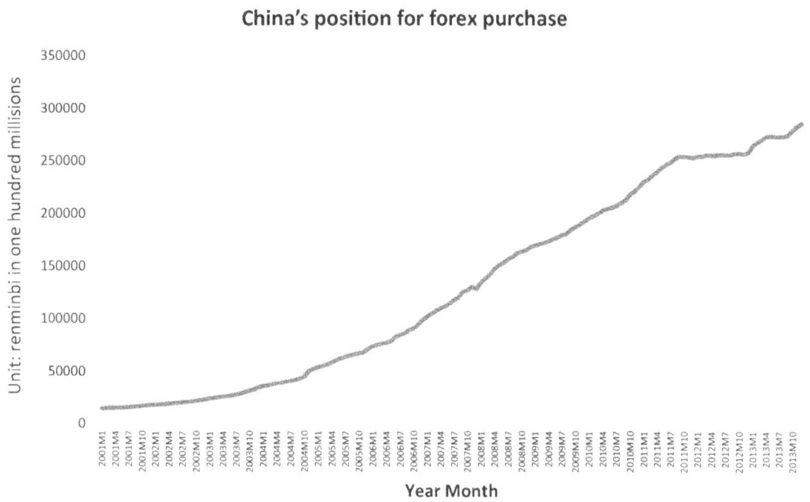

Fig. 4.3 China's position for forex purchase, from 2001 to 2013. *Source* PBOC Financial Survey and Statistics Department

manage both the RMB exchange rate and domestic money supply during this period of time.

The traditional open market operation of PBOC refers to repo transaction and spot bond trading.[21] The former includes repo and reverse repo in the primary market. PBOC's repo would sell securities to commercial banks, thus reducing reserves in the banking system and tightening money supply, and then after a specified period of time repurchase the securities and inject liquidities. On the contrary, reverse repo would initially add reserves and later drain them. The latter includes PBOC's spot bond purchase and spot bond sale in the secondary market. The spot bond purchase would directly inject base money to the market, while the spot bond sell would withdraw.

Although repo transaction and spot bond trading were highly flexible and effective in adjusting the base money, they were ultimately constrained by the limited amounts of securities and bond assets held by the central bank, which could not meet up with the increasing demand for sterilization of position for forex purchase after 2002.[22] Therefore, the PBOC invented a new tool for open market operation: the central bank bill. Central bank bills are short-term bonds (with term to maturity no more than three years, usually no more than one year) issued by PBOC in the national

[21]Repo is short for repurchase agreement, which is a transaction concluded on a deal date between two parties. Spot bond trading refers to a contract of buying or selling bonds on the spot date.

[22]People's Bank of China, "Monetary Policy Implementation Report 2003Q2", retrieved from http://www.pbc.gov.cn/zhengcehuobisi/125207/125227/125957/126021/2835159/201509081057 2487467.pdf.

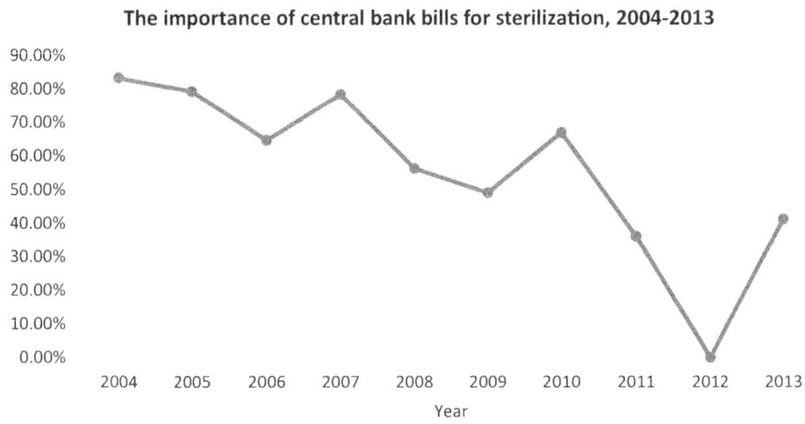

Fig. 4.4 The importance of central bank bills for sterilization, from 2004 to 2013. *Source* Author's own elaboration based on PBOC's open market operation announcements

inter-bank bond market.[23] On 24 September 2002, the PBOC converted all the undue repo, in the form of PBOC's assets held by commercial banks, to central bank bills, in the form of PBOC's liabilities. It was manifestly stated that the purpose of PBOC's conversion was to make more room for repo in future open market operations.[24] More importantly, on 22 April 2003, the PBOC began to directly issue central bank bills, which means the PBOC formally sought to sterilize the position for forex purchase through the issuance of central bank liabilities.[25] After this, the central bank bills were used as the main open market operation for sterilization of position for forex purchase, while spot bond trading was seldom used and repo transaction was used as supplementary short-term liquidity managements (see Appendix B).

If we denote the importance of central bank bills for sterilization as the proportion of central bank bill issuance in the total open market operations to drain liquidity, we may see from Fig. 4.4 that the values were all above 60% before 2008, which implies that the central bank bills played a pivotal role in the time period.

In addition to open market operations, it is also necessary to examine the required reserve ratio to grasp the full picture of PBOC's monetary policy implementation. The adjustment of required reserve ratio changes the amount of funds available for commercial banks to make loans with, which affects both base money and money

[23]Ibid, pp. 4–5.

[24]People's Bank of China, "Monetary Policy Implementation Report 2002Q4", retrieved from http://www.pbc.gov.cn/zhengcehuobisi/125207/125227/125957/126024/2899201/2015090810535810379.pdf.

[25]People's Bank of China, "Monetary Policy Implementation Report 2003Q2", retrieved from http://www.pbc.gov.cn/zhengcehuobisi/125207/125227/125957/126021/2835159/2015090810572487467.pdf; "Zhou Xiaochuan: open market operations play an important role", *Xinhua*, 16 June 2006, retrieved from http://news.xinhuanet.com/fortune/2005-06/15/content_3086465.htm.

multiplier. Therefore, the required reserve ratio adjustment causes more immediate and intense effects on money supply.

Western central banks generally prefer open market operations to required reserve ratio (actually it is rarely used) in terms of money supply adjustment. However, the PBOC used required reserve ratio as a frequent and regular tool for money supply adjustments after 2005 (see Appendix C). The PBOC altered (raised) the required reserve ratio three times in 2006, ten times in 2007, eight times in 2008, six times in 2010 and seven times in 2011. The required reserve ratio climbed from 7.5% in mid-year 2006 to an unprecedented 21.5% in mid-2011. The extremely unusual adjustments of required reserve ratio implied that the open market operation alone could not meet up with the increasing demand for sterilization of position for forex purchase. In retrospect, Zhou Xiaochuan made it clear that the main tasks and challenges of China's monetary policy in the twenty-first century were to manage the exchange rates by intervention in the foreign exchange rate market and to sterilize excess liquidity by open market operations and required reserve ratio adjustments simultaneously, but what he did not specify was that PBOC's monetary policy autonomy was heavily constrained.[26]

To summarize, the PBOC faced an increasing policy dilemma in simultaneously maintaining the gradually appreciated RMB exchange rates and controlling the domestic money supply, in the circumstance of persistent current account surplus and capital inflows. The rigid exchange rate regime with limited flexibility considerably eroded the central bank's monetary policy autonomy. The challenge was particularly daunting, with hot money inflows that speculated the RMB's gradual and steady appreciation after PBOC's announcement of exchange rate reform on 21 July 2005, which required the PBOC to engage in larger scale intervention in the inter-bank foreign exchange market and sterilization in the domestic money market. On the one hand, the PBOC issued central bank bills to commercial banks, which involved straightforward commercial bank purchase of interest-bearing papers issued by the PBOC. On the other, the PBOC raised the required reserve ratio, and the share of deposits that commercial banks must place at the central bank. Both methods sought to sterilize the increasing position for forex purchase through expansion of central bank liabilities. However, despite these endeavors, the money supply growth was still beyond PBOC's control, which remained at very high levels and ultimately caused inflations in the time period. In a nutshell, with the overriding policy target of gradual and continued RMB appreciations, PBOC's ability to control the money supply and hence to conduct domestic monetary policy have been significantly circumstanced.

---

[26]"Zhou Xiaochuan: The main characteristics of China's monetary policy in the new millennium", *SINA Finance*, 18 January 2013, retrieved from http://finance.sina.com.cn/money/bank/bank_yhfg/20130118/103214330306.shtml?wbf=more.

4.4 Re-emergence of External Pressure for Accelerated RMB Appreciation in 2007

With softened international pressure and MOFCOM's sustained resistance, the RMB only appreciated 3.3%, from 8.07 to 7.81, against the dollar in 2006. The 3.3% appreciation in the 2006 was modest, and China's current account surplus continued to grow rapidly in 2006, which reignited external pressure for accelerated RMB appreciation in 2007.

The US Congress set off another wave of targeting China's exchange rate policy in the first half of 2007, which was quite similar to the 2005 case. On the one hand, Congressmen were unsatisfied that China carried out the exchange rate reform in the extremely gradual way. Not only was the appreciation of the RMB exchange rate considered to be slow, but also the flexibility of the RMB exchange rate was rather limited. On the other hand, the US began to face a new round of economic recession when elements of the financial crisis became visible during 2007. American Congressmen once again tried to scapegoat China's currency for domestic economic slowdown.

There were five bills in 2007, all of which were introduced in the first half of the year. The first bill (H. R. 321) introduced on 9 January 2007 was a duplicate bill of the Currency Harmonization Initiative Through Neutralizing Action Act of 2005.[27] It once again requested the Treasury to analyse China's exchange rate policy and to report the rate of misalignment. The second bill (H. R. 782) and the fourth bill (S. 796) both named as Fair Currency Act of 2007, as well as the fifth bill (H. R. 2942) named as Currency Reform for Fair Trade Act of 2007, are very similar to the United States Fair Currency Practices Act of 2006.[28] Though the bills highlighted China's massive intervention in the foreign exchange market to keep its currency undervalued, it did not include any strict clause such as retaliatory tariffs on China's

---

[27]The U.S. Congress, "H. R. 321 Currency Harmonization Initiative Through Neutralizing Action Act of 2005: To require the Secretary of the Treasury to analyze and report on the exchange rate policies of the People's Republic of China, and to require that additional tariffs be imposed on products of that country on the basis of the rate of manipulation by that country of the rate of exchange between the currency of that country and the United States dollar", 9 January 2007, retrieved from https://www.congress.gov/110/bills/hr321/BILLS-110hr321ih.pdf.

[28]The U.S. Congress, "H. R. 782 Fair Currency Act of 2007: To amend title VII of the Tariff Act of 1930 to provide that exchange-rate misalignment by any foreign nation is a countervailable export subsidy, to amend the Exchange Rates and International Economic Policy Coordination Act of 1988 to clarify the definition of manipulation with respect to currency, and for other purposes", 31 January 2007, retrieved from https://www.congress.gov/110/bills/hr782/BILLS-110hr782ih.pdf; The U.S. Congress, "S. 796 Fair Currency Act of 2007: To amend title VII of the Tariff Act of 1930 to provide that exchange-rate misalignment by any foreign nation is a countervailable export subsidy, to amend the Exchange Rates and International Economic Policy Coordination Act of 1988 to clarify the definition of manipulation with respect to currency, and for other purposes", 7 March 2007, retrieved from https://www.congress.gov/110/bills/s796/BILLS-110s796is.pdf; The U.S. Congress, "H. R. 2942 Currency Reform for Fair Trade Act of 2007", 28 June 2007, retrieved from https://www.congress.gov/110/bills/hr2942/BILLS-110hr2942ih.pdf.

products. The most severe one was the third bill (H. R. 1002), which again included a potential punitive clause that a retaliatory tariff of 27.5% would be imposed on all China's products entering the US if China continued to manipulate its currency.[29] This is similar to the three bills (S. 14, S. 295 and H. R. 1575) of 2005, which included the punitive measure of 27.5% tariff.

Though the Congress's pressure on the RMB issue regained momentum in the first half of 2007, it could be seen that most of the bills did not add new points because both the accusations and the proposed measures were basically reproduction of previous bills. All the five bills in 2007 cited economic estimations that the RMB was undervalued against the dollar by as much as 40%, which remained unchanged compared with the first bill of 2003 regardless of the fact that the RMB had been appreciated 5.1% (from 8.28 to 7.61) until mid-2007, which rendered the criticisms in 2007 less compelling. Furthermore, the law of diminishing marginal utility applied to the bills and resolutions in 2007, which means they did not impose as intense pressure as those in 2005 did on China's exchange rate policy.

With the growing pressure from Congress, the Treasury's stance on China's exchange rate policy became tougher as well, which could be seen from the blunter language of Treasury's Reports. The comparison of 2006 and 2007 Treasury's Reports would reveal the evolution towards Treasury's stronger criticism and bolder arguments. Specifically, the Treasury still used "limited exchange rate flexibility" and "China's cautious approach to exchange rate reform" in the December 2006 Report.[30] However, it was only in June 2007 that for the first time, the Treasury came to the conclusion that "the Chinese currency is undervalued" and propose that "China should not hesitate any longer to take far more vigorous action to rebalance its economy, promote immediate RMB movement to tackle the currency's undervaluation, and achieve far greater flexibility in the exchange rate regime."[31] In the December 2007 Report, the Treasury further criticized "the substantial undervaluation of the renminbi (RMB)" and urged that "China should significantly accelerate the appreciation of the RMB's effective exchange rate."[32] Henry Paulson, who succeeded John Snow as the Treasury Secretary in mid-2006, also continued to "press

---

[29]The U.S. Congress, "H. R. 1002: To authorize appropriate action if the negotiations with the People's Republic of China regarding China's undervalued currency and currency manipulation are not successful", 12 February 2007, retrieved from https://www.congress.gov/110/bills/hr1002/BILLS-110hr1002ih.pdf.

[30]U.S. Department of the Treasury, "Report to Congress on International Economic and Exchange Rate Policies", December 2006, retrieved from https://www.treasury.gov/resource-center/international/exchange-rate-policies/Documents/Dec2007-Report.pdf, pp. 2 and 25–28.

[31]U.S. Department of the Treasury, "Report to Congress on International Economic and Exchange Rate Policies", June 2007, retrieved from https://www.treasury.gov/resource-center/international/exchange-rate-policies/Documents/2007_FXReport.pdf, pp. 2 and 32.

[32]U.S. Department of the Treasury, "Report to Congress on International Economic and Exchange Rate Policies", December 2007, retrieved from https://www.treasury.gov/resource-center/international/exchange-rate-policies/Documents/Dec2007-Report.pdf, pp. 2 and 34.

the Chinese to increase the flexibility of their exchange rate in the short term and to transition to a market-determined exchange rate in the medium term" on various occasions in 2007.[33]

With regard to the IMF, one may identify the same trend of more severe pressure. It became clear that the IMF was under growing American pressure to declare the RMB "fundamentally misaligned", which worsened China's relationship with the IMF substantially in 2007.[34] Finally, Beijing took the unusual step of voting against the adoption of the 2007 Decision on Bilateral Surveillance, which was seen as the culmination of a US-led international campaign. It withdrew from the bilateral surveillance process during 2007–08. To summarize, external pressure on the part of the US government and the IMF played an agenda-setting role to push China's leaders to accelerate the exchange rate reform in 2007, which was similar to the case in 2005. However, to explain the timing and pathway of China's exchange rate reform in 2007, one also needs to further explore China's domestic politics.

4.5 MOFCOM's Shifted Priority in 2007

Domestically, one of the most important changes in the level II game was MOFCOM's shifted priority in 2007. The MOFCOM used to be a vocal opponent of RMB appreciation and persistent advocate for export sectors' interests. However, the MOFCOM softened its resistance to RMB appreciation in 2007, as its main task changed from maintaining export growth to reducing excessive trade surplus.

One reason for MOFCOM's shifted priority in 2007 was that Chinese exporters faced unprecedented trade frictions in 2006, which placed enormous pressures on the MOFCOM to settle those trade disputes and preserve the interests of export industries.[35] Bo Xilai pointed out that China's excessive trade surplus was detrimental to both domestic economic development and foreign trade relations. He commented that "the expanding trade surplus had evolved into a prominent problem" as it triggered more frequent trade frictions.[36] In the National Commercial Work Conference on 15 January 2007, Bo explicitly stated that reducing trade surplus was the top priority of the year's foreign trade development and saw it as an opportunity for China to

[33]U.S. Department of the Treasury, "Transcript of U.S. Delegation Press Conference Second Meeting of the U.S.-China Strategic Economic Dialogue", 23 May 2007, https://www.treasury.gov/press-center/press-releases/Pages/hp421.aspx; U.S. Department of the Treasury, "Remarks by Treasury Secretary Henry M. Paulson, Jr. at the Heritage Foundation Lee Lecture: China and the Strategic Economic Dialogue", 5 June 2007, retrieved from https://www.treasury.gov/press-center/press-releases/Pages/hp439.aspx.

[34]See, for example, Walter (2014), p. 136; Foot and Walter (2011), pp. 113–116.

[35]"'Made in China' suffered from frequent trade frictions in 2006", *China Qiao Wang*, 28 December 2006, retrieved from http://www.chinaqw.com/tzcy/rdts/200612/28/56204.shtml.

[36]"Trade surplus a prominent problem—Bo", *China Daily*, 15 January 2007, retrieved from http://www.chinadaily.com.cn/china/2007-01/15/content_783951.htm.

upgrade its lower value-added processing trade and optimize export structure.[37] One week later, Fu Ziying, the Assistant Minister of Commerce, echoed Minister Bo's emphasis on the international trade balance, and suggested that exchange rate, export tax rebate and processing trade policy could be used to achieve the goal in the 5th Annual Meeting of Chinese Import and Export Enterprises.[38]

Moreover, a research report by the MOFCOM Research Institute further confirmed MOFCOM's changing stance on RMB appreciation. Firstly, the report admitted that RMB was widely conceived to be undervalued and put aside the disputes on the level of misalignment. Secondly, the report recognized the important role of exchange rate leverage in relieving international trade imbalances and speculative foreign exchange influx. Thirdly, the report claimed that the RMB exchange rate would face greater pressure to appreciate in the future and suggested "moderate appreciation", which means that the RMB exchange rate continued upward adjustments in an incremental and controllable manner. Specifically, the research report suggested that the RMB could appreciate 9–10% until the end of 2007.[39]

The other reason for MOFCOM's shifted priority in 2007 was that it would be more in line with the consensus reached in the Central Economic Work Conference at the end of 2006. The Central Economic Work Conference is an annual meeting that reviews economic performance of last year, analyses current economic situation, and sets the tone for macroeconomic policies and priorities in economic work next year. As it is convened by the Central Committee of the Communist Party and the State Council, it is the highest-ranking economic meeting.

At the Central Economic Work Conference at the end of 2006, the Chinese leadership reached a general consensus that the principal challenge for China's international balance of payments was no longer shortage of foreign exchange but the trade surplus and foreign exchange reserves. Therefore, promoting the international balance of payments was set to be an important task of macroeconomic control in 2007.[40] Furthermore, the 2006 Central Economic Work Conference demonstrated that China's top leaders stressed not only rate but also quality of economic growth. The tone for macroeconomic policies in 2007 was set as "good and fast economic development" and emphasis was placed on balanced and coordinated development. It was the first time that good quality of economic development came before fast

[37]"Bo Xilai: cutting trade surplus as the top priority for foreign trade development this year", *Xinhua*, 15 January 2007, retrieved from http://news.xinhuanet.com/fortune/2007-01/15/content_5608411.htm.

[38]Ministry of Commerce, "The new situation and tasks of China's foreign trade", 23 January 2007, retrieved from http://zhs.mofcom.gov.cn/article/xxfb/200701/20070104304587.shtml.

[39]Ministry of Commerce, "How to deal with the challenge of RMB appreciation for foreign trade and economic development", 3 March 2007, retrieved from http://binchuan.mofcom.gov.cn/aarticle/xglj/200803/20080305408267.html.

[40]"Promoting the international balance of payments is an important task of macroeconomic control", *People's Daily*, 14 December 2006, retrieved from http://finance.people.com.cn/GB/71364/5165799.html.

growth speed.[41] Although the central government's statements contained no direct deployment of further RMB exchange rate reform, the 2006 Central Economic Work Conference also provided significant political space for the advocates of exchange rate reform, as the RMB exchange rate was an important part of the toolkit to achieve the macroeconomic goal.

4.6 PBOC's Advocate for Exchange Rate Flexibility and Appreciation in 2007

MOFCOM's shifted priority on the balance of international payments and the central leadership's emphasis on economic balancing provided significant political space for advocates of exchange rate reform. Furthermore, as mentioned above, the PBOC encountered great difficulties in managing the gradually appreciated RMB exchange rates and controlling the domestic money supply simultaneously, under the circumstance of persistent current account surplus and capital inflows. The PBOC faced increasing and enormous inflationary pressure in 2007, and all the major monetary tools, including open market operations, required reserve ratio and interest rate, were used to fight inflation. For instance, the PBOC kept the "prudent monetary policy" in the first half of 2007, while it changed the stance and adopted the "moderately tight monetary policy" in the third quarter of 2007.[42] The required reserve ratios and the benchmark deposit and lending rates were raised ten times and five times respectively in 2007.[43] Under these circumstances, the PBOC more actively advocated to push forward exchange rate reform for greater flexibility and faster appreciation of the RMB exchange rate in 2007.

Zhou Xiaochuan expressed severe concern regarding China's domestic excess liquidity, and declared that the RMB exchange rate flexibility should be expanded if China's trade surplus continued to grow at the Bank for International Settlements conference in January 2007.[44] One week later, Hu Xiaolian, the deputy governor of the PBOC and the director of SAFE, advocated to promote the balance of international

[41] See, for example, "Central Economic Work Conference emits the new signal of China's economy in 2007", *People's Daily*, 8 December 2006, retrieved from http://finance.people.com.cn/GB/1045/5142837.html; "The new goal of Chinese economy: good, fast and balanced", *People's Daily*, 8 December 2006, retrieved from http://finance.people.com.cn/GB/1045/5142351.html.

[42] People's Bank of China, "2007 First Quarter Monetary Policy Implementation Report", 10 May 2007, retrieved from http://www.pbc.gov.cn/eportal/fileDir/history_file/files/att_11627_1.pdf; People's Bank of China, "2007s Quarter Monetary Policy Implementation Report", 8 August 2007, retrieved from http://www.pbc.gov.cn/eportal/fileDir/history_file/files/att_11628_1.pdf; People's Bank of China, "2007 Third Quarter Monetary Policy Implementation Report", 8 November 2007, http://www.pbc.gov.cn/eportal/fileDir/history_file/files/att_11629_1.pdf.

[43] People's Bank of China, "2007 Fourth Quarter Monetary Policy Implementation Report", pp. 8–9, 22 February 2008, retrieved from http://www.pbc.gov.cn/eportal/fileDir/history_file/files/att_11630_1.pdf.

[44] "Zhou Xiaochuan: RMB exchange rate flexibility will be expanded", *Xinhua*, 15 January 2007, retrieved from http://news.xinhuanet.com/fortune/2007-01/15/content_5607297.htm.

payments at the foreign exchange management conference, and the central bank decided to further increase the RMB exchange rate flexibility at the PBOC Work Conference.[45] In March 2007, Zhou Xiaochuan stated that exchange rate policy, as a tool of price lever, would play a complementary role in the economic restructuring and trade balancing at the press conference of the annual NPC meeting.[46] A few days later, Zhou expressed the message that China's exchange rate policy would be more market-oriented: "RMB exchange rate will depend on market supply and demand and there is no pre-determined target level."[47] Yi Gang, the assistant governor of the PBOC, explicitly pointed out that greater exchange rate flexibility and RMB appreciation could help to curb domestic inflation and enhance the autonomy and effectiveness of monetary policy.[48] Yu Yongding continued to advocate that RMB appreciation would achieve the result of "killing two birds with one stone": RMB appreciation would thus help to reduce both domestic inflation and current account surplus.[49]

Considering all the factors at home and abroad, China took the first major step on 18 May 2007 to make the RMB a more flexible currency by loosening its daily trading limits after the 21 July 2005 reform. The PBOC announced that "as of 21 May 2007, the RMB-dollar trading band in the inter-bank spot foreign exchange market will be expanded form 0.3 to 0.5%, namely, the daily RMB-dollar trading band may be floated within the 0.5% range of the middle price of the dollar against the RMB."[50] On the day of the announcement, Zhou reiterated that RMB exchange rate would be increasingly flexible and determined by market supply and demand.[51] Theoretically, the widened RMB-dollar trading band would allow more flexibility and faster appreciation of the RMB exchange rate. However, in practice, Fig. 4.5 shows that RMB was indeed more flexible, in that it fluctuated more volatilely against the dollar, but there was little evidence of faster RMB appreciation immediately after the 18 May 2007 announcement. The RMB exchange rate did not increase the pace of appreciation until October 2007. The reason for this will be elaborated in more detail in the following section.

---

[45]"The PBOC declared to further increase the RMB exchange rate flexibility", *Xinhua*, 21 January 2007, retrieved from http://news.xinhuanet.com/fortune/2007-01/21/content_5633583.htm.

[46]"Bo Xilai and Zhou Xiaochuan answered journalists' questions on trade cooperation and monetary policy", *Xinhua*, 12 March 2007, retrieved from http://news.xinhuanet.com/misc/2007-03/12/content_5833049_3.htm.

[47]"Zhou Xiaochuan: RMB exchange rate will be determined by market supply and demand", *SINA Finance*, 21 March 2007, retrieved from http://finance.sina.com.cn/roll/20070321/00041276796.shtml.

[48]Yi (2009).

[49]Yu (2007).

[50]People's Bank of China, "Announcement of the People's Bank of China on expanding the floating range of RMB-dollar trading price in the inter-bank spot foreign exchange market", 18 May 2007, retrieved from http://www.pbc.gov.cn/bangongting/135485/135491/135597/999532/index.html.

[51]"Zhou Xiaochuan: RMB exchange rate will be increasingly flexible", *Xinhua*, 18 May 2007, retrieved from http://news.xinhuanet.com/video/2007-05/18/content_6118128.htm.

Fig. 4.5 RMB exchange rate against the US dollar in 2007. *Source* PBOC—Figures—RMB exchange rate against the US dollar, http://www.pbc.gov.cn/rmyh/108976/109428/index.html

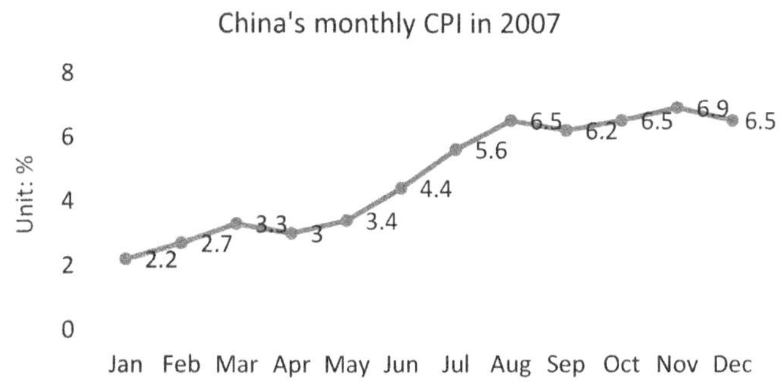

Fig. 4.6 China's monthly CPI in 2007 *Source* IMF International Financial Statistics

4.7 All-In to Fight Inflation

In spite of all the endeavors to contain inflation, China still faced rising inflationary pressure in 2007. There were debates of "too little pork" versus "too much money" over the reasons of rising inflation.[52] Yet if one understands the causal mechanism of PBOC's increasing policy dilemma mentioned above, they would be more likely to support the "too much money" hypothesis in explaining the Chinese inflationary cycle in 2007. Figure 4.6 shows the rising trend of China's CPI in 2007. In particular,

[52]See, for example, Pettis (2008), pp. 42–45.

CPI reached 3% (the alert line of inflation) after March 2007 and remained above 5% (the line of severe inflation) in the second half of 2007.

Under the circumstance, the PBOC expressed serious concerns with inflation on various occasions, not only in monetary policy implementation reports but also in officials' public remarks. The PBOC recognized that the continuous rising of trade surplus and CPI exacerbated the inflationary expectations and intensified the inflationary pressure.[53] Zhou said that he was worried about inflation, and pointed out that central bank would target inflation at the Bank for International Settlements Conference in September 2007.[54] When he was interviewed by Financial News, Zhou further stressed that exchange rate policy and interest rate policy, the two tools of price lever, should coordinate to stabilize inflationary expectations.[55] Furthermore, after the three hikes of CPI in the third quarter, the PBOC made a policy proposal to the State Council: to allow the RMB to appreciate at a faster rate in order to contain inflation.[56] The proposal was also confirmed by the 2007 third quarter monetary policy implementation report, which for the first time purported that "currency appreciation is conducive to curb domestic inflation".[57]

The severe situation of inflationary cycle and PBOC's firm suggestion produced a clear shift in exchange rate strategy in late 2007. China's top leadership seemed to accept PBOC's basic arguments to regard inflation as the most severe problem to tackle and to use currency appreciation as a tool to fight inflation, which was confirmed by two most important meetings—the Central Politburo meetings and the Central Economic Work Conference.

The Central Politburo usually holds meetings on economic situation and work twice a year, one in the middle of the year and the other at the end of the year. In the July 2007 meeting, the Central Politburo recognized the several problems of China's economy and proposed "to prevent relatively fast economic growth from becoming overheated", which was made as the top priority of macroeconomic management. Specifically, efforts should be made to ease the growth of investment, credit expansion, CPI and trade surplus.[58] However, during the November 2007 meeting, the Central Politburo further emphasised inflation control. The top priorities of macroeconomic management changed from one prevention to two preventions: "to prevent

[53]People's Bank of China, "2007 Third Quarter Monetary Policy Implementation Report", 8 November 2007, p. 31, retrieved from http://www.pbc.gov.cn/eportal/fileDir/history_file/files/att_11629_1.pdf.

[54]"Zhou Xiaochuan: worried about China's inflation", *Xinhua*, 11 September 2007, retrieved from http://news.xinhuanet.com/fortune/2007-09/11/content_6701378.htm.

[55]"Zhou Xiaochuan: to stabilize inflationary expectations", *Xinhua*, 15 November 2007, retrieved from http://www.china.com.cn/economic/txt/2007-11/15/content_9230584.htm.

[56]Interview_25092015.

[57]People's Bank of China, "2007 Third Quarter Monetary Policy Implementation Report", 8 November 2007, p. 34, retrieved from http://www.pbc.gov.cn/eportal/fileDir/history_file/files/att_11629_1.pdf.

[58]"Hu Jintao presided over the Central Politburo meeting to analyze the current economic situation and work", *Xinhua*, 26 July 2007, retrieved from http://news.xinhuanet.com/2007-07/26/content_6434538.htm.

relatively fast economic growth from becoming overheated and to prevent structural price increases from turning into significant inflation".[59]

At the Central Economic Work Conference at the end of 2007, the top leadership reaffirmed that inflation prevention was the next year's top priority.[60] Monetary policy and exchange rate policy would go hand in hand to achieve the goal. On the one hand, the PBOC announced that it would shift to a tight monetary policy next year, which was a significant change of monetary policy, as the last time when China adopted a tight monetary policy was ten years ago during the 1997–98 Asian Financial Crisis.[61] On the other hand, RMB appreciation was used as another tool to help China expand its imports and curb inflation. To summarize, the Central Economic Work Conference expressed the messages that inflation was the primary concern of current macroeconomic management, and that monetary tightening and RMB appreciation would be the most effective ways to fight inflation.[62]

Under these circumstances, RMB appreciated at a significantly faster pace in the fourth quarter of 2007 (see Fig. 4.5). The RMB appreciated 6.9% against the dollar from 7.807 to 7.305 in the year of 2007; it appreciated 2.8% against the dollar from 7.511 to 7.305 in the four quarter, account for 40% of the total appreciation in 2007. The widened RMB-dollar trading band allowed greater exchange rate flexibility and the rate of RMB appreciation sped up considerably during the latter part of 2007.

4.8 Concluding Remarks

This chapter has examined the subsequent development of China's exchange rate reform from July 2005 to 2007. With softened international pressure and MOFCOM's sustained resistance, the RMB exchange rate appreciated in a gradual manner after the July 2005 announcement. However, the PBOC faced increasing difficulties to preserve the gradually and continuously appreciated RMB exchange rate and to maintain the monetary policy autonomy simultaneously, under the circumstances of rising trade surplus and capital inflows.

Following this, the US government and the IMF were increasingly dissatisfied with the little progress of China's exchange rate reform, and the external pressure regained momentum in 2007, which once again played an agenda-setting role to push China's leaders to accelerate the exchange rate reform. However, to explain

---

[59] "Central Politburo holds a meeting to analyze the current economic situation and next year's economic work", *Xinhua*, 27 November 2007, retrieved from http://news.xinhuanet.com/newscenter/2007-11/27/content_7156005.htm.

[60] "Prevention of significant inflation as priority of macroeconomic management", *People's Daily*, 6 December 2007, retrieved from http://finance.people.com.cn/GB/6621769.html.

[61] "PBOC: to implement a tight monetary policy next year", *People's Daily*, 6 December 2007, retrieved from http://finance.people.com.cn/GB/6618610.html; "Chinese monetary policy change", *People's Daily*, 6 December 2007, retrieved from http://finance.people.com.cn/GB/6618613.html.

[62] "Monetary tightening and RMB appreciation as the most effective ways to fight inflation", *People's Daily*, 7 December 2007, http://finance.people.com.cn/GB/6627311.html.

the timing and pathway of China's exchange rate reform in 2007, one also needs to further explore China's domestic politics. On the one hand, the MOFCOM shifted its priority to trade surplus reduction in 2007, as Chinese exporters faced unprecedented trade frictions in 2006. On the other hand, the PBOC more actively advocated to push forward exchange rate reform for greater flexibility under inflationary pressure.

On 18 May 2007, China took the first major step to make the RMB a more flexible currency by widening the RMB-dollar trading band. The RMB did not begin to appreciate in a faster pace until the late 2007. The shift in exchange rate policy would not have been possible without the severe situation of the inflationary cycle in the second half of 2007 and the consensus reached by the Chinese leadership to make inflation prevention as the top priority in the fourth quarter of 2007. The next chapter will continue to examine the accelerated (but short-lived) exchange rate reform and how interest groups and local governments fit in to influence the exchange rate policy making in 2008.

Chapter 5
The Back and Forth of RMB Exchange Rate Reform in Turbulent Times, 2008–2010

Chapter 4 has examined the development of China's exchange rate reform from July 2005 to 2007. With softened international pressure and MOFCOM's sustained resistance, the RMB exchange rate appreciated in a gradual manner after the July 2005 announcement, and PBOC's monetary policy autonomy was severely eroded, as the central bank needed to maintain the gradually and continuously appreciated exchange rate. The situation changed dramatically in 2007. Internationally, the US government and the IMF were increasingly impatient and critical of the slow progress of China's exchange rate reform. Domestically, in the face of growing trade friction, the MOFCOM shifted its priority to trade surplus reduction and the PBOC more actively advocated to push forward exchange rate reform for greater flexibility under the inflationary pressure. Under these circumstances, the Chinese leadership decided to widen the RMB-dollar trading band to make the RMB into a more flexible currency on 18 May 2007 and the RMB appreciate against the dollar in a faster pace in the late 2007.

In the period from July 2005 to 2007, there was little pressure from export interest groups in China's exchange rate policy making. China's exports grew by 28.4%, 27.1% and 25.9% respectively in the years from 2005 to 2007.[1] There was no sharp decline in exports, as opponents of RMB exchange rate reform had feared. While the voices opposing appreciation were temporarily silenced, they had not disappeared. Opponents pointed out that although exports had continued to grow, the rate of growth had slowed, and the effects brought by RMB appreciation were to blame. Exporters became strongly opposed to the RMB appreciation in early 2008, as the pace of appreciation had accelerated. In truth, RMB appreciation was only one of a number of different factors that were squeezing these industries. Other policy changes, such as cuts in export tax rebates and the new labor contract law, as well as the simultaneous declines in the domestic stock and property markets, compounded

[1]National Bureau of Statistics of China, available from http://data.stats.gov.cn/easyquery.htm?cn=C01.

Z. Wang, *The International Political Economy of China's Exchange Rate Policy Making*, https://doi.org/10.1007/978-981-33-4578-2_5

their problems. Nevertheless, exchange rate appreciation became the main focus of exporters' hostility in 2008. Since the MOFCOM placed its priority on trade surplus reduction and its stance towards RMB appreciation had changed in 2007, the only alternative for the exporters at this juncture was to mobilize resources to lobby against the rapid RMB appreciation and seek policy adjustment.

Based on questionnaire surveys and semi-structured interviews, this chapter focuses on the Fujian province as a case study and explores the three main methods of export lobbying in the level III game: first guanxi-based lobbying through local governments, second guanxi-based lobbying through local offices of central governmental agencies, and third lobbying through trade associations. It argues that the exporters' lobbying imposed considerable pressure on the central government's exchange rate policy making in the first half of 2008. Confronted with pressure from businesses, the top leadership conducted intensive research and investigation in early July 2008, and finally decided to roll out rescue policies. The market-oriented RMB exchange rate reform beginning from 21 July 2005 was halted in the second half of 2008, and China returned to the de facto dollar-pegged exchange rate regime in the turbulent times of the global financial crisis. Therefore, this chapter provides a nuanced explanations of export lobbying in the level III game and the dynamics of central-local interactions in China's exchange rate policy making in 2008.

5.1 The International and Domestic Context in 2008

After China announced the exchange rate reform on 21 July 2005, Congress's pressure on China's currency gradually waned, and the Treasury commended China's move, which was similar to the case after PBOC's announcement of 18 May 2007 exchange rate reform. There was no Congress bill on the RMB issue in the second half of 2007 and only single one (S. 2813) in the year of 2008. The bill named China Currency Manipulation Act of 2008 mandated the Treasury to deal with China's currency manipulation, including making a determination, setting benchmarks and timeframes, initiate bilateral negotiations with China and coordinate with the IMF to address the RMB misalignment and US-China trade imbalance.[2] In the December 2007 and May 2008 Reports, the Treasury recognized that the RMB appreciation accelerated against the dollar in the second half of 2007 and the pace of appreciation increased further in the early months of 2008.[3] The Treasury regarded China's recent acceleration in RMB appreciation as a welcome development and encouraged

[2]The U.S. Congress, "S. 2813 China Currency Manipulation Act of 2008: To require the Secretary of the Treasury to take action with respect to currency manipulation by the People's Republic of China and for other purposes", 3 April 2008, retrieved from https://www.congress.gov/110/bills/s2813/BILLS-110s2813is.pdf.

[3]U.S. Department of the Treasury, "Report to Congress on International Economic and Exchange Rate Policies", December 2007, retrieved from https://www.treasury.gov/resource-center/international/exchange-rate-policies/Documents/Dec2007-Report.pdf; U.S. Department of the Treasury, "Report to Congress on International Economic and Exchange Rate Policies", May 2008,

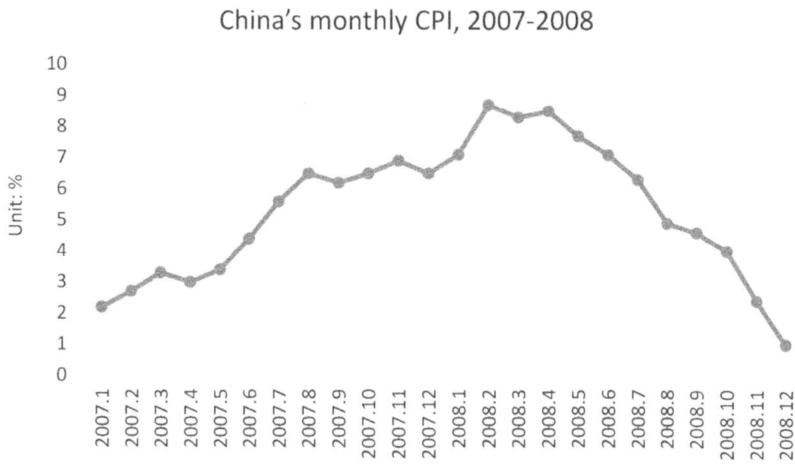

Fig. 5.1 China's monthly CPI, from 2007 to 2008. *Source* IMF, International Financial Statistics

China to continue the exchange rate reform. Overall, the international discussions and criticism of Chinese exchange rate policy were significantly lower after the 18 May 2007 reform, especially in the few months preceding the 2008 global financial crisis.

The softened international pressure in 2008 implies that the Chinese leadership would make exchange rate policy decisions mainly based on the conditions of domestic political economy. Though China's top leadership reached the consensus to treat inflation as the most severe problem and used both tight monetary policy and currency appreciation to fight inflation, the CPI remained high above 5%, the line of severe inflation, from mid-2007 to mid-2008. Figure 5.1 shows that inflation was even more severe in the first half of 2008 than in 2007.

With mounting inflationary pressure, the PBOC implemented the tight monetary policy by raising the required reserve ratio five times by 3% (see Appendix C) and allowed the RMB a faster rate of appreciation in the first half of 2008. As the central bank, the PBOC naturally placed its top priority to control the inflation.[4] Yu Yongding expressed the view that the goal of exchange rate stability should be subordinated to the goal of inflation control. He explained that the central bank should implement tight monetary policy to fight inflation and the preconditions of effective tight monetary policy were capital control and exchange rate flexibility (that

retrieved from https://www.treasury.gov/resource-center/international/exchange-rate-policies/Documents/052008_report.pdf.

[4]People's Bank of China, "2008 First Quarter Monetary Policy Implementation Report", retrieved from http://www.pbc.gov.cn/eportal/fileDir/history_file/files/att_11631_1.pdf, p. II.

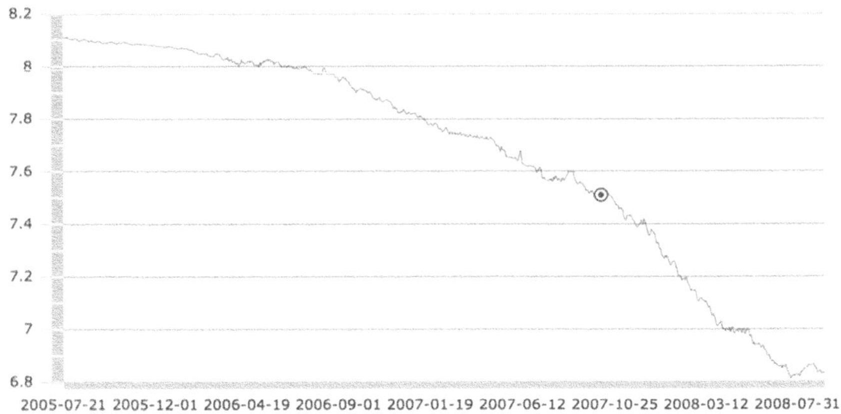

Fig. 5.2 RMB exchange rate against the US dollar, 21 July 2005 to 31 July 2008. *Source* PBOC Monetary Policy Department

allows currency appreciation).[5] When asked whether the central bank appreciated the currency to curb inflation, Zhou Xiaochuan did not deny it, but explained it in a subtler way:

> It is not necessary to see the aim of exchange rate adjustment is to curb inflation. However, the direction is right in the angle of analysis … Specifically, the increased exchange rate flexibility and appreciation is to improve the market-oriented exchange rate formation mechanism. In the angle of analysis, the accelerated RMB appreciation helps to control inflation.[6]

On the other hand, with a growing current account surplus, the MOFCOM continued to soften its resistance to RMB appreciation in 2008. The MOFCOM abandoned its emphasis on exchange rate stability and placed importance on exchange rate marketization. Faced with the demand to accelerate appreciation to reduce trade surplus, Minister Chen Deming responded firmly that it was unreasonable to require RMB devaluation based purely on trade surplus. He reaffirmed that China would not deliberately pursue trade surplus, and recognized both the positive and the negative effects of RMB appreciation on China's economy. He further pointed out that no one, including the PBOC governor, could manipulate the exchange rate; instead, the RMB exchange rate adjustment should follow the market rule.[7]

Under these circumstances, the RMB continued the trend of appreciation after the fourth quarter of 2007. Figure 5.2 shows the RMB exchange rate against the dollar after the 21 July 2005 reform. It may be seen that China's exchange rate appreciated

[5]"Yu Yongding: RMB appreciation will certainly help to curb inflation", *Xinhua*, 18 March 2008, retrieved from http://finance.qq.com/a/20080318/002158.htm.

[6]"Heads of NDRC, MOF and PBOC answer journalists' questions", The National People's Congress of the People's Republic of China, 6 March 2008, retrieved from http://www.npc.gov.cn/npc/zhibo/zzzb3/node_363.htm.

[7]"Chen Deming: China does not deliberately pursue trade surplus", *Xinhua*, 12 March 2008, retrieved from http://news.xinhuanet.com/fortune/2008-03/12/content_7775367.htm.

gradually against the dollar for more than two years. The substantial and faster RMB appreciation only happened in the period from October 2007 to July 2008, when the Chinese leadership concentrated their attention and spared no effort to fight inflation. More specifically, the RMB appreciated 9.8%, from 7.51 to 6.84, against the dollar in the ten months, which was even larger than the previous total RMB appreciation (8.0%, from 8.11 to 7.51) for more than two years.

It is also worth pointing out that exchange rate was not the only tool being used to curb inflation and reduce the trade surplus. The government cut export tax rebates for many commodities in 2007.[8] Moreover, the new labour law and stricter environmental regulations further lowered many exporters' profits.[9] Last but not least, the simultaneous decline in the domestic stock and property markets in 2008 reduced their profits from non-trade-related investments.[10] Faced with the various problems, Chinese exporters fell into a difficult position and grew hostile to exchange rate appreciation in 2008.

Based on an in-depth case study in the Fujian province, the following section will elaborate the difficult situation of export enterprises and their corresponding response. The data mainly comes from questionnaire surveys and interviews conducted in Fujian province. The researcher distributed 98 questionnaires to export entrepreneurs, and 63 valid responses were collected for analysis. The researcher also arranged 22 semi-structured interviews with export entrepreneurs, association representatives and local government officials at different levels. Interviews typically lasted from one to two hours, and many sources were interviewed multiple times. In order to protect the anonymity of sources, they are cited in the notes as "Interviews with dates".

---

[8]The MOF announces that starting from 1 July 2007, China will cut or eliminate export tax rebates for 2831 commodities representing 37% of the total number of items listed on customs tax regulations. China abolished export tax rebates on 553 "highly polluting products that consume heavy amounts of energy and resources" such as salt, cement, and liquefied petroleum gas, and reduced tax rebate on exports of 2268 commodities which "tend to cause trade frictions". See "Ministry of Finance and State Administration of Taxation's announcement on lower export tax rebate rates of some commodities", State Taxation Administration, 19 June 2007, retrieved from http://www.chinatax.gov.cn/n810341/n810765/n812176/n812778/c1194297/content.html.

[9]The NPC Standing Committee passes the new labour contract law that requires employers to provide written contracts to their workers, restricts the use of temporary labourers and makes it harder to lay off employees. See "Labour Contract Law enacted by the Standing Committee of the National People's Congress and implemented since 1 January 2008", *Xinhua*, 29 June 2007, retrieved from http://news.xinhuanet.com/legal/2007-06/29/content_6308311.htm and http://news.xinhuanet.com/legal/2007-06/30/content_6311563.htm.

[10]See, for example, "Earnings up, prices down: risk aversion hits Chinese stocks", *The Economist*, 19 March 2008, retrieved from http://www.economist.com/node/10881471; "Boom to bust: China's property bubble is about to burst", *The Economist*, 20 June 2008, retrieved from http://www.economist.com/node/11605123; "China's economy hits the wall", *Financial Times*, 15 December 2008, retrieved from http://www.ft.com/cms/s/0/a1ff5944-cac6-11dd-87d7-000077b07658.html#axzz3zs3Qxv4x.

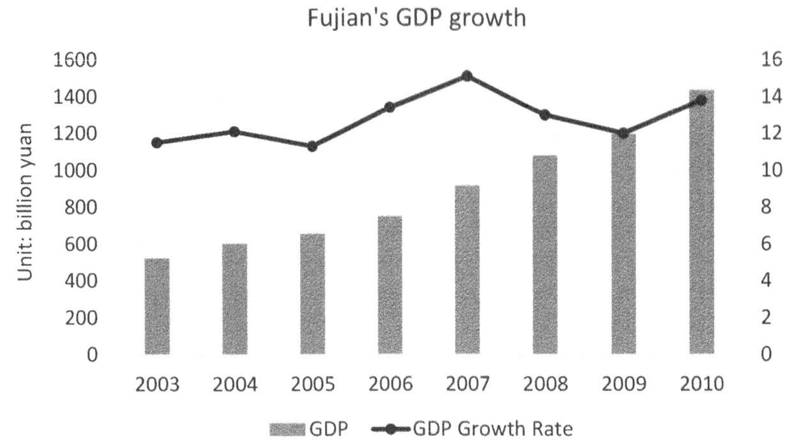

Fig. 5.3 Fujian's GDP growth, from 2003 to 2010. *Source* Fujian Provincial Statistics of Economic and Social Development, Fujian Provincial Bureau of Statistics, http://www.stats-fj.gov.cn/

5.2 Exporters Got into Trouble and Fought Back

The author has selected the Fujian province as a typical case study because it is one of the fastest growing provinces based on export-oriented industrialization in China's coastal region. Fujian lies on the southeast coast of China and faces the Taiwan Strait. Fujian's favorable geographical position is conducive to the dynamics of the local economy. It is one of the most affluent provinces, with many industries spanning tea production, garments and sporting goods. Moreover, Fujian was one of the first few provinces where special economic zones were established. The special arrangements that Fujian obtained for its fiscal relationship with the central government in the 1980s were also crucial for laying the foundations for export growth in the 1990s and 2000s, alongside infrastructure investment and preferential policies of tax and land.[11] Figure 5.3 shows that Fujian's GDP grew at double digit rates from 2003 to 2010. Figure 5.4 shows Fujian's export and import from 2003 to 2010. The exports increased at faster rates than imports after 2003. However, Fujian, like other export-oriented provinces, faced enormous difficulties in maintaining the momentum of export growth in 2008 and 2009. Therefore, it is particularly worthwhile investigating how exporters in Fujian responded to the exchange rate policy at a difficult time.

[11]See, for example, Nishitateno (1983); Pak (1997); Ge (1999).

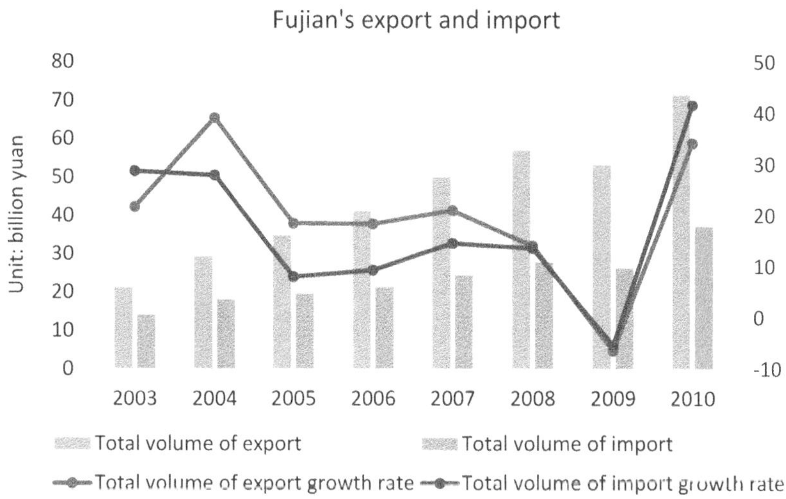

Fig. 5.4 Fujian's export and import, from 2003 to 2010. *Source* Fujian Provincial Statistics of Economic and Social Development, Fujian Provincial Bureau of Statistics, http://www.stats-fj.gov.cn/

5.2.1 Evidence from Questionnaire Surveys

Figure 5.5 shows that the dollar played a dominant role as a vehicle currency in international trade, according to the questionnaires collected from Fujian's entrepreneurs. More than three-quarters (49 out of 63) of the export enterprises in Fujian responded that they used dollar as the main currency for international trade settlement. Thus, their business was undeniably affected by the RMB exchange rate against the dollar. Figure 5.6 shows that around four in five export enterprises in Fujian responded that their business was subject to RMB exchange rate fluctuations.

Figure 5.7 demonstrates the response number of Fujian's enterprises that were greatly affected by RMB exchange rate fluctuations. As to the question "In which year(s) your enterprise was significantly affected by the RMB exchange rate fluctuations?", there were small numbers (2 and 3) of respondents in the first two years of exchange rate reform as the RMB exchange rate appreciated in a gradual manner, whereas there were more responses (17) in 2007 with the exchange rate reform accelerated. The response number (41) peaked in 2008, suggesting that the unfavorable conditions of export enterprises were exacerbated by the rapid appreciation of RMB.

Figure. 5.8 shows the measures taken by export entrepreneurs in a time of volatile exchange rate fluctuations. On the one hand, the enterprises mainly used financial instruments to reduce exchange risk at their own end. It was less feasible for the Fujian export enterprises to shift the cost to their trading partners or to upgrade their products to control their cost, as most of them were labor-intensive in the middle and low-end markets. On the other hand, they were more inclined to communicate

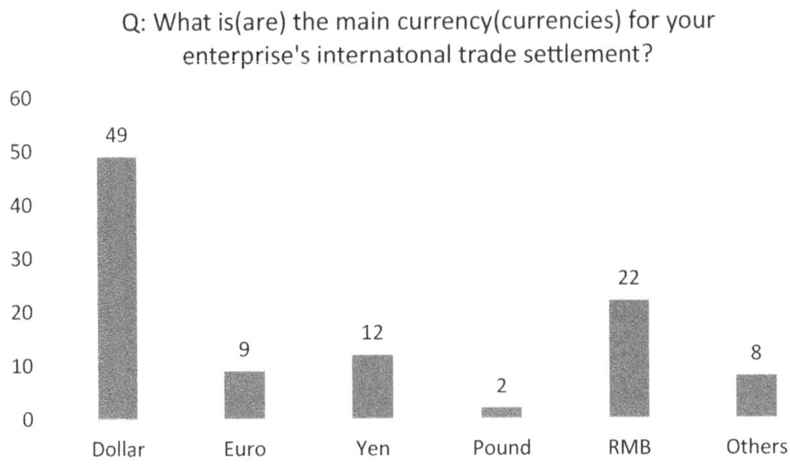

Fig. 5.5 The responses of 63 Fujian entrepreneurs to the question "What is (are) the main currency (currencies) for your enterprise's international trade settlement?" *Source* Author's own elaboration based on questionnaire data

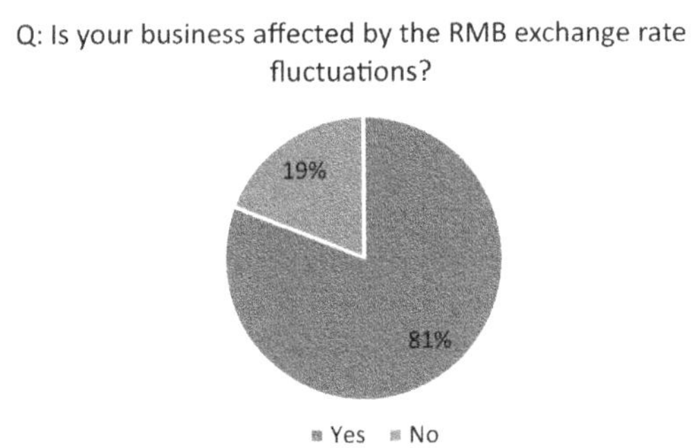

Fig. 5.6 The responses of 63 Fujian entrepreneurs to the question "Is your business affected by the RMB exchange rate fluctuations?" *Source* Author's own elaboration based on questionnaire data

with trade associations and local governments in order to seek exchange rate policy adjustment, which would be elaborated in more detail afterwards.

The questionnaires further explored the degree of difficulty and effectiveness with which the export entrepreneurs communicated with local governments and trade associations in a time of volatile exchange rate fluctuations. According to the responses of export entrepreneurs, Figs. 5.9 and 5.10 together show that it was easier and more effective for them to communicate with trade associations, whereas it was more difficult and less effective to do so with local governments. The reasons for this will be explored in more depth in the following sections.

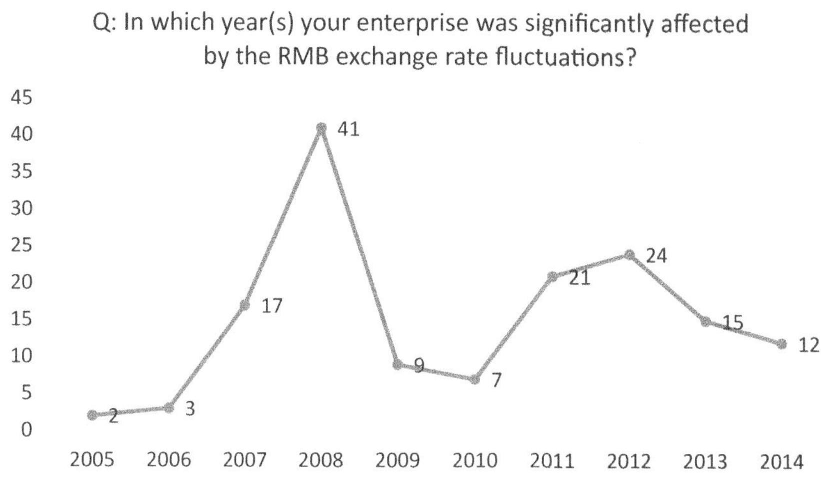

Fig. 5.7 The responses of 63 Fujian entrepreneurs to the question "In which year(s) your enterprise was significantly affected by the RMB exchange rate fluctuations?" *Source* Author's own elaboration based on questionnaire data

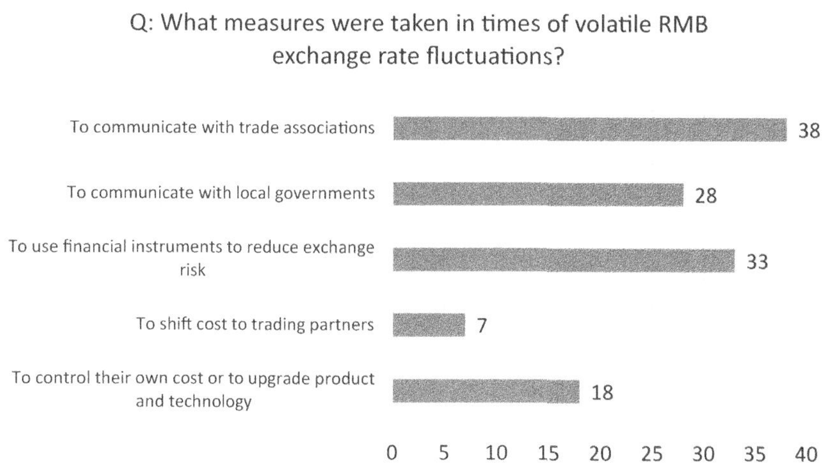

Fig. 5.8 The responses of 63 Fujian entrepreneurs to the question "What measures were taken in times of volatile RMB exchange rate fluctuations?" *Source* Author's own elaboration based on questionnaire data

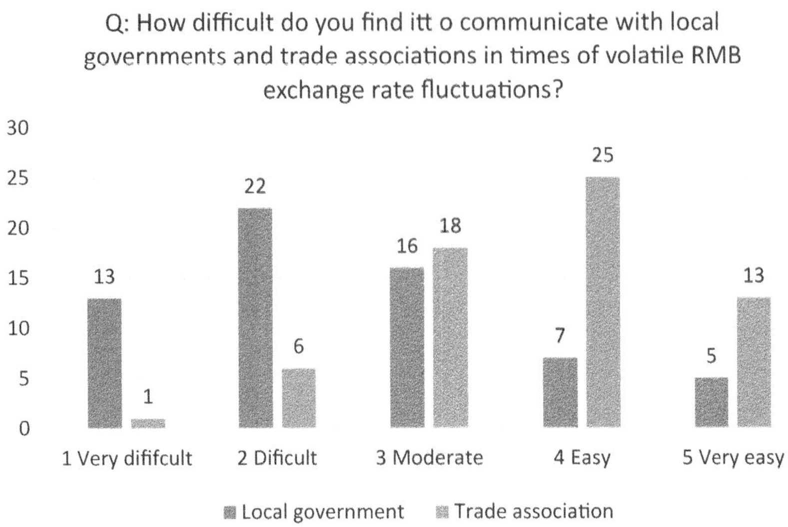

Fig. 5.9 The responses of 63 Fujian entrepreneurs to the question "How difficult do you find it to communicate with local governments and trade associations in times of volatile RMB exchange rate fluctuations?" *Source* Own elaboration based on questionnaire data

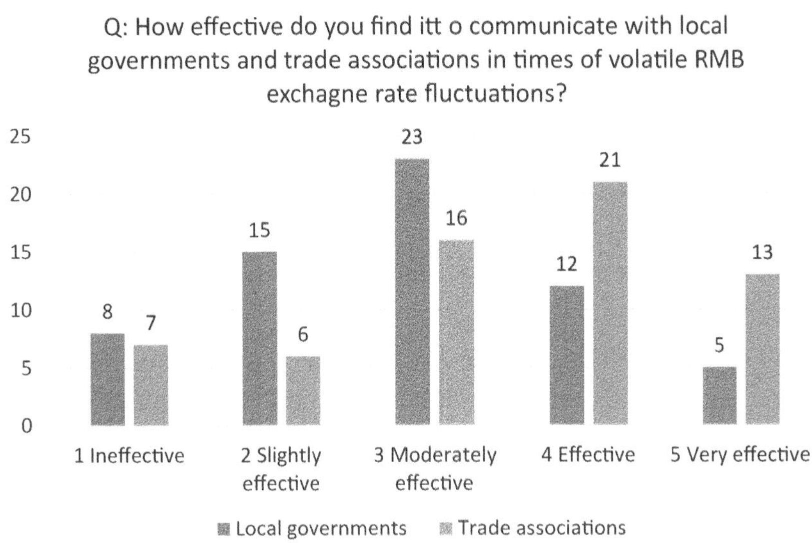

Fig. 5.10 The responses of 63 Fujian entrepreneurs to the question "How effective do you find it to communicate with local governments and trade associations in times of volatile RMB exchange rate fluctuations?" *Source* Author's own elaboration based on questionnaire data

5.2.2 Evidence from Semi-Structured Interviews

Semi-structured interviews with Fujian entrepreneurs confirmed their difficult export situation in the first half of 2008. For example, one export enterprise CEO at Jinjiang[12] said that their business relied heavily on the orders from the US and faced the challenge of losing proposition in 2008. He also recalled the loss-making business in the first quarter of 2008:

> The RMB exchange rate against the dollar was around 7.4 in February 2008, but it quickly appreciated to around 7.2 in March 2008 when the enterprise received the payment. The business was six hundred thousand dollars and the loss incurred by RMB appreciation was twelve thousand dollars. Even though they had considered the exchange rate factor, it was still very difficult for contract pricing under the circumstance that the RMB appreciation was continuous. If the contract pricing was too high, foreign trade partners would not accept it; if too low, the enterprise suffered from the exchange rate loss.[13]

One official at Quanzhou Chamber of Commerce for Import and Export suggested that many labor-intensive export enterprises fell into a dilemma in the face of currency appreciation and cuts in export rebates, as they had limited bargaining power: to raise the prices could lead to loss of orders, whereas not to raise the prices may lead to their own enormous loss.[14] This was why there was a small number (7 out of 63) of entrepreneurs who chose to take the measure of shifting costs to trading partners in times of volatile RMB exchange rate fluctuations (see Fig. 5.8). Furthermore, most interviewees explicitly stated or implied that the continued currency appreciation imposed a far more negative impact on business than the export rebate cut did. As one export entrepreneurs said:

> With every two percent cut of export rebate, the enterprise's profit would drop around one percent. However, the RMB appreciated 6.5% against the dollar, giving rise to around 10% profit loss in 2007. The RMB appreciation was even faster in 2008, which led to around one third profit loss. Therefore, the accelerated RMB appreciation dragged his enterprise into a deep crisis in 2008.[15]

It is also worth noting that the new labor contract law, effective from 1 January 2008, further increased costs for employers by raising the requirements for severance pay, which imposed additional pressure on China's export enterprises. One official at Quanzhou Municipal Bureau of Commerce commented that the rigid rising labor costs resulted in many multinational companies at Fujian moving their production lines to Southeast Asian countries such as Vietnam and Cambodia.[16] More specifically, Chinese textile and garment exports to the US fell by 1.68% and 7.74% respectively, while Vietnamese textile and garment exports to the US increased 29.69% and

[12]Jinjiang is a county-level city of Quanzhou, and Quanzhou is a prefecture-level city of Fujian province.

[13]Interview_24082015.

[14]Interview_26082015.

[15]Interview_04092015.

[16]Interview_08082015.

33.06% respectively in the first quarter of 2008.[17] As many interviewees confirmed, China's demographic dividend was diminishing and rising labor costs were the heavy burden of many labor-intensive industries after 2007.[18]

During the author's interviews, only one interviewee at a comprehensive high-tech company that combined research, production, marketing, service and export trading stated that "the company's strategy in response to the crisis was to reduce or even stop producing those low-tech and low value-added products and to focus on producing those higher value-added and high-end products in the difficult time."[19] In contrast, a great number of interviewees explicitly stated that labor-intensive industries, particularly textile enterprises and garment manufacturers, found it difficult to upgrade production lines or transfer rising costs to trade partners, and that they had no other choice but to seek policy adjustment in times of extreme difficulty.[20]

Against this backdrop, the only alternative for export companies at this juncture was to mobilize resources to influence central government's exchange rate policy, in order to prevent the RMB from appreciating, or at least from rising too quickly. The following sections of the chapter will elaborate the three main methods of export lobbying: first, guanxi-based lobbying through local governments, second guanxi-based lobbying through local offices of central governmental agencies, and third lobbying through trade associations. The concept of lobbying herein refers to any effort used to influence policy, and more specifically, the central government's exchange rate policy making.

5.2.3 *Guanxi-Based Lobbying Through Local Governments*

In the face of the worsening export situation, the direct way of exporters' lobbying was to communicate with the local governments and local offices of central governmental agencies so as to seek for exchange rate policy change. Exporters made use of their connections and relationships (guanxi) and focused their lobbying efforts on the local governments where they were concentrated.[21] Entrepreneurs discussed their difficulties with municipal government officials and pressed them to persuade Beijing to stop the currency appreciation.

Guanxi-based lobbying is not reported in Chinese newspapers or periodicals. Meanwhile, there are no records or documents on business lobbying in the Chinese

---

[17] IMF Direction of Trade Statistics, available from https://discover.ukdataservice.ac.uk/catalogue/?sn=4745.

[18] Interview_15082015; Interview_18082015; Interview_21082015; Interview_24082015; Interview_15092015.

[19] Interview_15082015.

[20] Interview_10082015; Interview_13082015; Interview_18082015; Interview_22082015 (1); Interview_04092015; Interview_06092015.

[21] For a wide-ranging discussion of guanxi, see Gold et al. (2002).

statistics system and other government statistics.[22] Therefore, it has to be studied through interviews. During my field trip in Jinjiang, many garment and shoe exporters there mentioned that they had ties (guanxi) with the Jinjiang municipal county-level government and ensured that the government officials got to know their opposition to the worsening exchange rate situation in a time of crisis.[23] One official at Jinjiang Municipal Bureau of Commerce also confirmed that many local export entrepreneurs communicated their difficulties with them in formal and informal ways: the formal way was to disclose their accounting statements to them, while the informal way was to treat local government leaders to dinner and to make them aware of the enterprises' difficulties.[24]

As China's political system evaluated the local cadre primarily in terms of local economic performance, it created strong incentives for the local government leaders to ensure local economic growth.[25] In response to these complaints and pressures from the local entrepreneurs, the local government officials visited the local garment and shoe manufactories from time to time, usually every month in the first half of 2008, to find out about their production and operation. Based on field investigations, the local government officials in Jinjiang and Quanzhou tried to persuade the provincial government to help the local export-oriented business. Fujian provincial politicians then pushed their case with the central government, advising the leadership that more favorable exchange rate and export rebate policies were necessary to prevent mass bankruptcies and social unrest. For instance, one interviewee from the Jinjiang Municipal Bureau of Commerce revealed that the Fujian provincial economic report submitted to the State Council in early 2008 suggested that:

> It is imperative to stabilize the foreign trade policy, particularly the exchange rate policy. The RMB appreciation should slow down moderately. Industrial transformation and upgrading are necessary, but should be pushed in a steady way. In the process government should implement large amounts of investment funds to support R&D and innovation. Meanwhile, the process of export structure adjustment should be market-oriented, rather than based on the administrative emphasis on high-end technology. It is important to prevent the rapid shrinking of traditional labor-intensive exports, which may trigger a large number of business failures and corresponding unemployment.[26]

The fieldwork further sheds light on the nature of the relationship between local politics and local economic actors. This suggests that the provincial government in many ways is not really local in any meaningful way, and that really "local" politics takes place at the prefecture and county levels. Brown recognizes that "local officials were on the front line in relationships between one of the most difficult groups in contemporary China, the farmers, and the state."[27] This is true for prefecture

[22] Kennedy (2009), p. 196.

[23] Interview_22082015 (1); Interview_22082015 (2); Interview_24082015.

[24] Interview_20082015.

[25] For more in-depth discussions of China's cadre management at the local level, see Edin (2003a) and Edin (2003b).

[26] Interview_20082015.

[27] Brown (2014), p. 93.

and county-level governments. The provincial government is responsive to the local lower-level government and passes information (including the issues and problems of local politics) to the central government. Yet the real interaction between state and non-state actors typically takes place at a much lower level of the administrative hierarchy.

5.2.4 *Guanxi-Based Lobbying Through Local Offices of Central Governmental Agencies*

Besides lobbying the local government, exporters could also make use of their connections (guanxi) to discuss their difficulties with local officials of central government agencies, particular MOFCOM, and pressed them to influence central government's exchange rate policy. The local officials of MOFCOM served as middlemen to pass along the concerns of China's export enterprises to the MOFCOM and further to the State Council. "The lobbying groups organized in the form of MOFCOM's regional branches exerted a very strong influence on the key officials in MOFCOM and State Council, and they usually exaggerated the negative impacts of RMB appreciation on China's export sector, hence constraining the policy options of the State Council," noted a professor of political economy from Xiamen University.[28]

As with the local government leaders, the political achievements of officials in the MOFCOM's regional branches depended at least in part on the flourishing of China's export sector.[29] In the first half of 2008, several MOFCOM's regional branches, including but not limited to Jiangsu, Guangdong, Shanghai and Liaoning, conducted field research to empirically analyze the impact of RMB appreciation on different industries in different regions. The research reports generally echoed local interests and became important policy inputs for the central government's exchange rate policy making. For instance, the Jiangsu report emphasized that the textile and garment export sectors could no longer bear the continued RMB appreciation in the second half of 2008:

> In the following six months, a 6.15% appreciation of RMB against the dollar would impose serious impacts on the textile and garment export enterprises in Jiangsu. First, the textile and garment export growth would decrease to zero. Second, there would be significant decline in profits of textile and garment export enterprises. A large number of enterprises would collapse, thereby affecting employment and social stability. If there were no relevant

[28] Interview_28072015.

[29] MOFCOM's local branch at the provincial level is called Shangwuting; MOFCOM's local branch at the municipal level is called Shangwuju.

support policies, the continued RMB appreciation would bring enormous downside risks to exports of textile and garment industry.[30]

The Guangzhou report also confirmed the negative impact of RMB appreciation on export enterprises: "with every 1% of RMB appreciation against the dollar, the total exports of Guangdong province would drop 2.37%, the exports of general trade enterprises would drop 5.79% and the exports of process trade enterprises would drop 1.44%."[31] It was also explicitly suggested that "the exchange rate reform should proceed as gradually as possible, rather than in one step, so that export enterprises would gradually raise risk awareness and then establish and improve the exchange rate risk prevention mechanism."[32]

However, it is worth pointing out that although the guanxi-based lobbying through local governments and local offices of central governmental agencies was direct and straightforward, it took a considerable amount of time to influence central government's exchange rate policy making. As confirmed by several interviewees, the various levels of local governments in China's administrative divisions became the major obstacle.[33] It was conventional wisdom that it was easier to engage with the lower levels of local governments directly and more difficult to reach the higher levels of local governments. However, it definitely took time to transfer information from county-level or municipal governments to provincial governments, and further to the central government. For instance, the RMB began to appreciate against the dollar at a faster pace in the fourth quarter of 2007. The Fujian provincial government's economic report was drafted in May 2008, which took more than half a year in total. The reports on RMB appreciation and enterprise competitiveness by MOFCOM's regional branches came even later. The reports were drafted in the second quarter of 2008, and the final versions did not get published until October 2008. Therefore, many export entrepreneurs also lobbied through trade association to seek more timely policy rescue from the central government.

---

[30] Ministry of Commerc, "RMB appreciation and enterprise competitiveness: empirical analysis of mechanical and electrical industries and textile and garment industries in Jiangsu", 1 October 2008, retrieved from http://kjxh.mofcom.gov.cn/article/r/200811/20081105883828.shtml.

[31] Ministry of Commerce, "RMB appreciation and enterprise competitiveness: empirical analysis of labour-intensive industries and processing trade industries in Guangdong", 1 October 2008, retrieved from http://kjxh.mofcom.gov.cn/article/r/200811/20081105883925.shtml.

[32] Ibid.

[33] Interview_02082015; Interview_18082015; Interview_26082015; Interview_04092015. Moreover, the vertical configuration of Chinese governments is more conducive to top-down administrative governance rather than bottom-up political participation. See, for example, Tsui and Wang (2008); Wang (2014).

5.2.5 Lobbying Through Trade Associations

The other more effective way used by the export companies was to lobby the central government or government departments through trade associations. Trade associations for labor-intensive enterprises began to lobby for slower RMB appreciation and cuts of export rebate rates in the early 2008. They argued that if the government did not take any measure, large quantities of labor-intensive enterprises would go bankrupt, thousands of workers would be laid off, and the social stability would therefore be threatened. As one of the most severely hit industries, the textile industry was a typical example of this case.

As confirmed by several interviewees, the textile and garments exporters in Fujian began to actively seek policy adjustments through two trade associations: Fujian Textile Industry Association (FTIA) and Fujian Chamber of Commerce for Import and Export (FCCIE). FTIA established itself as a bridge between government and enterprises.[34] On the one hand, FTIA conveyed the national economic policies to the member enterprises; on the other hand, FTIA represented the interests of member enterprises, and communicated more effectively with governments and other organizations. More importantly, FTIA collaborated horizontally with trade associations in other provinces, such as Jiangsu Textile Association and Guangdong Textile Association, to jointly collect the information that the local export enterprises faced enormous difficulties in the face of currency appreciation and export rebate cuts and reflect the situation to the corresponding higher organization.[35]

In response to the appeals of local textile trade associations, China National Textile & Apparel Council (CNTAC), as the national textile industry association centred at Beijing, formed six research teams to tour six typical provinces to survey the situations of the local textile industries in early March 2008. The six provinces were Jiangsu, Fujian, Zhejiang, Shandong, Guangdong, and Hebei, whose textile exports represented 85% of the total. After the survey, CNTAC representatives concluded that the profit margin of two-thirds of the textile enterprises was only 0.62%, and that each province's textile industry was facing imminent danger, which would jeopardize the jobs of about 15 million people.[36] After that, they summarized the situation in a report and submitted it directly to the State Council. CNTAC proposed 2% rollback of the export tax rebate rate of textile industry to 13 and 4% adjustment of the export tax rebate rate of apparel industry to 15%, so as to give the textile industry a chance to weather the difficulties.[37]

---

[34]"Introduction to Fujian Textile Industry Association", retrieved from http://www.afta.org.cn/about.asp.

[35]Interview_03082015.

[36]"Textile industry faces imminent danger", *SINA Finance*, 22 March 2008, retrieved from http://finance.sina.com.cn/chanjing/b/20080322/14554655553.shtml.

[37]"The first step in textile industry rescue: rollback the export tax rebate rate 2%", *SINA Finance*, 1 August 2008, retrieved from http://finance.sina.com.cn/roll/20080801/02045154886.shtml.

The other channel of lobbying was through chambers of commerce. FCCIE was established in 2003 to represent the interests of member enterprises and to promote the development of international trade in Fujian.[38] According to a FCCIE official, the representatives in the FCCIE mainly included entrepreneurs from export companies as well as retired governmental officials who previously held senior-level positions in the MOFCOM or provincial level Bureau of Commerce. The former ministerial and provincial government officials often used their informal patronage networks and other political resources to lobby for policies in favour of their interests.[39] They could not only communicate with the incumbent provincial level government leaders, but also put the case forward to higher chamber of commerce.

In response to the appeals of local chambers of commerce, China Chamber of Commerce for Import and Export of Textile and Apparel (CCCT) started investigation on the situation of textile industry in February 2008 and submitted its report to the MOFCOM in early May, recommending an adjustment of textile trade policy. The report argued that if the government stayed aloof, large amounts of small and medium enterprises would go bankrupt, thousands of workers would be laid off, and the livelihoods of the 20 million people employed in the textile industry would be threatened.[40] CCCT requested that the best outcome would be to increase the export rebate rate to 17%.[41]

The efforts of textile trade associations and chambers of commerce were successful. Their research reports on the situations of local textile industry finally got a response from the central government. In late April 2008, Zhang Xiaoqiang, a deputy director of NDRC, argued that "China's labor-intensive industries are the driving force for employment, which also helps increase farmers' income. It is impossible for China to completely abandon comparative advantage of cheap labour in the short term. Close attention must be paid to the current status of labor-intensive industries."[42] Fu Ziying, a vice-minister of MOFCOM, also proposed that "China must stabilize exports of labor-intensive industries, especially the steady growth of textile and garment trade, to allow time for product upgrade and industrial transformation."[43] In late May, China's Ministry of Industry and Information Technology issued an opinion letter which strove to the alleviate the difficulties of textile industry, and also sought suggestions and recommendations from NDRC, MOFCOM, PBOC, CNTAC and other organizations. The recommendations mainly referred to adjusting

---

[38]"Introduction to Fujian Chamber of Commerce for Import and Export", retrieved from http://www.fjiec.com/Aboutus.asp?Title=%C9%CC%BB%E1%BC%F2%BD%E9.

[39]Interview_08082015; Interview_26082015.

[40]"Textile industry 'rescue' will increase the export tax rebate rate", *WANGYI Finance*, 22 June 2008, retrieved from http://money.163.com/08/0627/09/4FEFSPRA00252G50.html.

[41]"The first step in textile industry rescue: rollback the export tax rebate rate 2%", *SINA Finance*, 1 August 2008, retrieved from http://finance.sina.com.cn/roll/20080801/02045154886.shtml.

[42]"MOFCOM: China must stabilize the exports of labour-intensive industries", *CAIJING*, 28 April 2008, retrieved from http://www.caijing.com.cn/2008-04-28/100058661.html.

[43]Ibid.

the export tax rebates to the previous level and taking measures to slow down the RMB appreciation, so as to relieve the difficult situations of the textile and garment industry.[44]

5.3 The Top Leadership Concerned

The central government faced considerable pressure to raise export rebate rates and maintain the stability of RMB exchange rate. Furthermore, information from various channels on decline of exports, unfavorable employment situation, and failure of businesses frequently reached the central government. This was no longer merely an economic problem, but rather an issue of political stability, because unemployment in the coastal industries would intensify the problem of the tide of migrant labors returning to their hometowns, which may give rise to social unrest.

As a result, the top leadership held several internal meetings to discuss the issue and finally decided to tour the key manufacturing centres in the coastal provinces. Particular attention was paid to the textile industry. Intensive research and investigation began in early July 2008. Premier Wen Jiabao went on an inspection trip to Jiangsu and Shanghai on 4–6 July. Wen was particularly concerned with the textile industry. He personally visited the Wuxi No. 1 Cotton Mill, where local governments arranged meetings between Wen and entrepreneurs from the electronic and textile industries. Wen heard about their difficulties and discussed ways to overcome the difficulties with the heads of enterprises.[45]

The then vice-president Xi Jinping, the former Governor of Fujian province and Party Secretary of Zhejiang province, expressed sympathy for the exporters during his visit to Guangdong province on 4–5 July. After Xi learned that some enterprises experienced a substantial decline in production because of the weakening foreign demand and rising oil and raw material prices, he explicitly called for ministerial and provincial government officials who accompanied him to implement policies to help out these industries.[46]

The vice-premier Li Keqiang and Minister of Commerce Chen Deming went on an inspection trip to Zhejiang, with a particular focus on the performance of export-oriented enterprises on 6–8 July. In the economic performance symposium that included representatives of both enterprises and government departments, Li

---

[44] "Textile export tax rebate rollback pending, a weather vane for renminbi exchange rate", *The Economic Observer*, 6 June 2008, retrieved from http://www.eeo.com.cn/eeo/jjgcb/2008/06/09/102552.shtml.

[45] "Wen Jiabao stressed to promote sound and rapid economic development when inspecting Jiangsu and Shanghai", *Xinhua*, 6 July, 2008, retrieved from http://news.xinhuanet.com/newscenter/2008-07/06/content_8499192.htm.

[46] "Xi Jinping inspected Guangdong documentary", *IFENG*, 7 July 2008, retrieved from http://news.ifeng.com/mainland/special/xijinpingshenzhen/content-4/detail_2008_07/07/788396_0.shtml.

listened to the entrepreneurs talking about their difficulties and stated that officials at various levels of government should help address the difficulties, especially those of small and medium enterprises.[47]

The vice-premier Wang Qishan also went on an inspection trip to Shandong on 3–5 July to investigate the situation and difficulties of export enterprises. He demanded that the relevant governmental departments should help export companies over the difficulties in a time of crisis and that enterprises should upgrade products and improve competitiveness.[48]

Based on intensive research and investigation in early July 2008, the top leadership was convinced that China's export situation was severe and that prompt counter measures should be taken. In the July 2008 Central Politburo meeting, the Central Politburo members recognized the dramatic change of China's economic fundamentals, incurred by the several problems of domestic severe natural disasters[49] and the international financial crisis. Although emphasis was still placed on inflation control, the other top priority of macroeconomic management was switched from "preventing relatively fast economic growth from becoming overheated" to "maintaining steady and relatively fast growth of the economy".[50] On the one hand, the PSC instructed the PBOC to stop the fast RMB appreciation in the middle of July. On the other hand, the PSC also required the MOF to adjust the export rebate rates for the most difficult industries, such as textiles and apparels, in late July.[51]

5.4 Stagnation of RMB Exchange Rate Reform, July 2008 to June 2010

Under the guidance of PSC, there was a significant change in exchange rate policy in the third quarter of 2008, according to the PBOC monetary policy implementation reports. The third-quarter monetary policy implementation report did not mention, as most previous reports did, the use of the market mechanism in deciding the value

---

[47] "Li Keqiang visits Zhejiang to investigate the economic performance", *China News*, 8 July 2008, retrieved from http://news.china.com.cn/txt/2008-07/09/content_15977912.htm.

[48] "Wang Qishan's three-day inspection to Yantai and Weihai: hot money, renminbi, and enterprises", *IFENG*, 10 July 2008, retrieved from http://news.ifeng.com/mainland/200807/0710_17_644323.shtml.

[49] A magnitude 7.9 earthquake struck Wenchuan in Sichuan province on 12 May 2008. The Sichuan Wenchuan Earthquake is the largest earthquake in PRC's history in terms of socio-economic losses. See "Sichuan Wenchuan Earthquake", *Xinhua*, retrieved from http://www.xinhuanet.com/politics/kzjz.

[50] "Central Politburo holds a meeting to analyze the current economic situation and next year's economic work", *Xinhua*, 25 July 2008, retrieved from http://news.xinhuanet.com/newscenter/2008-07/25/content_8770081.htm.

[51] The MOF announces that starting from 1 August 2008, China will raise export rebates for textile and apparel from 11 to 13% and increase export rebate for bamboo products to 11%. See "Ministry of Finance and State Administration of Taxation's announcement on lower export tax rebate rates of some commodities", State Taxation Administration, 30 July 2008, retrieved from http://www.chinatax.gov.cn/n810341/n810765/n812171/n812700/c1191582/content.html.

Fig. 5.11 RMB exchange rate against the US dollar, from 1 July 2008 to 1 January 2009. *Source* PBOC Monetary Policy Department

of the RMB. Instead, the third-quarter report described the exchange rate policy as "maintaining the RMB exchange rate stable"[52]—a striking departure from "continuing to enhance the RMB exchange rate flexibility"[53] in the first-quarter and second-quarter reports.

As Fig. 5.11 shows, the PBOC stopped the RMB appreciation in mid-July 2008 and depreciated the currency until mid-August 2008. After that, the RMB experienced some two-way fluctuations but the band was very limited. The RMB exchange rate against the dollar remained stable at around 6.83 by the end of 2008. During several periods of RMB depreciation, there existed widespread speculation that China would promote exports through currency devaluation, to which China's top leadership expressed firm opposition. The PBOC responded to the market panic that the RMB exchange rate would not continue to devalue.[54] The MOFCOM Minster Chen Deming also remarked that he would not expect to promote exports through currency devaluation and the recent RMB exchange rate fluctuations were completely normal.[55] Wen Jiabao further asserted that China had no intention to pursue trade surplus and would keep its currency at the reasonable and stable level.[56]

However, before we come to the conclusion that the level III game provided the most important source for the stagnation of China's exchange rate reform in the second half of 2008, it is necessary to emphasize that the interest group lobbying and

[52]People's Bank of China, "2008 Third Quarter Monetary Policy Implementation Report", retrieved from http://www.pbc.gov.cn/eportal/fileDir/history_file/files/att_11633_1.pdf, p. 6.

[53]People's Bank of China, "2008 First Quarter Monetary Policy Implementation Report", retrieved from http://www.pbc.gov.cn/eportal/fileDir/history_file/files/att_11631_1.pdf, p. 9; People's Bank of China, "2008 s Quarter Monetary Policy Implementation Report", retrieved from http://www.pbc.gov.cn/eportal/fileDir/history_file/files/att_11632_1.pdf, p. 10.

[54]"The PBOC responds to RMB hitting the decline limit: the exchange rate will not continue to devalue", *Xinhua*, 3 December 2008, retrieved from http://news.xinhuanet.com/finance/2008-12/03/content_10449602.htm.

[55]"MOFCOM minister: recent RMB exchange rate fluctuations 'completely normal'", *Xinhua*, 4 December 2008, retrieved from http://news.xinhuanet.com/fortune/2008-12/04/content_10457783.htm.

[56]"Wen Jiabao defends the RMB exchange rate policy", The Financial Times Chinese, 30 January 2009, retrieved from http://www.ftchinese.com/story/001024407?full=y.

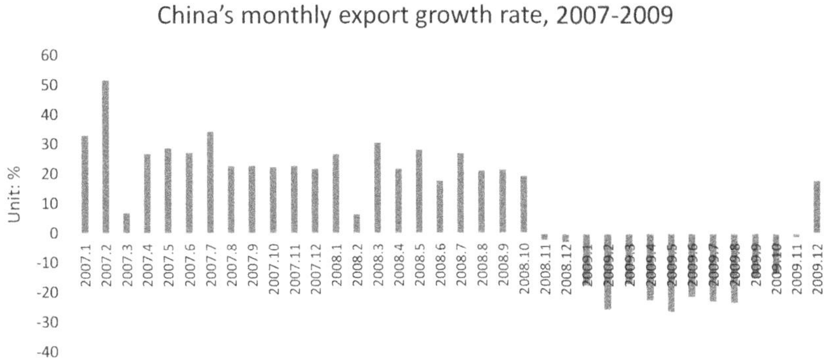

Fig. 5.12 China's monthly export growth rate, from 2007 to 2009. *Source* National Bureau of Statistics of PRC

the policy adjustment of both exchange rate and export rebate tax happened before the impact of the global financial crisis really hit, so that we can somehow separate the "normal" consequence of accelerated RMB appreciation out from the "extraordinary" consequence of the global financial crisis.[57] A comparison of China's export growth in the years of 2007–2009 would shed light on the different consequences. As Fig. 5.12 shows, China's export continued to grow in 2008, although the growth rate was lower than that in 2007. This is the "normal" consequences of accelerated RMB appreciation, and implies that the exporters perceived their difficult situation caused by the accelerated RMB appreciation, which has been discussed in detail in the Fujian case study, and that they lobbied based on this belief. Therefore, the stagnation of China's exchange rate reform in the second half of 2008 should be more a political analysis than an economic one.

By contrast, when it came to late 2008 and 2009, it was not just a matter of export growth declining, but of an actual fall in exports. While exports were growing by an average of more than 20% month on month for most of the year, in November 2008 they fell dramatically by 2.2%. Therefore, China's economy faced the external shock of the global financial crisis at the end of 2008, and the Chinese leadership rolled out a series of rescue policies, including the fiscal stimulus package and loose monetary policy in 2009. Amid turbulent times of global financial crisis, Chinese leaders stressed the top priority of "maintaining steady and relatively fast economic growth" at the Central Politburo meeting.[58] Furthermore, at the Central Economic Work Conference at the end of 2008, Chinese leaders reaffirmed the priority and

[57] The author thanks Shaun Breslin for his insight of the different consequences of the RMB appreciation and the global financial crisis.

[58] "Hu Jintao stressed to place stable and relatively fast economic growth as top priority", *Xinhua*, 29 November 2008, retrieved from http://news.xinhuanet.com/newscenter/2008-11/29/content_10431026.htm.

Fig. 5.13 RMB exchange rate against the US dollar, from 21 July 2005 to 18 June 2010. *Source* PBOC Monetary Policy Department

also discussed the exchange rate issue, explicitly stating that the RMB would remain stable, rather than depreciate substantially. There were mainly two reasons for this:

> First, substantial devaluation will result in asset prices plunge. It will cause large-scale foreign capital flight and more severe shock to the housing and stock markets, which is at odds with the current target of maintaining stability. Second, China's devaluation may lead to further depreciations of the neighbouring countries. It is neither conducive to Asia's financial stability nor conducive to enhancing the international status of the yuan.[59]

Under these circumstances, China's exchange rate remained stable at around 6.83 RMB/dollar. Extremely limited flexibility of the RMB exchange rate was allowed in 2009. China's leaders officially still claimed the exchange rate regime as managed floating, as they had done since 1994.[60] Yet practically, China returned to the de facto dollar-pegged exchange rate regime until June 2010 (see Fig. 5.13).

5.5 Implications of Exchange Rate Reform Stagnation

After China halted its exchange rate reform in the second half of 2008, many observers criticized the protectionist policy as a step back that could give rise to currency wars and exacerbate global imbalance.[61] In retrospect, China's exchange rate policy was

[59]"Central Economic Work Conference researches the exchange rate issue and RMB will not depreciate substantially", *People's Daily*, 10 December 2008, retrieved from http://finance.people.com.cn/GB/jinji/222/2322/8492789.html.

[60]Lionel Barber, "Transcript: Wen Jiabao", *Financial Times*, 2 February 2009, retrieved from http://www.ft.com/cms/s/0/795d2bca-f0fe-11dd-8790-0000779fd2ac.html#axzz4539B7huI.

[61]See, for example, "China's currency: a yuan-sided argument", *The Economist*, 18 November 2009, retrieved from http://www.economist.com/node/14901104; Martin Wolf, "Why China's exchange

a component of a policy package in response to the global financial crisis, which was not abnormal considering the unconventional monetary policies of the other major economies. Moreover, it did not constitute the final word on China's exchange rate reform, as China re-initiated the exchange rate reform in 2010. This will be discussed in more detail in the next chapter. Yet the stagnation of exchange rate reform suggested important implications of China's politics.

The short-lived acceleration of RMB appreciation in 2008 and China's return to the dollar-pegged exchange rate regime suggest that stability maintenance and short-term crisis management prevailed over long-term planning in the formation of economic policy. This does not mean that the Chinese leadership was short-sighted and lack of long-term thinking. Indeed, Chinese leaders were long aware of the disadvantages of over dependence on the export and the US dollar. They had also made a public commitment to addressing the economic imbalance. For example, Wen Jiabao had officially used very serious words such as "unstable, unbalanced, uncoordinated and unsustainable" to describe the conditions of China's economy, and stressed that China should restructure and rebalance its economy for sustainable growth.[62] In Wen's words:

> The unstable matter is that China has an excessively high investment growth rate, excessively large extension of credit, excessive liquidity of the currency, and *improper foreign trade and international payment* [emphasis added]. The unbalanced issue is that China has unbalanced development between urban and rural areas, between different regions, and between economic expansion and social progress. The uncoordinated matter is that the primary, secondary and tertiary industries are not coordinated, investment and consumption are not coordinated, and *China's economic growth relies too much on investment and export* [emphasis added]. The unsustainable issue is that China does not effectively address the issues related to energy saving, emission reduction and environmental protection. In order to achieve sustainable development, *China needs to boost domestic consumption* [emphasis added], push forward reform and opening-up, remove institutional obstacles, encourage intellectual and technological innovation, and make more efforts to save energy and reduce emissions.[63]

However, in practice, Chinese leaders were most concerned with social stability and obsessed with growth, often at the expense of economic rebalancing. The gradual, limited nature of China's exchange rate policy reform was a good illustration. The half-hearted reform was even more evident in times of crisis. China's response to both the 1997 Asian financial crisis and the 2008 global financial crisis resonated with this argument. With regard to the 1997 Asian financial crisis, Breslin argues

---

rate policy concerns us", *Financial Times*, 8 December 2009, retrieved from https://next.ft.com/content/afac7ada-e448-11de-bed0-00144feab49a; Martin Wolf, "How to fight the currency wars with stubborn China", *Financial Times*, 5 October 2010, retrieved from https://next.ft.com/content/52b8a8e4-d0b0-11df-8667-00144feabdc0; George Soros, "China must fix the global currency crisis", *Financial Times*, 7 October 2010, retrieved from https://next.ft.com/content/f4dd9122-d22a-11df-8fbe-00144feabdc0.

[62] "Premier Wen Jiabao Press Conference", State Council Bulletin, 16 March 2007, retrieved from http://www.gov.cn/gongbao/content/2007/content_595145.htm.

[63] Ibid.

that "the Chinese leadership's response to the regional crises [Asian financial crisis] illuminates their perceptions of the importance of export growth."[64] Specifically,

> China's leaders appear to have been very fearful of a global turndown in demand. For example, as the rate of the growth of exports slowed in the first third of 1997 in the wake of the Asian financial crisis, the minister in charge of foreign trade, Wu Yi, appeared on national television warning of the dangers of slowing growth rates for employment and social stability. This was not a case of exports actually declining – exports were still growing at over 11% over the previous years – but simply that they were not growing fast enough as far as the government was concerned.[65]

As to the 2008 global financial crisis, this had an immediate negative effect on Chinese exports and thus threatened China's economic trajectory significantly, revealing the vulnerability of export-oriented economic growth model. However, China's crisis response once again revealed the Chinese leadership's short-term prioritisation to preserve the growth and stability over the long-term economic rebalancing. Hung recognized that China's export-oriented industrialization faced enormous challenge and turned to debt-financed, state-driven investment to maintain the economic growth.[66] More critically, Jiang defined China's crisis response as "vulgarised version of Keynesianism" that "strengthened state monopolies and enriched the public sector at the expense of private businesses and consumer welfare, exacerbated the unbalanced and unsustainable elements in the economy, and created massive infrastructural and industrial over-capacity".[67]

To summarize, the stagnation of China's exchange rate during the turbulent times of 2008–2010 suggests that although Chinese leaders were aware of the negative impacts of China's asymmetrical external dependence, their immediate response in face of the global financial crisis and economic downturn was to spare no effort to maintain the economic growth, which provided important sources for social stability. The economic transition and rebalancing, which was conducive to China's economy in the long term, was often placed in secondary position.

5.6 Concluding Remarks

This chapter has closely examined the short-lived acceleration of RMB appreciation in the first half of 2008 and the stagnation of exchange rate reform from 2008 to 2010. It provides more nuanced explanations for export lobbying in the level III game and the dynamics of central-local interactions in China's exchange rate policy making in 2008. The typical case study in Fujian province suggests that exporters faced considerable difficulties and grew hostile to the RMB appreciation in 2008. They mobilized resources to lobby through local governments, local offices of central

[64] Breslin (1999), p. 1194.
[65] Breslin (2012), pp. 79–80.
[66] Hung (2012).
[67] Jiang (2015a), p. 361.

governmental agencies, and trade associations. The Chinese leadership could not afford to neglect local interests, as the export enterprises' difficult situation was not only an economic problem but also an issue related to social and political stability. China halted exchange rate reform in the second half of 2008, and further returned to the dollar-pegged exchange rate regime during the global financial crisis.

The empirical study clearly shows that Chinese leaders prioritized short-term growth and stability maintenance, which sacrificed the long-term interest of economic transition and rebalancing. Evidence in this chapter demonstrates that for this period, international pressure was very much relegated to secondary importance behind domestic pressure and considerations. China's interest group politics in the level III game provided the most important sources for China's exchange rate policy from 2008 to 2010.

With the benefit of hindsight, the stagnation of exchange rate reform was a temporary policy response to the global financial crisis. Chinese leaders bore the negative consequences of excessive external dependence in mind and intended to make some changes after China weathered the crisis. The next chapter will continue to explore the resumption of the RMB exchange rate reform in mid-2010 and China's effort to internationalize its currency to reduce the dependence on the US dollar.

Chapter 6
The Resumption of RMB Exchange Rate Reform and the Internationalization of RMB, 2010–2013

Chapter 5 has examined the interest group politics of exchange rate policy making between 2008 and 2010. Chinese exporters grew hostile to the accelerated RMB appreciation in early 2008. They waged lobbying campaigns through local governments, local offices of central governmental agencies and trade associations. Faced with considerable pressure, the Chinese leadership personally investigated several key manufacturing centers in the coastal provinces. They recognized the dramatic change of China's economic fundamentals and rolled out rescue policies for export sectors. On the one hand, the PSC instructed the MOF to adjust the export rebate rates for the most difficult industries such as textile and apparel in the late July 2008. On the other hand, the PSC required the PBOC to stop the fast RMB appreciation in the middle of July 2008 and China returned to the de facto dollar-pegged exchange rate regime amid the most turbulent times of global financial crisis. Empirical evidence suggests that China's interest group politics in the level III game provided the most important sources for China's exchange rate policy from 2008 to 2010.

This chapter will analyze the resumption of RMB exchange rate reform after June 2010. It will first examine external influence of the US Congress, the Treasury and the IMF on China's exchange rate reform in 2010. While Congress's influence on the RMB issue generally diminished over time after the global financial crisis, international criticism and pressure from the US administration and the IMF still played an important role of agenda-setting in China's exchange rate policy making in 2010. The second section describes the Chinese government's response to the external pressure on the RMB issue in 2010. The Chinese leadership stood firm against external pressure, as they did in 2005. Moreover, with less internal controversy within the central government (between PBOC and MOFCOM), Chinese leaders were more consistent in exchange rate policy in 2010. The third section combines the Chinese leadership's consensus to promote the internationalization of RMB and the domestic politics of exchange rate policy making. It argues that with the development of RMB internationalization and increasing openness of the capital account, a flexible exchange rate was the feasible choice to preserve the independence and effectiveness of Chinese monetary policy, which produced the Chinese leadership's consensus on

Z. Wang, *The International Political Economy of China's Exchange Rate Policy Making*, https://doi.org/10.1007/978-981-33-4578-2_6

the second round of RMB exchange rate reform. As the stability and predictability of RMB exchange rate was one of the most important attributes to improving confidence and promoting the international use of RMB, it determined the pathway of gradual and steady appreciation in the second round of RMB exchange rate reform.

6.1 The Mixed External Influence on the RMB Issue, 2008–2010

The analysis in Chap. 3 suggests that external influences of the US government and the IMF played an agenda-setting role in China's exchange rate policy making in 2005. With regard to the relationship between external pressure and China's second round of exchange rate reform from June 2010, there have been divisive debates among scholars and observers. For instance, on one side of the spectrum is the argument that the increasing US criticism of China's currency practices gives rise to China's exchange rate in June 2010 and the subsequent RMB appreciation.[1] At the other end of the spectrum is Ferguson's argument that "the dollar-RMB issue have already become essentially moribund" after the global financial crisis.[2] The section will offer empirical analyses of US Congress RMB-related bills and Treasury's Reports to Congress on International Economic and Exchange Rate as well as IMF's Consultation Reports with China. Based on documentary analysis, I will not entirely agree with either Lichtervelde's argument or Ferguson's without reservations. Instead, it will be argued that the Congress, the Treasury and the IMF imposed a mixed influence on China's currency after the global financial crisis. While Congress's influence on the RMB issue has generally diminished over time after the global financial crisis, international criticism and pressure from the US administration and the IMF still played an important role of agenda-setting in China's exchange rate policy making in 2010.

6.1.1 Congress's Influence on the RMB Issue Diminished

Congress relieved pressure on the RMB during the global financial crisis. There was only one bill (S. 2813) on the RMB issue during the period from 2008 to the first half of 2010. The China Currency Manipulation Act of 2008, introduced on 3 April 2008, mandates the Treasury to deal with China's currency manipulation, including deciding, setting benchmarks and timeframes, initiating bilateral negotiations with

[1] Lichtervelde (2012).

[2] Ferguson (2014), p. 123.

China and coordinating with the IMF to address RMB misalignment and US-China trade imbalance.[3]

A plausible explanation is that both the US and China, along with most of the world's countries, looked domestically to stabilize their own economies first and then re-examined the macroeconomic policies of other economies during the turbulent times of global financial crisis. As noted in the previous chapter, China first halted its currency's appreciation and adjusted export rebate rates for difficult export sectors, even before the global financial crisis really hit. Moreover, China rolled out a four-trillion-yuan stimulus package to expand domestic demand and stimulate economic growth at the end of 2008. For the US, the Congress enacted a number of bills, including but not limited to the Housing and Economic Recovery Act of 2008 (30 July 2008), the Emergency Economic Stabilization Act of 2008 (3 October 2008), and the American Recovery and Reinvestment Act of 2009 (17 February 2009), in order to save jobs and stop further economic deterioration.[4]

Despite there being no RMB-related bills between July 2008 and June 2010, it is worth noting that the RMB issue was still under Congress' scrutiny in the first half of 2010. In particularly, on 15 March 2010, a group of 130 House members signed a letter to the administration and urged the Treasury to name China as a currency manipulator in the next Treasury Report.[5] However, the letter was not as effective as those bills in 2005 with the threat of punitive duties. This may be seen from the Treasury's decision to delay the April 2010 Report before President Hu Jintao's April 2010 visit to Washington, which will be further discussed later on. Therefore, Congress' pressure on the RMB issue, even if somewhat gained momentum in the first half of 2010, was considered as limited.

Furthermore, there were still only two RMB-related bills (H. R. 6071 and H. R. 2909) after June 2010.[6] Neither bills added anything new to the previous bills, thereby producing a diminishing influence. The RMB issue generally slipped down

---

[3]The U.S. Congress, "S. 2813 China Currency Manipulation Act of 2008: To require the Secretary of the Treasury to take action with respect to currency manipulation by the People's Republic of China and for other purposes", 3 April 2008, retrieved from https://www.congress.gov/110/bills/s2813/BILLS-110s2813is.pdf.

[4]The U.S. Congress, "H.R.3221 Housing and Economic Recovery Act of 2008", 30 July 2008, retrieved from https://www.congress.gov/110/plaws/publ289/PLAW-110publ289.pdf; The U.S. Congress, "H.R.1424 Emergency Economic Stabilization Act of 2008", 3 October 2008, retrieved from https://www.congress.gov/110/plaws/publ343/PLAW-110publ343.pdf; The U.S. Congress, "H.R.1 American Recovery and Reinvestment Act of 2009", 17 February 2009, retrieved from https://www.congress.gov/111/plaws/publ5/PLAW-111publ5.pdf.

[5]Sharma (2010), p. 102.

[6]The U.S. Congress, "H. R. 6071 Emergency China Trade Act of 2010: To withdraw normal trade relations treatment from the products of the People's Republic of China, to provide for a balanced trade relationship between that country and the United States, and for other purposes", 30 July 2010, retrieved from https://www.congress.gov/111/bills/hr6071/BILLS-111hr6071ih.pdf; The U.S. Congress, "H. R. 2909 Emergency China Trade Act: To withdraw normal trade relations treatment from the products of the People's Republic of China, to provide for a balanced trade relationship between that country and the United States, and for other purposes", 13 September 2011, retrieved from https://www.congress.gov/112/bills/hr2909/BILLS-112hr2909ih.pdf.

the agenda in the US Congress after 2008, which was confirmed by the limited number of Congress bills on the RMB issue from 2008 to 2013. Considering all the Congress RMB-related bills during the period between 2003 and 2013 (see Appendix A), the argument is supported that the pressure from the US Congress on China's exchange rate policy has declined to near vanishing point over time. Therefore, the pressure from US Congress was very unlikely to be a significant factor in influencing China's exchange rate policy making in and after June 2010.

6.1.2 Treasury's and IMF's Pressure on the RMB Issue Intensified in 2010

As China's current account surplus and international reserves continued to grow in 2008, the Treasury's December 2008 Report remained critical of China's persistently undervalued RMB exchange rate and large interventions in the foreign exchange market. However, the April 2009 Report demonstrated substantial changes. The April 2009 Report recognized that the global economic and financial backdrop had changed dramatically, and did not criticize China's return to the dollar peg regime. Instead, the Report recognized that the RMB was the only emerging market currency strengthened against the dollar whereas most other emerging market currencies fell sharply. More specifically, the Treasury highlighted in the April 2009 Report the following factors:

> First, China has taken steps to enhance exchange rate flexibility. Officials acknowledged in January the need for greater flexibility and the need to allow the exchange rate to adapt to an equilibrium level. Second, the Chinese currency appreciated by 16.6% in real terms between the end of June 2008 and the end of February 2009. As the crisis intensified, the currency appreciated slightly against the dollar when most other emerging market currencies fell sharply. Third, official statistics suggest the pace of China's foreign exchange reserve accumulation slowed in the second half of last year. Fourth, China has enacted a large fiscal stimulus package – second in size to that of the United States in the G-20 – which should help spur domestic demand growth and help rebalance the Chinese economy.[7]

Such positive comments on China's policy response implied that the Treasury accepted China's halting of the RMB appreciation at a time of crisis, in comparison with other emerging countries devaluing their currencies. However, this does not mean that the Treasury would approve China halting the exchange rate reform forever. It should be noted that the Treasury insisted that China should continue to allow for greater flexibility of the RMB exchange rate. Treasury Secretary Geithner also reaffirmed the above key points in his statement to Congress on International Economic and Exchange Rate Policies.[8] The October 2009 Report further commended that

[7]U.S. Department of the Treasury, "Report to Congress on International Economic and Exchange Rate Policies", April 2009, retrieved from https://www.treasury.gov/resource-center/international/exchange-rate-policies/Documents/fxreportfinalfor%20webapril152009.pdf, p. 3.

[8]U.S. Department of the Treasury, "Statement by Treasury Secretary Timothy Geithner on Release of Semi-Annual Report to Congress on International Economic and Exchange Rate Policies", 15 April 2009, retrieved from https://www.treasury.gov/press-center/press-releases/Pages/tg90.aspx.

China's timely and aggressive fiscal and monetary policy stimulus resulted in a strong domestic economic recovery and a decline in its current account surplus, which also contributed significantly to recovery in global demand.[9]

However, the RMB issue intensified in early 2010. The US still struggled with sluggish economic growth and a high unemployment rate in the first half of 2010. In addition to pressure from the Congress, many western observers and analysts saw China's exchange rate policy as an important distortion in the world economy, which slowed the recovery of other economies worldwide, and proposed that China must revalue its currency to address the imbalance.

To name but a few, a report by John Williamson, an important figure with wide credibility amongst neoliberals, demonstrated that China's currency was substantially undervalued. More specifically, his report estimated that the RMB was about 25% undervalued in effective terms and about 40% undervalued in bilateral terms against the US dollar.[10] Based on the Report, C. Fred Bergsten, Director of Peterson Institute for International Economics, testified before the Committee on Ways and Means on 24 March 2010. He declared that the substantial undervaluation of the RMB was "a blatant form of protectionism" and recommended that the US Administration should label China as a "currency manipulator" in the next Treasury's Report and collaborate with the European countries as well as emerging market and developing economies in multilateral ways (through the IMF and the WTO) to remedy the situation promptly.[11] Added pressure also came from the Nobel-prize winning economist Paul Krugman. He suggested that Washington should take a tough attitude against Beijing, as the US had no reason to fear China.[12] He declared that "the U.S. Treasury Department must stop fudging and obfuscating" and "something must be done".[13]

Faced with mounting pressure, the US administration became increasingly critical of China's currency undervaluation and took action to demand Beijing to make policy changes. In February 2010, President Obama set the objective of the next year for China "to recognize that it is also in their interest to allow their currency to appreciate", expecting some "very serious" and "bumpy" negotiations.[14] Treasury Secretary Geithner discussed the exchange rate issue with Vice Premier Wang Qishan in their meeting, iterating that it was in China's own interest to move to a more flexible exchange rate.[15] Moreover, the Obama administration sought to make considerable use of multilateral channels like the G20 and the IMF to tackle the RMB issue. For

[9]U.S. Department of the Treasury, "Report to Congress on International Economic and Exchange Rate Policies", October 2009, retrieved from https://www.treasury.gov/resource-center/international/exchange-rate-policies/Documents/FX%20Report%20FINAL%20October%2015%202009.pdf.

[10]Williamson (2010).

[11]Bergsten (2010).

[12]Krugman (2010).

[13]Ibid.

[14]"Obama's corporate messaging", *Bloomberg*, 11 February 2010, retrieved from http://www.bloomberg.com/news/articles/2010-02-10/obamas-corporate-messaging.

[15]"Geithner, Wang exchange views on U.S.-China concerns", *Reuters*, 8 April 2010, retrieved from http://www.reuters.com/article/us-usa-china-currency-geithner-idUSTRE6373B720100408.

instance, Obama sent a letter to G20 nations ahead of the Toronto summit in June, which strived to reach a consensus on market-oriented exchange rates. He emphasised that "market-determined exchange rates are essential to global economic vitality" and "flexible exchange rates are necessary to support a strong and balanced global economy".[16] The IMF was particularly concerned with the overvalued dollar and undervalued RMB in 2010. "The Chinese renminbi has depreciated in real effective terms in tandem with the US dollar and is assessed to be substantially undervalued from a medium-term perspective," noted an IMF official in the G20 ministers meeting in Seoul.[17]

Similar to the case in 2005, despite increasing political pressure in the US to confront Beijing over the value of the RMB, it was quite obvious that the US administration sought a resolution to address the currency issue with Beijing without serious US-China confrontation. Similar to his predecessor John Snow, Geithner responded that mounting public pressure and labelling China as a currency manipulator would not help address the RMB issue. Therefore, the Treasury finally decided to delay the April 2010 Report, originally scheduled for release on 15 April and before President Hu Jintao's April 2010 visit to Washington, which highlighted the Obama administration's effort to maintain the US-China relations.[18]

To summarize, the Congress, the Treasury and the IMF imposed mixed pressure on China's currency in 2010. While Congress's influence on the RMB issue diminished over time after the global financial crisis, international criticism and pressure from the US administration and the IMF on the RMB undervaluation gained momentum in the first half of 2010. Similar to the case in 2005, external pressure played an agenda-setting role, which meant that China's leaders found it impossible to avoid the RMB exchange rate issue. The next section will discuss China's response to the increasing demand for RMB revaluation in 2010.

6.2 China's Response to the External Pressure on the RMB Issue in 2010

This section will analyze China's response to the mounting external pressure in 2010. Compared with the case in 2005, the Chinese leadership showed some similarities and more differences in responding to the external pressure for China's currency revaluation in 2010. On the one hand, what remained the same was that China's

[16]"Obama's letter to the Group of 20 countries on financial and foreign exchange reform", *Reuters*, 18 June 2010, retrieved from http://www.reuters.com/article/g20-obama-letter-idUSN1811668220100618; "Obama urges G20 to boost demand: White House releases letter ahead of Toronto summit", *Financial Times*, 18 June 2010, retrieved from https://next.ft.com/content/10f0ebec-7aca-11df-8549-00144feabdc0.

[17]"IMF says Chinese currency substantially undervalued", *Reuters*, 1 March 2010, retrieved from http://www.reuters.com/article/us-imf-g-idUSTRE6204QY20100301.

[18]"Is China a currency manipulator?", Council on Foreign Relations, 15 April 2010, retrieved from http://www.cfr.org/china/china-currency-manipulator/p21902.

leaders stood firm against the external pressure and refused the rhetoric of China as the cause of global imbalance and the responsibility to revalue its currency. On the other hand, it could be recognized that there was much less internal controversy within the Chinese central government, and the Chinese leadership was more consistent in their exchange rate policy in 2010.

6.2.1 Standing Firm to the External Pressure

The Chinese leadership did not wish to show any sign of weakness under international pressure. Chinese leaders consistently opposed the international criticism that the RMB was substantially undervalued, and stated that wrongful accusations and pressure would not help solve the RMB issue. Not to mention the lower-level government and departmental officials,[19] Premier Wen Jiabao straightforwardly retorted that the RMB exchange rate was not undervalued in his answer to a *Financial Times* journalist in the press conference at the close of NPC.[20] Wen repeated the official wordings that "we will continue the managed floating exchange rate regime based on market supply and demand and maintain the stability of the RMB at a reasonable and balanced level."[21] Furthermore, Wen complained about the demands for Beijing to revalue its currency. He asserted that "we object to mutual criticisms between countries and tough measures to force a country to revalue its currency, which are definitely not conducive to the RMB exchange rate reform",[22] which echoed his "exchange rate—sovereignty"[23] statement in 2005.

Resonating with Wen's remarks, a few days later the PRC's Embassy in the US reprinted on the official website a review article "The Yuan Scapegoat", originally published in the Wall Street Journal, to explicitly demonstrate the Chinese government's stance.[24] It directly pointed out that the US was more wrong than China in fighting a currency war, which might give rise to "beggar-thy-neighbour currency

---

[19] See, for example, Edward Wong and Mark Landler, "China rejects U.S. complaints on its currency", *New York Times*, 4 February 2010, retrieved from http://www.nytimes.com/2010/02/05/world/asia/05diplo.html; "Qin Gang: RMB exchange rate is not the main cause of Sino-US trade imbalance", *Xinhua*, 18 March 2010, retrieved from http://news.xinhuanet.com/world/2010-03/18/content_13196329.htm.

[20] "Premier Wen Jiabao Press Conference", *Xinhua*, 14 March 2010, retrieved from http://www.xinhuanet.com/politics/2010lh/zljzh_index.htm.

[21] Ibid.

[22] Ibid.

[23] "Wen Jiabao: exchange rate reform is China's sovereignty and not subject to external pressure", *Xinhua*, 17 May 2005, retrieved from http://news.xinhuanet.com/fortune/2005-05/17/content_2964746.htm.

[24] "The Yuan Scapegoat", Embassy of People's Republic of China in the United States of America, retrieved from http://www.china-embassy.org/eng/xw/t674124.htm; "The Yuan Scapegoat: The U.S. establishment flirts with a currency and trade war with China", *The Wall Street Journal*, 18 March 2010, retrieved from http://www.wsj.com/articles/SB10001424052748704743404575127511778280940.

protectionism".[25] Therefore, it warned the US not to make the RMB into a scapegoat and risk a trade war with China. In referring to Japan's experience in the 1980s and 1990s, it argued that China was right to resist the external criticism and pressure to avoid the negative effects of a large revaluation on China's economic growth.

Moreover, in a bilateral meeting between President Barack Obama and President Hu Jintao at Washington, Hu particularly stressed that the RMB exchange rate reform would not be advanced under external pressure.[26] He pointed out the general principle of China's exchange rate reform:

> China stands firm in the direction of promoting the RMB exchange rate reform, which is based on the needs of China's economic and social development. Moreover, specific reform measures should be considered according to the development and changes of the world's as well as China's economic situation.[27]

6.2.2 MOFCOM and PBOC in the Same Boat

While the Chinese leadership stood against the external pressure in 2010 as firmly as they did in 2005, two prominent differences could be identified between the 2005 and the 2010 cases. First and foremost, there existed much less internal controversy within the Chinese central government with regard to the exchange rate policy. Chapter 3 has elaborated the internal battle of the PBOC vis-à-vis the MOFCOM over the RMB exchange rate reform. The PBOC advocated a more flexible exchange rate for more monetary autonomy, whereas the MOFCOM, with more political clout, maintained that exchange rate stability was crucial for China's growth and employment. The limited nature of the 2005 exchange rate reform was largely a result of compromise between the two previously divided central government agencies. However, when it came to 2010, the two agencies both held the position that a stable exchange rate was necessary in turbulent times, and that the RMB exchange rate alone was not responsible for the trade imbalance.

For instance, Zhou Xiaochuan said that the excessive demand for RMB appreciation from the US did not help in the Inter-American Development Bank Meeting.[28] In the NPC and CPPCC Meetings Zhou explained China's exchange rate policy in detail:

> Since July 2005, China has adopted the managed floating exchange rate system based on market supply and demand with reference to a basket of currencies and maintained the stability of the RMB at a reasonable and balanced level. However, it does not rule out some special policies in some special periods, such as the special exchange rate formation

---

[25]Ibid.

[26]"Hu Jintao: the RMB exchange rate reform will not be advanced by any external pressure", *Xinhua*, 13 April 2010, retrieved from http://news.xinhuanet.com/fortune/2010-04/13/c_1229512.htm.

[27]Ibid.

[28]"Zhou Xiaochuan: The 'noise' of RMB appreciation does not help", *Xinhua*, 24 March 2010, retrieved from http://news.xinhuanet.com/fortune/2010-03/24/content_13233276.htm.

mechanism in the global financial crisis, which is a component of the policy package to cope with the crisis.[29]

Yi Gang, the deputy governor of PBOC, also reaffirmed Wen's non-undervaluation argument and Zhou's explanation of China's exchange rate policy. Yi said that China would improve the RMB exchange rate formation mechanism and the RMB exchange rate would be kept stable at the proper and balanced level in the process.[30]

With regard to MOFCOM's stance on exchange rate policy, when asked to comment on the pressure to label China as a currency manipulator, the MOFCOM Minister Chen Deming fought back that it was the American export control policy against China that worsened the trade imbalance.[31] He emphasized that "the RMB exchange rate is not a panacea" and RMB revaluation alone could not resolve the Sino-US trade imbalance.[32] Furthermore, Chen complained that since 2007 the US had separated China and imposed additional sets of export control to China, including computers, civil aviation technology, Computer Numerical Control machines and many components.[33] He further remarked that the US trade protectionism was unfair not only to China, but also to the American manufacturers and exporters, which was negative for the American employment and economic growth.[34]

More importantly, the MOFCOM withdrew its opposition to exchange rate reform and stressed proper pace of proceeding, which was consistent with MOFCOM's shifted priority of surplus reduction after 2007. One official at the MOFCOM Comprehensive Department noted:

> The MOFCOM did not strongly oppose the exchange rate reform in the internal meetings in 2010. Instead, the MOFCOM insisted that exchange rate reform should be carried out at the right pace, under the guidance of Premier Wen Jiabao's three principles of own initiative, controllability and gradualism. For example, the MOFCOM faced enormous pressure in 2010 and 2011, particularly after the G20 agreed on the guidelines to measure economic external imbalances. Therefore, we also supported the market-oriented exchange rate reform and the internal dissent was not as much as the outside world speculated.[35]

In summary, the disagreement between the PBOC and the MOFCOM on exchange rate policy was far less in 2010 than in 2005. On the one hand, the PBOC reiterated the necessity of exchange rate stability in 2010, which was different from the active

---

[29] "Zhou Xiaochuan: RMB exchange rate policy will remain targeted and flexible", *Xinhua*, 6 March 2010, retrieved from http://news.xinhuanet.com/video/2010-03/06/content_13109474.htm.

[30] "Yi Gang: RMB appreciation is determined by the market", *Xinhua*, 9 March 2010, retrieved from http://news.xinhuanet.com/fortune/2010-03/09/content_13131254_4.htm.

[31] Ministry of Commerce, "Chen Deming delivers a speech at the 2010 China Development Forum", 21 March 2010, retrieved from http://www.mofcom.gov.cn/aarticle/ae/ai/201003/20100306831415.html.

[32] "Chen Deming: the RMB exchange rate is not a 'panacea'", *Xinhua*, 31 March 2010, retrieved from http://news.xinhuanet.com/fortune/2010-03/31/content_13272655.htm.

[33] Ministry of Commerce, "Chen Deming delivers a speech at the 2010 China Development Forum", 21 March 2010, retrieved from http://www.mofcom.gov.cn/aarticle/ae/ai/201003/20100306831415.html; for a detailed historical account of the US-China trade relations, see Meijer (2016).

[34] Ibid.

[35] Interview_25092015.

advocate of exchange rate reform in 2005. On the other hand, the MOFCOM was not firmly against the exchange rate reform in 2010, which was also different from the powerful resistance in 2005.

6.2.3 The Chinese Leadership More Consistent in the Exchange Rate Reform Policy

Chapter 3 has analyzed that in the case of 2005 exchange rate reform, the PBOC and the MOFCOM were in polar opposite positions and the Chinese leadership swung back and forth with difficulties to reconcile the interests of all parties. The situation changed considerably in 2010. With less internal controversy within the central government, the Chinese leadership was more consistent in its exchange rate policy.

More specifically, in the case of 2005, though China's leaders made public commitments to exchange rate reform, they said on various occasions that no specific timetable or schedule would be provided and even stated that the exchange rate reform would be postponed. PBOC's announcement of RMB exchange rate reform on 21 July 2005 turned out to be unexpected. However, when it came to 2010, the Chinese leaders, including the heads of MOFCOM and PBOC, agreed on the general direction of market-oriented exchange reform, which was confirmed by several MOFCOM and PBOC officials.[36] In early March 2010, the PBOC Governor Zhou suggested that China would eventually abandon the peg and manage the exit strategy carefully in the NPC press conference. "If we are to exit from unconventional policies and return to conventional policies, we must be extremely prudent about our choice of timing," Zhou noted, "this also includes the RMB exchange rate policy."[37] When asked subsequently about his views on the RMB exchange rate, the MOFCOM Minister Chen confirmed that Zhou's message represented Chinese government's position on exchange rate policy.[38] In April 2010 there were already several sources that revealed China's readiness to resume exchange rate reform.[39] After this, the

[36]Interview_25092015; Interview_19092015; Interview_26092015.

[37]"NDRC, MOF, MOFCOM and PBOC press conference on enhancing and improving macroeconomic management", Ministry of Finance of People's Republic of China, 6 March 2010, retrieved from http://www.mof.gov.cn/gongzhongcanyu/tuwenzhibo/ft100306lianghui03.html.

[38]Ibid.

[39]See, for example, Jamil Anderlini, "Beijing lays ground for renminbi shift: China could widen daily trading band for currency", *Financial Times*, 6 April 2010, retrieved from https://next.ft.com/content/64c4bd04-4193-11df-865a-00144feabdc0; "Over to you, China", *The Economist*, 8 April 2010, retrieved from http://www.economist.com/node/15868014; Huang (2010).

Chinese officials, particularly from the PBOC, continued to signal the readiness to resume the exchange rate reform sooner rather than later.[40]

To summarize, this section has elaborated Chinese government's response to the mounting international criticism and pressure in the first half of 2010. The Chinese leadership stood firm to the external pressure and emphasized that politicization of the RMB exchange rate would not help address the issue. The PBOC and the MOFCOM were not divergent in terms of the exchange rate reform, and there was less internal controversy within the central government. Therefore, the Chinese leadership was more consistent in its exchange rate policy. However, it remained a question as to why the domestic politics of exchange rate policy making in 2010 was different from that in 2005. The next section will discuss the relationship between the exchange rate reform and the internationalization of RMB, which will provide answers to the unsolved puzzle.

6.3 The RMB Exchange Rate Reform and the Internationalization of RMB, 2010–2013

To examine the relationship between exchange rate reform and the internationalization of RMB, I will begin by exploring the origins of RMB internationalization. The internationalization of RMB was at first China's response to the global financial crisis, in order to relieve concerns over foreign asset losses and reduce exchange rate risk. It was then also regarded as a way to advance the reform on capital control and domestic financial market, including the RMB exchange rate reform. This section will argue that the Chinese leadership's consensus to promote the internationalization of RMB explains the domestic politics of exchange rate policy making in 2010, in which there was less internal controversy within the central government.

6.3.1 The Origins of RMB Internationalization

After the outbreak of the global financial crisis, China was increasingly concerned with the profound flaws in the current international monetary system, which was dominated by the US dollar as the international reserve currency. China suffered from losses of foreign reserves, owing to the quantitative easing (QE) by the US Federal Reserve. China's concern with the dollar hegemony and intention to reform the international monetary system were evident in the landmark essay titled "Reflections on the reform of the international monetary system" by the PBOC Governor Zhou

[40]"FACTBOX-Forecasts for the yuan rate and regime", *Reuters*, 5 May 2010, retrieved from http://www.reuters.com/article/china-yuan-forecasts-idUSYUANVIEW20100505; "FACTBOX-Forecasts for the yuan rate and regime", *Reuters*, 11 June 2010, retrieved from http://www.reuters.com/article/china-yuan-forecasts-idUSYUANVIEW20100611.

in March 2009.[41] Referring to the Triffin Dilemma,[42] Zhou focused on the problem of relying on credit-based national currencies as the major international reserve currencies:

> Issuing countries of reserve currencies are constantly confronted with the dilemma between achieving their domestic monetary policy goals and meeting other countries' demand for reserve currencies. On the one hand, the monetary authorities cannot simply focus on domestic goals without undertaking their international responsibilities; on the other hand, they cannot pursue different domestic and international objectives at the same time. They may either fail to adequately meet the demand of a growing global economy for liquidity as they try to ease inflationary pressure at home, or create excess liquidity in the global economy by overly stimulating domestic demand.[43]

The solution, according to Zhou, was to establish a reserve currency that "is disconnected from individual nations and is able to remain stable in the long run, thus removing the inherent deficiencies caused by using credit-based national currencies".[44] He further suggested that the Special Drawing Right (SDR), as "a super-sovereign reserve currency", could be "the light in the tunnel for the reform of the international monetary system".[45] Zhou proposed a shift away from the dollar and instead the use of the SDR. Specifically, Zhou argued that "special consideration should be given to giving the SDR a greater role, as the SDR has the features and potential to act as a super-sovereign reserve currency."[46]

In retrospect, Zhou was right to point out the problem of the dollar-dominant international monetary system, while he underestimated the institutional limitations and political obstacles that prevented the SDR from challenging the dollar.[47] Zhou's call for SDRs as the super-sovereign reserve currency eventually lost momentum, and the Chinese leadership turned to promote the diversification of international monetary system, thereby reducing the reliance on the dollar.

For instance, President Hu Jintao stressed the need to improve the international monetary system and diversify the world's reserve currencies. He suggested that all parties work out the timetable and roadmap on the basis of full consultation at the 2009

[41] Zhou Xiaochuan, "Reflections on the reform of the international monetary system", People's Bank of China, 23 March 2009, retrieved from http://www.pbc.gov.cn/hanglingdao/128697/128719/128772/825742/index.html.

[42] Triffin pointed out the monetary system based on the currency of one country could not sustainably deliver both liquidity and confidence in the 1960s. Specifically, the continuous growth of world economy demanded a steady stream of dollars, which required the US to run balance of payment deficits. However, excessive US deficits would erode people's confidence in the dollar's value (convertibility into gold at fixed price at that time). This inherent conflict of the dollar's role as the world's reserve currency and the declining confidence in the dollar within the postwar international monetary system was termed as the Triffin Dilemma. See, for more detail, Triffin (1961).

[43] Ibid.

[44] Ibid.

[45] Ibid.

[46] Ibid.

[47] See, for example, Ly (2012); Chin (2014).

Table 6.1 The roles of international currency

Function level	Medium of exchange	Unit of account	Store of value
Private	Transactions currency	Denomination currency	Asset currency
Official	Intervention currency	Anchor currency	Reserve currency

Source Cohen (1971) *The Future of Sterling as an International Currency*, London: Macmillan, pp. 13–23

G20 London Summit.[48] At the opening ceremony of Bo'ao Forum in April 2009, Premier Wen Jiabao continued to advocate implementing the consensus reached at the G20 London Summit and advancing the reforms of international financial system. More specifically, Wen proposed "to increase the representation and voice of emerging markets and developing countries, to strengthen the supervision on macroeconomic policies of the major reserve currency issuing economies, and to promote the diversification of international monetary system."[49] One of the most important ways to diversify the international monetary system was to promote the international use of the RMB as a matter of course. My interviews with PBOC officials also confirmed the central importance of the global financial crisis in stimulating the RMB internationalization.[50] Starting from mid-2009, China promoted the RMB internationalization as an effort to diversify the international monetary system, which will be discussed in further detail as follows.

6.3.2 Towards RMB Internationalization

To understand the development of RMB internationalization, Cohen's analysis of the six roles of international currency provides a useful point of departure.[51] Table 6.1 shows the three functions of currency and how an international currency is used at both official and private levels. It is worth noting that the six roles of international currency are ideal types for the convenience of analysis whereas in reality some of them cannot be separated. For instance, a central bank's foreign reserves could also be used for foreign exchange intervention, so an international currency undeniably serves the functions of intervention currency and reserve currency simultaneously. With the benefit of hindsight, the RMB internationalization has been pursued along

[48]"Clearer 'roadmap' for RMB internationalization", *Xinhua*, 3 April 2009, retrieved from http://news.xinhuanet.com/newscenter/2009-04/03/content_11126968.htm.

[49]"Wen Jiabao addresses opening ceremony of Boao Forum", *Xinhua*, 18 April 2009, retrieved from http://www.hq.xinhuanet.com/focus/2009-04/18/content_16292111_1.htm.

[50]Interview_17092015; Interview_19092015.

[51]Cohen (1971).

Table 6.2 Cross-border RMB current-account settlement (classified by trade types). Unit: one hundred million yuan

	2009	2010	2011	2012	2013
Trade settlement amount	36	5064	20800	29409	46300
– Trade in goods	N/A	N/A	N/A	20642	30200
– Trade in services	N/A	N/A	N/A	8765	16100

Source Author's own elaboration based on PBOC Monetary Policy Implementation Report, available from http://www.pbc.gov.cn/zhengcehuobisi/125207/125227/125957/index.html

two tracks: to develop the RMB as an international trade and investment currency (see Appendix E) and as an intervention and reserve currency (see Appendix F).

The Chinese leadership promoted the international use of its own currency to settle cross-border trade beginning from 2009. Beijing gradually widened the range of trade transactions, in which there were three stages of development. First, on 8 April 2009, the State Council executive meeting decided to implement the pilot RMB cross-border trade settlement at Shanghai and four cities (Guangzhou, Shenzhen, Zhuhai and Dongguan) in Guangdong.[52] Second, on 22 June 2010, the State Council approved that the RMB cross-border trade settlement within the pilot areas be expanded to 20 provinces, and that the overseas coverage be expanded from Hong Kong, Macao and ASEAN to all countries and regions.[53] By the end of 2010, the number of Chinese pilot enterprises had risen from the initial 365 firms to more than 67,000.[54] Third, on 23 August 2011, PBOC, MOF, MOFCOM, General Administration of Customs, State Administration of Taxation, China Banking Regulatory Commission jointly announced the "Notice on Expanding the RMB Cross-border Trade Settlement Areas", which approved that the RMB cross-border trade settlement be expanded to the whole country.[55]

Table 6.2 shows that the use of the RMB as a trade settlement currency increased rapidly between 2009 and 2013. Table 6.3 shows that the RMB payments were consistently larger than RMB receipts in the trade settlement, which partly suggests that the RMB was favourable asset to the foreign trading partners and the RMB cross-border trade settlement was indeed conducive to RMB internationalization.

[52]"The State Council executive meeting decided to implement the pilot RMB cross-border trade settlement at Shanghai and four cities in Guangdong", *Xinhua*, 8 April 2009, retrieved from http://news.xinhuanet.com/newscenter/2009-04/08/content_11151247.htm.

[53]"The pilot RMB cross-border trade settlement expanded to 20 provinces", *Xinhua*, 22 June 2010, retrieved from http://news.xinhuanet.com/fortune/2010-06/22/c_12248526.htm.

[54]People's Bank of China, "2010 Fourth Quarter Monetary Policy Implementation Report", 30 January 2011, retrieved from http://www.pbc.gov.cn/eportal/fileDir/image_public/UserFiles/goutongjiaoliu/upload/File/2010%E5%B9%B4%E7%AC%AC%E5%9B%9B%E5%AD%A3%E5%BA%A6%E4%B8%AD%E5%9B%BD%E8%B4%A7%E5%B8%81%E6%94%BF%E7%AD%96%E6%89%A7%E8%A1%8C%E6%8A%A5%E5%91%8A.pdf, p. 11.

[55]"The RMB cross-border trade settlement expanded to the whole country", *Xinhua*, 23 August 2011, retrieved from http://news.xinhuanet.com/2011-08/23/c_121900298.htm.

Table 6.3 Cross-border RMB current-account settlement (classified by payment and receipt). Unit: one hundred million yuan

	2009	2010	2011	2012	2013
Total amount of payments and receipts	36	5064	20800	28700	46300
– Payments	N/A	799	7704	13000	18800
– Receipts	N/A	4285	13096	15700	27500
Ratio of receipts to payments	N/A	1:1.5	1:1.70	1:1.20	1:1.46
Gap between receipts and payments	N/A	– 3506	– 5393	– 2700	– 8700

Source Author's own elaboration based on PBOC Monetary Policy Implementation Report, available from http://www.pbc.gov.cn/zhengcehuobisi/125207/125227/125957/index.html

To facilitate the cross-border RMB trade settlement, there were three main ways to develop international investment in RMB: cross-border bond investment, cross-border direct investment and cross-border security investment. Beijing has relied heavily on the special status of Hong Kong as an offshore RMB business hub.

First, after the China Development Bank issued the first overseas RMB bond (dim-sum bond) in 2007, the RMB bond issuance increased persistently, and particularly fast after the July 2010 liberalization of the conditions for bond issuers. The value of bonds issued in the second half of 2010 alone (38 billion yuan) equaled that of the previous three years combined.[56] The bond insurance markets have also expanded from Hong Kong to other financial centers including London, Singapore, Sydney and Luxembourg. For instance, HSBC issued the RMB-denominated bond in London on 18 April 2012, the first issue of RMB offshore bond outside Hong Kong, marking a milestone in London's efforts to become a center for offshore RMB trading alongside Hong Kong.[57]

Second, the PBOC announced "Measures for the administration on RMB settlement in foreign direct investment" to regulate foreign investors and banks to handle RMB settlement in foreign direct investment on 14 October 2011.[58] The rules enabled overseas enterprises, economic organization and individuals to apply to the commercial banks for settlement of their RMB denominated direct investment. Table 6.4 shows that cross-border RMB settlement of direct investment increased rapidly from 2011 to 2013.

Third, with regard to cross-border security investment, the RMB Qualified Foreign Institutional Investor (RQFII) scheme was launched on 16 December 2011 to allow overseas investors to establish RMB-denominated funds in Hong Kong for investment

56 Bowles and Wang (2013), p. 1368.

57 "HSBC issues the first RMB bond in London", *Xinhua*, 19 April 2012, retrieved from http://news.xinhuanet.com/finance/2012-04/19/c_123004520.htm.

58 "The PBOC issues a document to regulate foreign direct investment of RMB settlement business", *Xinhua*, 14 October 2011, retrieved from http://news.xinhuanet.com/fortune/2011-10/14/c_122158006.htm.

Table 6.4 Cross-border RMB capital-account settlement. Unit: one hundred million yuan

	2009	2010	2011	2012	2013
Direct investment amount	N/A	N/A	1109	2840	5337
– Foreign Direct Investment (FDI)	N/A	N/A	907	2536	4481
– Outward Direct Investment (ODI)	N/A	N/A	202	304	856
RMB Qualified Foreign Institutional Investor (RQFII)	N/A	N/A	107	670	1575

Source Author's own elaboration based on PBOC Monetary Policy Implementation Report, available from http://www.pbc.gov.cn/zhengcehuobisi/125207/125227/125957/index.html

in the mainland securities market.[59] RQFII can be seen as a measure to increase the internationalization of the RMB by facilitating a reverse flow of RMB investment back into the mainland. Table 6.4 also shows the rapid growth of RQFII programme from 2011 to 2013.

In addition to the effort to promote the international use of RMB to settle trade and investment, the PBOC also signed a number of bilateral currency swap agreements (see Appendix F) with other central banks or monetary authorities after 2009 to help the RMB become an official foreign exchange intervention currency and reserve currency. By the end of 2013, the PBOC had established bilateral currency swap arrangements with 23 foreign central banks or monetary authorities with a total volume of 2.55 trillion yuan. The bilateral currency swaps could provide liquidity not only in times of crisis but also in conventional times to facilitate the bilateral trade and investment, thereby promoting the development of RMB offshore markets. One PBOC official explained the mechanism as follows:

> The foreign importers of Chinese goods or foreign enterprises going to invest in China need to borrow money from their central bank if there is not enough RMB in the market. If the two central banks sign currency swap agreement, the foreign enterprise can get access to timely financing, thereby promoting the bilateral trade and investment.[60]

However, the interviewee also pointed out that the mechanism would only work under the condition that the RMB was used in the bilateral trade and investment (as denomination currency), which was largely determined by the choice of market participants.[61]

To summarize, the Chinese government actively promoted the international use of its own currency to settle the cross-border trade and investment after 2009. The PBOC has also signed a number of currency swaps to meet the overseas demand for RMB liquidity. The eye-catching development of RMB internationalization has convinced the leadership to make it into one of the most important national strategies in the 2010s. Therefore, it is essential to examine the RMB exchange rate reform in the backdrop of RMB internationalization, which will be discussed in the next part.

---

[59] "RQFII pilot regulation announced to facilitate overseas RMB investment in mainland securities market", *Xinhua*, 16 December 2011, retrieved from http://news.xinhuanet.com/fortune/2011-12/16/c_111251039.htm.

[60] Interview_17092015.

[61] Interview_17092015.

6.3.3 *Explaining the RMB Exchange Rate Reform Under the Context of RMB Internationalization*

As mentioned in the previous section, there was very limited controversy within Chinese central government in terms of the RMB exchange rate reform and Chinese leaders were consistent in the exchange rate policy in the case of 2010. Based on the analysis of the development of RMB internationalization, this part will argue that the Chinese leadership's consensus to promote the internationalization of RMB explains the domestic politics of exchange rate policy making in 2010.

China has become not only the world's largest exporter of manufactured goods but the second-largest economy since 2010. The size of the economy, coupled with a diversified trade structure and relatively high growth rate, has provided much of the groundwork for internationalizing the RMB. However, economic size alone is not enough to make RMB a competitive international currency. Setting aside the problem of political determinants for the moment, economists have identified three key factors—confidence, liquidity and transactional networks—to be key economic determinants of international currencies.[62] China's economic size and Chinese government's efforts to push forward the international use of RMB are definitely conducive to the confidence and transactional networks of RMB, while the liquidity problem, including the existence of well-developed and open financial markets, remains the most difficult to overcome.

With the wisdom of hindsight, the Chinese government followed a unique approach to internationalizing the RMB, promoting the international use of RMB under the conditions of unconvertible RMB and capital account control at an early stage. However, with the deepening of RMB internationalization, the demand for RMB investment and capital account liberalization naturally arose. According to Mundell's theory of impossible trinity, a monetary authority cannot have fixed exchange rate, capital mobility, and independent monetary policy at the same time.[63] With the development of RMB internationalization and increasing openness of capital account, a flexible exchange rate was the feasible choice to preserve the independence and effectiveness of Chinese monetary policy, which produced the Chinese leadership's consensus on the second round of RMB exchange rate reform. My interview with one official at the MOFCOM Comprehensive Department confirmed the finding. In addition to the notes on MOFCOM's stance on the 2010 exchange rate reform, the official at the MOFCOM Comprehensive Department made the following comments:

> With regard to the general direction of market-oriented exchange reform, I think the top leadership had no objection, including the MOFCOM and PBOC leaders. However, in the view of MOFCOM, PBOC's goal of exchange rate reform remained a puzzle. Specifically, we were not clear whether the continued RMB appreciation after June 2010 was to promote the internationalization of RMB or to promote the market-determined exchange rate mechanism. In my personal perspective, a strengthened currency does not necessarily contribute to the

[62] Helleiner (2008).

[63] Mundell (1963).

> internationalization of RMB. The comprehensive national strength that builds on economic, political and military progress is the fundamental determinant of RMB internationalization. Even if a small country has a strong currency, it cannot become an international currency. If our economy falls into trouble owing to the improper exchange rate policy, the RMB would lose the foundations of a strong currency, let alone internationalization. Therefore, the MOFCOM consistently stress the importance of gradual RMB appreciation.[64]

Change eventually came on 19 June 2010. Approved by the State Council, the PBOC announced to further reform the RMB exchange rate regime based on the measures taken in 2005.[65] According to the announcement, continued emphasis would be placed to reflecting market supply and demand with reference to a basket of currencies and the exchange rate floating bands would remain the same as previously announced in the inter-bank foreign exchange market. The second round of exchange rate reform policy could be interpreted as a hybrid outcome of both external influences from the Western countries and internal needs of the RMB internationalization. On the one hand, international criticism and pressure from the US administration and the IMF still played an important role of agenda-setting in China's exchange rate policy making in 2010. On the other hand, the Chinese central government reached the consensus that a more flexible exchange rate was necessary for further internationalizing its currency.

Furthermore, like the first round of the exchange rate reform, the key principle of gradualism was repeatedly emphasized. According to the MOFCOM Comprehensive Department's official, although the MOFCOM did not oppose market-oriented exchange rate reform, it still underlined the relative stability of RMB exchange rate, which was conducive to RMB internationalization. Moreover, on the second day of PBOC's announcement, the PBOC spokesman addressed that China would keep the exchange rate stable and prevent large fluctuations. [66] Zhou Xiaochuan also publicly expressed in the 2010 Annual Meetings of the IMF and the World Bank that China's exchange rate reform would be in gradual manner and would not take the so-called "shock therapy".[67]

Figure 6.1 shows RMB's gradual and steady appreciation after PBOC's announcement of the second round of exchange rate reform. The stability and predictability of the RMB exchange rate was one of the most important attributes in improving the confidence and promoting the international use of RMB. Furthermore, the exchange rate reform proceeded in the market-oriented direction. It is noteworthy that the PBOC announced on 14 April 2012 that "the RMB-dollar trading band in the interbank spot foreign exchange market will be expanded form 0.5 to 1%, namely, the

---

[64] Interview_25092015.

[65] People's Bank of China, "To further promote the reform of RMB exchange rate formation mechanism and enhance the RMB exchange rate flexibility", 19 June 2010, retrieved from http://www.pbc.gov.cn/bangongting/135485/135491/135597/1002571/index.html.

[66] People's Bank of China, "The PBOC spokesman answers journalists' question on further promotion of the RMB exchange rate formation mechanism", 20 June 2010, retrieved from http://www.pbc.gov.cn/bangongting/135485/135491/135597/1002568/index.html.

[67] "Zhou Xiaochuan: China will reform gradually and refuse the 'shock therapy'", *Xinhua*, 9 October 2010, retrieved from http://news.xinhuanet.com/fortune/2010-10/09/c_12641215.htm.

Fig. 6.1 RMB exchange rate against the US dollar, from 18 June 2010 to 31 December 2013. *Source* PBOC Monetary Policy Department

daily RMB-dollar trading band may be floated within the 1% range of the middle price of the dollar against the RMB."[68] At the same time, the PBOC made some adjustment to its sterilization operation in the foreign exchange market, considerably reducing the foreign exchange intervention.[69] It can be seen from Fig. 6.1 that the RMB exchange rate experienced more two-way fluctuations after May 2012, which also reduced the inflow of hot money. This was different from the continuous one-way appreciation in the first round of exchange rate reform between 2005 and 2008.

To summarize, this part of the chapter has argued that with the development of RMB internationalization and increasing openness of capital account, a flexible exchange rate was Chinese government's feasible choice to maintain independent and effective monetary policy. The PBOC announced further reform the RMB exchange rate formation mechanism in June 2010 and the second round of exchange rate reform proceeded in the market-oriented direction in a gradual manner after then.

[68]People's Bank of China (2012).

[69]People's Bank of China, "2012s Quarter Monetary Policy Implementation Report", 2 August 2012, pp. 14–15, retrieved from http://www.pbc.gov.cn/eportal/fileDir/image_public/UserFiles/goutongjiaoliu/upload/File/2012%E5%B9%B4%E7%AC%AC%E4%BA%8C%E5%AD%A3%E5%BA%A6%E4%B8%AD%E5%9B%BD%E8%B4%A7%E5%B8%81%E6%94%BF%E7%AD%96%E6%89%A7%E8%A1%8C%E6%8A%A5%E5%91%8A.pdf.

6.3.4 Alternative Explanations

It is worthwhile to note that two other seemingly plausible factors could also explain the Chinese leadership's decision to carry out the 2010 exchange rate reform. The first argument is to facilitate the economic transition and rebalancing. There is no denying that Hu and Wen had the long-standing desire to rebalance China's economy away from heavy reliance on exports towards consumption. It is also analytically true that a more flexible and appreciated RMB exchange rate would be conducive to China's economic restructuring, as the exchange rate was an important price mechanism to help transform the Chinese export-oriented economy to a domestic consumption-driven economy. However, as mentioned in Chap. 5, the Chinese leadership placed priority on growth and stability and often place economic reforms in secondary place. Therefore, the limited nature of exchange rate policy reform also had a limited impact on the economic transition.

Empirical data is consistent with this argument. Figures 6.2 and 6.3 show ratios of China's current account to GDP and consumption to GDP respectively between 2005 and 2013. On the one hand, though the RMB consistently appreciated against the dollar between 2005 and 2007, the ratio of China's current account to GDP was on the rise. The ratio of China's current account to GDP decreased slightly in the year of 2008, when the RMB appreciated in a faster pace in the first half of 2008. On the other hand, we could not see any trend in consumption growth during the whole period of time. Therefore, it is suggested that the first round of exchange rate reform had a limited impact to facilitate China's economic transition from export-oriented towards consumption-driven.

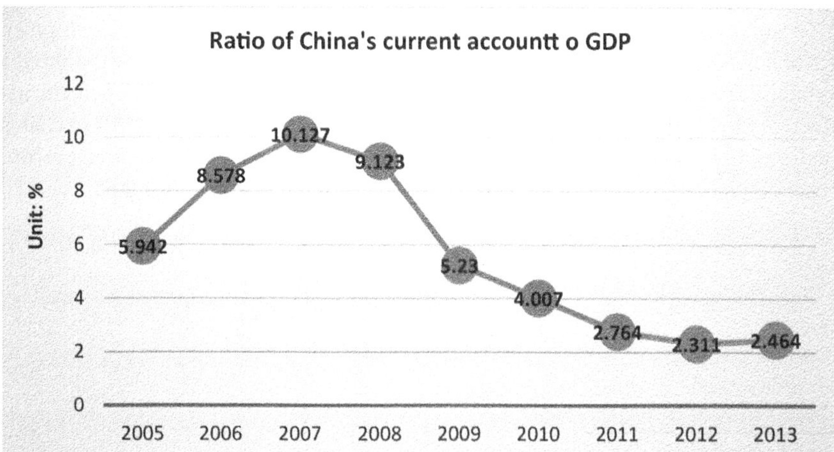

Fig. 6.2 Ratio of China's current account to GDP, from 2005 to 2013. *Source* IMF World Economic Outlook, https://www.imf.org/external/pubs/ft/weo/2016/01/weodata/index.aspx

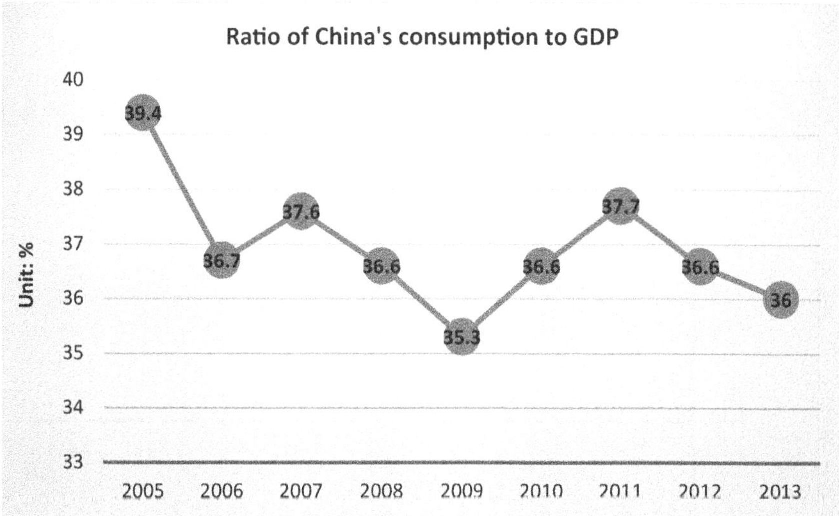

Fig. 6.3 Ratio of China's consumption to GDP, from 2008 to 2013. *Source* World Bank Data, available from http://data.worldbank.org/indicator/NE.CON.PETC.ZS

Furthermore, China's current account surplus experienced a notable reduction in 2009, largely due to the negative impact of the global financial crisis. Then China's external trade steadily became more balanced after 2009. It was not of great necessity to seek trade surplus reduction through exchange rate appreciation from 2010 to 2013. With the benefit of hindsight, there is also little evidence to suggest that the second round of exchange rate reform would be conducive to boost the domestic consumption (see Fig. 6.3). China's transformation into a consumer-driven economy is a rather complex issue that exchange rate appreciation alone cannot resolve.

What of the hypothesis that China's exchange rate reform policy in 2010 was driven by the goal of inflation control? According to this argument, greater exchange rate flexibility and RMB appreciation could help to enhance the autonomy and effectiveness of monetary policy and curb domestic inflation. Chinese policy makers, especially the PBOC officials, recognized the benefits of exchange rate flexibility. However, careful analysis of China's CPI data (see Fig. 6.4) shows that there is little support for this argument as well. China's annual CPI is 1.8% in 2005 and 3.3% in 2010. The data suggests that inflation was not a serious problem in the two years, when the RMB exchange rate reform initiated. Though it is more plausible to speculate that the PBOC widened the RMB-dollar trading band two times aiming at inflation control in 2007 and 2012, there is a lack of empirical evidence to suggest that the Chinese leadership launched the exchange rate reform in order to moderate inflation in 2005 and 2010.

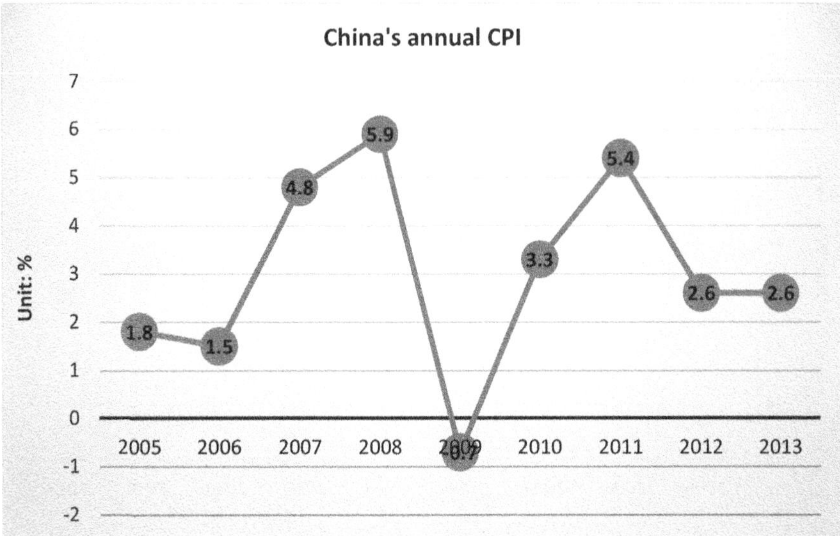

Fig. 6.4 China's annual CPI, from 2007 to 2013. *Source* World Bank Data, http://data.worldbank.org/indicator/FP.CPI.TOTL.ZG/countries/CN?display=graph

6.4 Concluding Remarks

This chapter has examined the resumption of RMB exchange rate reform, beginning from June 2010. As with Chap. 3, the level I game and level II game should be combined to explain the Chinese leadership's decision to continue the exchange rate reform in 2010. On the one hand, analysis of US Congress RMB-related bills and Treasury's Reports to Congress on International Economic and Exchange Rate as well as IMF's Consultation Reports on China demonstrates that external criticism and pressure still played an important role of agenda-setting in China's exchange rate policy making in 2010. On the other hand, the Chinese leadership stood firm to the external pressure, with less internal battles within the central government (between PBOC and MOFCOM). The Chinese leadership was consistent in the RMB exchange rate reform policy in 2010, in which the RMB internationalization played the role of "intervening variable".

The Chinese leadership promoted international use of its own currency to settle the cross-border trade beginning from 2009. Beijing not only gradually widened the range of trade transactions but also facilitated the development of RMB international investment. Moreover, China's central bank signed bilateral currency-swap agreements with a number of central banks and monetary authorities to expand the use of the RMB in international trade and financial transactions. With the development of RMB internationalization and an increasing openness of capital account, a flexible exchange rate was the feasible choice to preserve the independence and effectiveness of Chinese monetary policy, which produced the Chinese leadership's consensus on the RMB exchange rate reform in 2010. As the stability and predictability of RMB exchange rate was one of the most important attributes in improving the confidence and promoting the international use of RMB, it determined the pathway of gradual and steady appreciation in the second round of RMB exchange rate reform.

Chapter 7
Conclusion

This book has striven to enhance the understanding of the nature and mechanism of China's exchange rate policy making, notably during the Hu-Wen administration. It has sought to address the research questions raised in the introduction by examining the international political economy of China's exchange rate policy making from a theoretical and an empirical perspective. This concluding chapter firstly summarizes the theoretical framework and the empirical findings of the book. It then relates China's exchange rate reforms to the wider context of China's politics. The empirical studies of China's exchange rate reform from 2002 to 2013 have suggested that the Hu-Wen administration's governance was characterized by consensus-building collective leadership and they placed priority on economic growth and social stability. The last section delineates the implications of this study for future research.

7.1 Theoretical Framework and Empirical Findings

With China's economic rise, and particularly owing to its massive international trade surplus with the rest of the world, the exchange rate of its currency has come under increasing scrutiny in the new millennium. Based on the revision and synthesis of existing CPE and IPE approaches, this book proposes that an IPE approach that bridges international politics and domestic politics is best suited to explain the development of China's exchange rate policy. By specifically examining the external factors and domestic sources of China's exchange rate policy, the book further develops a three-level game framework for China's exchange rate policy making to address the first research question: "What factors determine China's exchange rate policy making from 2002 to 2013?" It is argued that China's central decision makers strove to reconcile international pressures, domestic ministerial interests and domestic interest groups when making RMB exchange rate policies. More specifically, the three-level game framework examines the Chinese leadership's negotiations with the international bargainers at the international level (level I), negotiations

Z. Wang, *The International Political Economy of China's Exchange Rate Policy Making*, https://doi.org/10.1007/978-981-33-4578-2_7

between central government's ministries at the central governmental level (level II) and negotiations with the domestic interest groups and local governments at the local level (level III).

However, the applicability of the adapted three-level game framework and the relative importance of the three level games remain a puzzle, which needs to be further examined in empirical studies. After offering a theoretical review, revision and synthesis, the book provides in-depth empirical studies on China's exchange rate policy from 2002 to 2013. Empirical studies address the following research questions raised in the introduction: What accounts for the two phases of dollar-pegged exchange rate regime? What are the key causes of the three turning points of exchange rate policy change? How to explain the gradual, rather than one-off, pattern of the RMB appreciation?

The first answer to these questions is that the book shows how the level I game played an agenda-setting role in China's exchange rate policy making before the 2005 exchange rate reform. External pressure mainly from the US government and the IMF began to gain momentum in 2003. Faced with international concerns, Chinese leaders made a public commitment to the international society to carry out exchange rate reform in 2004. However, internal struggles in China's central government explained why the Chinese leadership did not make a final decision and exchange rate reform was delayed. External pressure on China's exchange rate policy reached its apex in the first half of 2005, which forced the Chinese leadership to put exchange rate reform clearly on the policy agenda. However, to explain the specific pathway of China's exchange rate reform, one needs to further explore China's domestic politics.

Second, the level II game determined the limited scope of the initial reform in July 2005 and the subsequent gradual RMB appreciation from 2005 to 2007. Two key ministries with competing preferences were divided internally in China's central government. PBOC's officials were particularly interested in exchange rate reform, which would endow them with more monetary policy autonomy. Nevertheless, PBOC's position was challenged by the MOFCOM, which preferred a fixed (and undervalued) RMB exchange rate. The MOFCOM, with their constituencies within China's state-owned enterprises and a more politically powerful Minister (Bo Xilai), was more influential over the central government's decision-making than the PBOC. As a result of compromise, PBOC's wish for exchange rate flexibility was granted, but was considerably qualified to satisfy MOFCOM's concerns. The initial RMB appreciation was limited to 2.1% against the dollar, and the pace of subsequent appreciation was to be relatively stable and slow. After July 2005, the PBOC faced an increasing policy dilemma in simultaneously maintaining the gradually appreciated RMB exchange rates and controlling the domestic money supply, where there were persistent current account surplus and capital inflows.

Third, the level III game provided the most important sources for the stagnation of China's exchange rate reform in 2008, and China returned to the de facto dollar-pegged exchange rate regime during the global financial crisis. China faced rising inflationary pressure in 2007 and the Chinese leadership made inflation prevention the top priority in the fourth quarter of 2007. RMB appreciation was used as one of the tools to help China expand its imports and curb inflation. RMB appreciated at a significantly faster pace in the fourth quarter of 2007 and the first half of 2008. Exporters became strongly opposed to RMB appreciation in 2008. They lobbied through local governments, local offices of MOFCOM, and trade associations to impose considerable pressure on the central government. Confronted with pressure from businesses, the top leadership conducted intensive research and investigation in early July 2008 and finally decided to roll out rescue policies. The market-oriented RMB exchange rate reform beginning from 21 July 2005 was halted in the second half of 2008, and China returned to the de facto dollar-pegged exchange rate regime in turbulent times of the global financial crisis.

Fourth, the level I game once again played an agenda-setting role in the 2010 exchange rate reform, but the level II game was important as well, resulting in the Chinese leadership allowing the RMB to appreciate against the dollar in a gradual and steady manner. While the Congress's influence on the RMB issue generally diminished over time after the global financial crisis, international criticism and pressure from the US administration and the IMF gained momentum in the first half of 2010. The Chinese leadership stood firm to the external pressure and emphasized that what it called the "politicization" of the RMB exchange rate would not help to address the issue. The PBOC and the MOFCOM were not divergent in terms of the exchange rate reform and there was less internal controversy within the central government in 2010. Therefore, the Chinese leadership was more consistent on exchange rate policy. The underlying reason was that, with the development of RMB internationalization and increasing openness of the capital account after 2009, a flexible exchange rate was Chinese government's feasible choice to maintain independent and effective monetary policy. As the stability and predictability of RMB exchange rate was one of the most important attributes in improving confidence and promoting the international use of RMB, it determined the pathway of gradual and steady appreciation in the second round of RMB exchange rate reform.

Last, the empirical studies respond to the question as to why China's exchange rate policy making is a three-level game rather than a two-level one. Of course, this could be treated simply as a modified two-level game. However, the suggestion here is that the difference between the two domestic games is so great that it is better conceived of as two separate negotiations, rather than two parts of the same domestic game. Though the MOFCOM strongly advocated for the interests of export sectors in 2005 and 2006, there were few signs of direct lobbying from export enterprises after the initiation of exchange rate reform. In contrast, when it came to 2008, export enterprises lobbied through local governments, local offices of MOFCOM, and trade associations to impose considerable pressure on the central government. The level II game and the level III game were so different that they cannot be simply treated as the same domestic game. The empirical studies generally validate the applicability of the adapted three-level game framework of China's exchange rate policy making.

To sum up, this book examines the international political economy of China's exchange rate policy making from a theoretical and an empirical perspective. The three-level game framework and the empirical studies provide a richer portrait of the dynamism and complexity of China's exchange rate policy making in the Hu-Wen era. The book has clearly shown that China's central decision makers strove to reconcile international pressures, domestic ministerial interests and domestic interest groups when making RMB exchange rate policies. To explain the last research question "why have some policy preferences prevailed in policy making at the expense of others during different periods of time?" in the introduction, the author will further discuss the relationship between China's exchange rate reforms and the nature of China's politics.

7.2 The Bigger Picture: China's Exchange Rate Reforms and the Nature of China's Politics

The introduction of this book established a view of Chinese politics in the Hu-Wen era that informs this research project. The empirical studies of China's exchange rate policy making in the Hu-Wen era meanwhile suggested that China's economic reforms were literally a non-linear process, in which both international and domestic political powers influenced the timing and drove the pace of exchange rate reforms. Though the overall direction of China's exchange rate reform was towards greater liberalization, there was limited evidence to suggest that Chinese leaders had a long-term grand strategy for economic reform. The stagnation of China's exchange rate reform from 2008 to 2010 clearly shows that the process did not proceed in a smooth manner but with twists and turns along the way. This section will explore this contingency by discussing the relationship between China's exchange rate policy making and the nature of China's politics.

As has been argued, international pressure played an agenda-setting role in China's exchange rate policies in both 2005 and 2010. In particular, exchange rate reform was unlikely to happen in 2005 without the mounting external pressure, considering the fact that the MOFCOM was far more politically powerful than the PBOC in China's central government. The MOFCOM had serious concerns about the potential negative effects of RMB appreciation. After the reform announcement in 2005, both the PBOC and the MOFCOM kept a close eye on the impacts of RMB appreciation on China's exports, which implied that the Chinese leadership took a very cautious approach toward the exchange rate reform. There is no denying that the increasing scale of China's engagement with the world economy in the twenty-first century meant that international interests were much more entangled in China's domestic politics. However, the book demonstrates that the evolution of China's exchange rate reform was still largely determined by China's domestic politics. As Naughton notes:

> China's enduring 'gradualist' approach to transition obviously suits the needs of its authoritarian leaders. More interesting is that the concrete policy content of China's transition – which differed dramatically in different periods – can also be traced to the changing nature of power and strategic calculations of leaders within the authoritarian system.[1]

China's exchange rate reform policies were decided by top leaders in the authoritarian political system, and as a result exchange rate reforms were closely related to

[1] Naughton (2008), p. 91.

the political system and the needs of political leaders in the system. Despite different exchange rate reform policies in the different periods of time, the author holds the view that it is still possible to reach some conclusions as to the relationship between China's exchange rate policy making and the nature of China's politics in the Hu-Wen era.

First and foremost, the fundamental reason for the important role of level II game between the MOFCOM and the PBOC in China's exchange rate policy making throughout the research time frame was that China's politics was characterized by collective leadership in the Hu-Wen era, and arguably more so than ever before. The introduction has elaborated the fact that Hu and Wen did not enjoy as much political capital and/or authority as their predecessors. Moreover, with continuous reform and opening up from Deng to Hu, China's economy was much more complex and China had an increasingly pluralist society—clearly not a fully liberal one with the levels of plurality associated with democratic states, but certainly more plural than before. Lynch notes that "China is increasingly pluralistic and will continue to become even more so as long as the economy continues to grow on the basis of being market oriented."[2] And as Miller argues, "the problems of governing an increasingly globally interdependent and market-driven economy and a correspondingly more complex and sophisticated society required a politics of expertise,"[3] in particular the (international) economic expertise from the empowered ministries and agencies.

Therefore, China's changing political-socioeconomic landscapes determined the growing importance of ministerial politics in China's economic policy making, and more specifically, the bargaining game between the MOFCOM and the PBOC in China's exchange rate policy making. As noted by Downs in 2009, "policymaking overall has been moving towards greater pluralization over the past decade" and "as a result, more voices are being heard, but that means decision making is becoming more contentious and protracted."[4] The inputs for exchange rate policy deliberations in the central government mainly came from government agencies, notably the MOFCOM and the PBOC. Therefore, bureaucratic politics played a key role in China's exchange rate policy making.

It also suggests that Hu and Wen exercised effective governance by maintaining a politics of consensus in China's central government, which was consistent with the "consensus-building collective leadership"[5] style of Hu-Wen administration outlined in the introduction. Despite MOFCOM and PBOC's conflicting preferences over exchange rate policy, the empirical studies demonstrated that their competition generally remained behind closed doors in the central government. Once the top leadership made the final exchange rate policy decision, government agencies would adhere to the principle and implement the policy, which is the main characteristic of Leninist

[2]Lynch (2015), p. 76.
[3]Miller (2011), p. 532.
[4]Downs (2009), p. 137.
[5]Miller (2009), p. 61.

democratic centralism or consultative Leninism/authoritarianism.[6] PBOC's endeavor to preserve the gradual RMB appreciation in the first round of exchange rate reform provided firm support to this argument. Therefore, it may be concluded that Hu and Wen maintained effective governance by consensus building, which was adapted to the China's changing political-socioeconomic landscapes in the twenty-first century. As Lynch notes:

> China today is a kaleidoscopically plural society – although still, to be sure, always subject to the Leninist state's discipline should the leaders decide, for whatever reason, to crack down, either on a whole category of activity/discourse or on a particular person who has irritated a local tyrant.[7]

Second, the nature of China's exchange rate reform, characterized by gradualism and incrementalism, suggested that stability maintenance and short-term crisis management prevailed over long-term planning in the formation of economic policy. Many observers and analysts recognized Hu-Wen's shifted priority to sustainable development and social development after the leadership transition in 2002. For instance, Liew and Wu argue that: "There is without doubt a fundamental shift in emphasis between the Jiang Zemin-Zhu Rongji and the Hu Jintao-Wen Jiabao leadership. While the former leadership was deeply concerned with engaging the global economy, the latter is more concerned with poverty and income inequality, especially in the countryside and western China."[8]

Moreover, the first two public visits by Hu Jintao as general secretary were not to the modern and prosperous cities of Shanghai or Shenzhen but rather to Xibaipo (a village in Hebei) and Inner Mongolia. Particularly, Hu Jintao put forward the "scientific development outlook" in the Third Plenary Session of the 16th CCP Central Committee in 2003, which aimed to address the problems including the widening gap between urban and rural development, the uneven development among China's regions, the pursuit of economic growth at the sacrifice of environmental sustainability, and the imbalance between export-driven growth and domestic consumption.[9]

However, with the wisdom of hindsight, Hu's proposal of a scientific development outlook was not translated into concrete measures. China's first round of exchange rate reform from 2005 to 2008 could be one of the best footnotes to this argument. Effective exchange rate reform could have contributed to economic rebalancing by making exports more expensive and imports cheaper, thereby alleviating the export surge and stimulating domestic consumption.[10] However, as Chap. 6 shows, the ratio of China's current account to GDP was on the rise, while that of consumption to GDP

---

[6]For Leninist democratic centralism, see Waller (1981). For consultative Leninism/authoritarianism, see Tsang (2009); He and Thøgersen (2010).

[7]Lynch (2015), p. xii.

[8]Liew and Wu (2007), p. 206.

[9]"Third Plenary Session of the 16th CCP Central Committee articulated scientific development outlook", *Xinhua*, 4 August 2012, retrieved from http://news.xinhuanet.com/politics/2012-08/04/c_112623819.htm.

[10]Lardy (2012).

was in decline generally from 2005 to 2008. On the one hand, the limited nature of the 2005 exchange rate reform and the subsequent gradual RMB appreciation was dedicated to continuing export growth. On the other hand, the acceleration of RMB appreciation in the last quarter of 2007 and first half of 2008 was short-lived owing to the intensive local lobbying and the top leadership's severe concerns about employment and stability. Therefore, in spite of Hu-Wen's official rhetoric of people's orientation and economic rebalancing, Chinese policymakers in reality still placed priority on the coastal regions and acted out of an obsession with short-term growth, in order to preserve the CCP's legitimacy and social stability.

To summarize, the analysis of China's exchange rate reform suggests that it was in fact contingent, rather than inevitable, because of the complex array of interests in the policy making process. To address the research question "why have some policy preferences prevailed in policy making at the expense of others during different periods of time?", we have examined China's domestic politics in more depth. The empirical study of China's exchange rate reform from 2003 to 2013 confirms that the Hu-Wen administration's governance was characterized by consensus-building collective leadership and they placed priority to maintain economic growth and social stability.

7.3 Directions for Future Research

The book has made the first attempt to construct a three-level game framework to study China's exchange rate politics. The explanatory strengths of the theoretical framework have already been demonstrated in the empirical studies. However, it does not constitute the final word on the international political economy of China's exchange rate policy making. As far as the author is concerned, the book invites further research in the following two areas.

7.3.1 China's Exchange Rate Policy in the Xi Era

It is definitely worth examining China's exchange rate policy making after 2013. China's politics and economy have changed considerably since Xi Jinping and Li Keqiang succeeded Hu Jintao and Wen Jiabao. On the one hand, Xi seems to intend to reverse the trend of increasingly fragmented authority and to centralize the political power in China's central government. He has used the anti-corruption campaign to consolidate his authority.[11] He has also strengthened his own power by creating some Central Leading Groups and heading most of them, including the CLGFE, the Central Leading Group for Comprehensively Deepening Reform, and Central Leading Group

[11] See, for example, Fewsmith (2014); Brown (2015).

for National Defense and Military Reform.[12] On the other hand, China's economic growth has been slowing down, and Xi declared in 2014 that China entered a new phase of economic development— a "new normal". There are three characteristics of China's new normal economy: "first, the economy has shifted from the previous high speed to a medium-to-high speed growth; second, the economic structure is constantly improved and upgraded; and third, the economy is increasingly driven by innovation instead of input and investment."[13] Under the new circumstances, China's exchange rate policy has been changed accordingly.

As has been argued in Chap. 6, with the development of RMB internationalization and increasing openness of capital account, a flexible exchange rate was the best choice to preserve the independence and effectiveness of Chinese monetary policy. A more flexible RMB exchange rate was in turn conducive to the international use of RMB. More specifically, China's exchange rate experienced a depreciation tendency in the first half of 2014, which was unprecedented in the previous years. After this, two-way fluctuations of the RMB exchange rate was becoming the "new normal", which indicated that the Chinese currency become increasingly market-oriented.

In particular, the PBOC announced a further reform of the exchange rate system on 11 August 2015. The daily central parity quotes of the RMB exchange rate against the dollar were to take into consideration the closing rate of the previous day, the demand and supply of the foreign exchange market, and the exchange rates of the world's major currencies.[14] Then China Foreign Exchange Trade System, a division of PBOC, released the RMB exchange rate index to help guide market participants to refer not only the bilateral RMB/USD exchange rate but also effective exchange rate based on currency basket to judge the trend and strength of the RMB.[15] Moreover, RMB was included in IMF's SDR basket in December 2015, which reflected China's increasing financial integration and the growing international use of RMB.[16] According to the IMF's Annual Report on Exchange Arrangements and Exchange Restrictions in 2016, IMF changed China's classification from an arrangement in

---

[12]Heilmann and Stepan (2016).

[13]"Xi Jinping for the first time systematically elaborates the 'new normal'", Xinhua, 10 November 2014, retrieved from http://news.xinhuanet.com/politics/2014-11/10/c_127195118.htm.

[14]People's Bank of China, "PBOC's announcement on improving the central parity quotes of RMB exchange rate against the US dollar", 11 August 2015, retrieved from http://www.pbc.gov.cn/goutongjiaoliu/113456/113469/2927054/index.html; "China improves exchange rate formation system", *Xinhua*, 11 August 2015, retrieved from http://news.xinhuanet.com/english/2015-08/11/c_134503641.htm.

[15]Lin Jiang, "CFETS released the RMB exchange rate index", *Xinhua*, 12 December 2015.

[16]International Monetary Fund, "IMF survey: Chinese renminbi to be included in IMF's special drawing right basket", 1 December 2015, retrieved from https://www.imf.org/en/News/Articles/2015/09/28/04/53/sonew120115a.

which the flexibility of the RMB is limited vis-à-vis the US dollar to one in which more flexibility is allowed relative to a basket of currencies.[17]

It could be seen that in the Xi era China's politics becomes more authoritarian, while the economic policy (at least exchange rate policy) becomes more liberal. Here interesting questions arise: is there any relationship or contradiction between the more authoritarian political regime and more liberal economic policy? Moreover, will the CCP be able to address "the contradiction between China's increasingly pluralistic society and culture, on the one hand, and the authoritarian political structure, on the other"[18]? The slowing down of RMB internationalization and PBOC's moderation of capital outflows since the 2015 seem to support the argument that stability comes first while marketization is placed in secondary position. Future research to explore the questions in more depth will make an important contribution.

7.3.2 *Comparative Studies of Exchange Rate Policy Making*

The book also invites further exploration of generalizability of the three-level game framework to exchange rate policy making of other countries. For one example, comparative case studies on the yen and the RMB exchange rate policies could provide fruitful results. The yen adopted a fast appreciation approach after the 1985 Plaza Accord, while the RMB appreciation stuck to gradualism after the 21 July 2005 announcement. The comparative studies can figure out how different patterns of international-domestic interactions in Japan and China influence their distinctive approaches of currency appreciation.

As another example, Malaysia pegged the ringgit (Malaysia's official currency) to the dollar at 3.8 ringgit per dollar in the aftermath of the Asian financial crisis and ran continuous trade surpluses with the US in the 2000s. Interestingly, Malaysia shifted from the dollar-pegged regime to a managed floating system on 21 July 2005, exactly the same date when China announced the reform of China's exchange rate system. Here the questions arise: given Malaysia was a country with less economic impact and geopolitical independence compared with China, what were the roles of external factors for Malaysia's 2005 exchange rate reform? Whether, and if so how, domestic politics influenced the transition of the ringgit exchange rate regime? In short, the book invites future comparative case studies of exchange rate policy making to explore the way in which the international and domestic factors interact, what factors exert the most influences and the conditions under which they matter most in different countries.

---

[17]International Monetary Fund, "Annual Report on Exchange Arrangements and Exchange Restrictions 2016", 11 November 2016, https://www.imf.org/en/Publications/Annual-Report-on-Exchange-Arrangements-and-Exchange-Restrictions/Issues/2017/01/25/Annual-Report-on-Exchange-Arrangements-and-Exchange-Restrictions-2016-43741.

[18]Lynch (2015), p. 107.

In conclusion, this book makes a contribution by providing original and systematic research on China's exchange rate policy making in the Hu-Wen era. The book makes a modest theoretical contribution to the existing body of CPE and IPE literature by developing the three-level game framework to explain China's exchange rate policy making. More importantly, it provides substantial empirical evidence based on documentary analysis and primary data from interviews and questionnaire surveys. The empirical study provides a richer portrait of the dynamism and complexity of China's exchange rate policy making in the Hu-Wen era. The book invites further exploration of China's exchange rate policy in the Xi era and future comparative case study of exchange rate policy making.

Appendix A
US Congress Bills on the RMB Issue, 2003–2013

Date	Bill number	Full title	Sponsor
5 September 2003	S. 1586	To authorize appropriate action if the negotiations with the People's Republic of China regarding China's undervalued currency and currency manipulation are not successful	Charles E. Schumer
8 September 2003	S. 1592	Fair Currency Enforcement Act of 2003: "To require negotiation and appropriate action with respect to certain countries that engage in currency manipulation"	Joseph I. Lieberman
9 September 2003	S. RES. 219	"To encourage the People's Republic of China to establish a market-based valuation of the yuan and to fulfill its commitments under international trade agreements"	Lindsey Graham

(continued)

Z. Wang, *The International Political Economy of China's Exchange Rate Policy Making*, https://doi.org/10.1007/978-981-33-4578-2_1

(continued)

Date	Bill number	Full title	Sponsor
10 September 2003	H. R. 3058	Currency Harmonization Initiative through Neutralizing Action Act of 2003: "To require the Secretary of the Treasury to analyze and report on the exchange rate policies of the People's Republic of China, and to require that additional tariffs be imposed on products of that country on the basis of the rate of manipulation by that country of the rate of exchange between the currency of that country and the United States dollar"	Phil English
17 September 2003	H. CON. RES. 285	"Expressing the concern of the Congress regarding the detrimental impact on the United States economy of the manipulation by foreign governments of their currencies"	Donald A. Manzullo
8 October 2003	H. R. 3269	Currency Manipulation Prevention Act: "To require certain actions to be taken against countries that manipulate their currencies, and for other purposes"	John D. Dingell
20 October 2003	S. 1758	Currency Harmonization Initiative through Neutralizing Action Act of 2003: "To require the Secretary of the Treasury to analyze and report on the exchange rate policies of the People's Republic of China, and to require that additional tariffs be imposed on products of that country on the basis of the rate of manipulation by that country of the rate of exchange between the currency of that country and the United States dollar"	George V. Voinovich

(continued)

(continued)

Date	Bill number	Full title	Sponsor
21 October 2003	H. R. 3364	"To authorize appropriate action if the negotiations with the People's Republic of China regarding China's undervalued currency and currency manipulation are not successful"	Sue Wilkins Myrick
28 October 2003	H. RES. 414	"To encourage the People's Republic of China to fulfill its commitments under international trade agreements, support the United States manufacturing sector, and establish monetary and financial market reforms"	Phil English
6 November 2003	S. RES. 262	"To encourage the Secretary of the Treasury to initiate expedited negotiations with the People's Republic of China on establishing a market-based currency valuation and to fulfill its commitments under international trade agreements"	Olympia J. Snowe
22 July 2004	H. R. 4986	"To require the Secretary of the Treasury to analyze and report on the exchange rate policies of the People's Republic of China, and to require that measures consistent with the obligations of the United States under the World Trade Organization be taken to offset any disadvantage to United States producers resulting from China's exchange rate policies"	Mike Rogers

(continued)

(continued)

Date	Bill number	Full title	Sponsor
23 September 2004	H. CON. RES. 498	"Urging the President to take immediate steps to establish a plan to adopt the recommendations of the United States-China Economic and Security Review Commission in its 2004 Report to the Congress in order to correct the current imbalance in the bilateral trade and economic relationship between the United States and the People's Republic of China"	Timothy John
24 January 2005	S. 14	Fair Wage, Competition, and Investment Act of 2005: "To provide fair wages for America's workers, to create new jobs through investment in America, to provide for fair trade and competitiveness, and for other purposes"	Debbie Stabenow
26 January 2005	H. CON. RES. 33	"Urging the President take immediate steps to establish a plan to adopt the recommendations of the United States-China Economic and Security Review Commission in its 2004 Report to the Congress in order to correct the current imbalance in the bilateral trade and economic relationship between the United States and the People's Republic of China"	Tim Ryan
3 February 2005	S. 295	"To authorize appropriate action if the negotiations with the People's Republic of China regarding China's undervalued currency are not successful"	Charles E. Schumer
15 February 2005	S. 377	Fair Currency Enforcement Act of 2005: "To require negotiation and appropriate action with respect to certain countries that engage in currency manipulation"	Joseph I. Lieberman

(continued)

(continued)

Date	Bill number	Full title	Sponsor
6 April 2005	H. R. 1498	Chinese Currency Act of 2005: "To clarify that exchange-rate manipulation by the People's Republic of China is actionable under the countervailing duty provisions and the product-specific safeguard mechanisms of the trade laws of the United States, and for other purposes"	Tim Ryan
12 April 2005	H. R. 1575	"To authorize appropriate action if the negotiations with the People's Republic of China regarding China's undervalued currency and currency manipulation are not successful"	Sue Wilkins Myrick
17 May 2005	H. R. 2414	Currency Rate Adjustment and Trade Enforcement Act: "To require the Secretary of the Treasury to analyze and report on the exchange rate policies of the People's Republic of China, and to require that measures consistent with the obligations of the United States under the World Trade Organization be taken to offset any disadvantage to United States producers resulting from China's exchange rate policies"	Mike Rogers
21 June 2005	H. R. 3004	Currency Harmonization Initiative Through Neutralizing Action Act of 2005: "To require the Secretary of the Treasury to analyze and report on the exchange rate policies of the People's Republic of China, and to require that additional tariffs be imposed on products of that country on the basis of the rate of manipulation by that country of the rate of exchange between the currency of that country and the United States dollar"	Phil English

(continued)

(continued)

Date	Bill number	Full title	Sponsor
14 July 2005	H. R. 3283	United States Trade Rights Enforcement Act: "To enhance resources to enforce United States trade rights"	Phil English
14 July 2005	H. R. 3306	Fair Trade with China Act of 2005: "To amend the Tariff Act of 1930 and the Trade Act of 1974 to provide relief from certain practices by other countries, and for other purposes"	Charles B. Rangel
19 July 2005	S. 1421	United States Trade Rights Enforcement Act: "To enhance resources to enforce United States trade rights"	Susan M. Collins
28 July 2005	H. R. 3283	United States Trade Rights Enforcement Act: "To enhance resources to enforce United States trade rights"	Phil English
6 October 2005	S. RES. 270	"Expressing the sense of the Senate that the International Monetary Fund should investigate whether China is manipulating the rate of exchange between the Chinese yuan and the United States dollar"	Evan Bayh
28 September 2006	S. 3992	United States Fair Currency Practices Act of 2006: "To amend the Exchange Rates and International Economic Policy Coordination Act of 1988 to clarify the definition of manipulation with respect to currency, and for other purposes"	Jim Bunning

(continued)

(continued)

Date	Bill number	Full title	Sponsor
9 January 2007	H.R.321	Currency Harmonization Initiative Through Neutralizing Action Act of 2005: "To require the Secretary of the Treasury to analyze and report on the exchange rate policies of the People's Republic of China, and to require that additional tariffs be imposed on products of that country on the basis of the rate of manipulation by that country of the rate of exchange between the currency of that country and the United States dollar"	Phil English
31 January 2007	H. R. 782	Fair Currency Act of 2007: "To amend title VII of the Tariff Act of 1930 to provide that exchange-rate misalignment by any foreign nation is a countervailable export subsidy, to amend the Exchange Rates and International Economic Policy Coordination Act of 1988 to clarify the definition of manipulation with respect to currency, and for other purposes"	Tim Ryan
12 February 2007	H. R. 1002	"To authorize appropriate action if the negotiations with the People's Republic of China regarding China's undervalued currency and currency manipulation are not successful"	John M. Spratt
7 March 2007	S. 796	Fair Currency Act of 2007: "To amend title VII of the Tariff Act of 1930 to provide that exchange-rate misalignment by any foreign nation is a countervailable export subsidy, to amend the Exchange Rates and International Economic Policy Coordination Act of 1988 to clarify the definition of manipulation with respect to currency, and for other purposes"	Jim Bunning

(continued)

(continued)

Date	Bill number	Full title	Sponsor
28 June 2007	H. R. 2942	Currency Reform for Fair Trade Act of 2007: "To provide for identification of misaligned currency, require action to correct the misalignment, and for other purposes"	Tim Ryan
3 April 2008	S. 2813	China Currency Manipulation Act of 2008: "To require the Secretary of the Treasury to take action with respect to currency manipulation by the People's Republic of China and for other purposes"	Jim Bunning
30 July 2010	H. R. 6071	Emergency China Trade Act of 2010: "To withdraw normal trade relations treatment from the products of the People's Republic of China, to provide for a balanced trade relationship between that country and the United States, and for other purposes"	Brad Sherman
13 September 2011	H. R. 2909	Emergency China Trade Act: "To withdraw normal trade relations treatment from the products of the People's Republic of China, to provide for a balanced trade relationship between that country and the United States, and for other purposes"	Brad Sherman

Source Thomas Library of Congress, US Congress bills and resolutions, available from http://thomas.loc.gov/home/bills_res.html

Appendix B
PBOC's Open Market Operations, 2004–2013

Year, Quarter		Repo transactions	Reverse repo transactions	Spot bond purchase	Central bank bill issuance
2004	Total	3010	400	0	15072
	Q1	0	400	0	4352
	Q2	700	0	0	2390
	Q3	1710	0	0	2989.5
	Q4	600	0	0	5340.5
2005	Total	7230	380	0	27882
	Q1	550	380	0	7130
	Q2	900	0	0	6450
	Q3	3400	0	0	5350
	Q4	2380	0	0	8952
2006	Total	19900	1183	0	36510
	Q1	7040	1183	0	13200
	Q2	4150	0	0	9040
	Q3	6350	0	0	8162
	Q4	2360	0	0	6108
2007	Total	11185	900	6100	40680
	Q1	3400	900	0	18030
	Q2	0	0	0	7950
	Q3	750	0	6000	9910
	Q4	7035	0	100	4790
2008	Total	33260	0	0	42990

(continued)

Z. Wang, *The International Political Economy of China's Exchange Rate Policy Making*, https://doi.org/10.1007/978-981-33-4578-2_1

(continued)

Year, Quarter		Repo transactions	Reverse repo transactions	Spot bond purchase	Central bank bill issuance
	Q1	18350	0	0	17860
	Q2	5120	0	0	11530
	Q3	6010	0	0	9810
	Q4	3780	0	0	3790
2009	Total	41710	0	0	40260
	Q1	11150	0	0	4800
	Q2	11700	0	0	9300
	Q3	8700	0	0	12910
	Q4	10160	0	0	13250
2010	Total	20850	0	0	42360
	Q1	8930	0	0	14350
	Q2	5920	0	0	11680
	Q3	3430	0	0	12330
	Q4	2570	0	0	4000
2011	Total	24790	0	0	14020
	Q1	8150	0	0	3370
	Q2	5450	0	0	5860
	Q3	6290	0	0	1640
	Q4	4900	0	0	3150
2012	Total	9440	60380	0	0
	Q1	3980	3520	0	0
	Q2	5460	2140	0	0
	Q3	0	22930	0	0
	Q4	0	31790	0	0
2013	Total	7650	21660	0	5362
	Q1	2530	13440	0	0
	Q2	5120	170	0	1140
	Q3	0	4700	0	4008
	Q4	0	3350	0	214

Source Author's own elaboration based on open market operation announcements, PBOC Monetary Policy Department, available from http://www.pbc.gov.cn/zhengcehuobisi/125207/125213/125431/125469/index.html

Appendix C
Adjustments of Required Reserve Ratio (RRR), 2001–2013

Date	RRR before adjustment (%)	Adjustment range (%)	RRR after adjustment (%)
2012.5.18	20.5	-0.5	20.0
2012.2.24	21.0	-0.5	20.5
2011.12.5	21.5	-0.5	21.0
2011.6.20	21.0	0.5	21.5
2011.5.18	20.5	0.5	21.0
2011.4.21	20.0	0.5	20.5
2011.3.25	19.5	0.5	20.0
2011.2.24	19.0	0.5	19.5
2011.1.20	18.5	0.5	19.0
2010.12.20	18.0	0.5	18.5
2010.11.29	17.5	0.5	18.0
2010.11.16	17.0	0.5	17.5
2010.5.10	16.5	0.5	17.0
2010.2.25	16.0	0.5	16.5
2010.1.18	15.5	0.5	16.0
2008.12.25	16.0	-0.5	15.5
2008.12.05	17.0	-1.0	16.0
2008.10.15	17.5	-0.5	17.0
2008.06.07	16.5	1.0	17.5
2008.05.20	16.0	0.5	16.5
2008.04.25	15.5	0.5	16.0
2008.03.18	15.0	0.5	15.5
2008.01.25	14.5	0.5	15.0

(continued)

Z. Wang, *The International Political Economy of China's Exchange Rate Policy Making*, https://doi.org/10.1007/978-981-33-4578-2_1

(continued)

Date	RRR before adjustment (%)	Adjustment range (%)	RRR after adjustment (%)
2007.12.25	13.5	1.0	14.5
2007.11.26	13.0	0.5	13.5
2007.10.25	12.5	0.5	13.0
2007.09.25	12.0	0.5	12.5
2007.08.15	11.5	0.5	12.0
2007.06.05	11.0	0.5	11.5
2007.05.15	10.5	0.5	11.0
2007.04.16	10.0	0.5	10.5
2007.02.25	9.5	0.5	10.0
2007.01.15	9.0	0.5	9.5
2006.11.15	8.5	0.5	9.0
2006.08.15	8.0	0.5	8.5
2006.07.5	7.5	0.5	8.0
2004.04.25	7.0	0.5	7.5
2003.09.21	6.0	1.0	7.0

Source RMB required reserve, PBOC Monetary Policy Department, available from http://www.pbc.gov.cn/zhengcehuobisi/125207/125213/125434/125798/index.html

Appendix D
Semi-structured Interview Questions

Semi-structured Interview Questions—Elites/Experts at Beijing

1. General questions:

   (1) What role did China play in the global political economy in the twenty-first century?
   (2) What role did China's currency play in the world economy in the twenty-first century?

2. More specific questions: the first group of questions is on the first round of exchange rate reform.

   (1) What do you think is the most important factor that pushed the China's central government to carry out the reform?
   (2) In your point of view, what factors influenced the RMB appreciation after the 21 July 2005 announcement?
   (3) After two years of gradual appreciation, the speed of RMB appreciation accelerated, especially in the first half of 2008. What do you think is the main consideration of the central government with regard to this policy change?

3. The second group of questions is on the stagnation of exchange rate reform from 2008 to 2010.

   (1) What do you think is the most important factor that influenced China's policy return to dollar-pegged exchange rate from July 2008 to June 2010?
   (2) What role could the domestic interest groups (local entrepreneurs and industry associations) play in lobbying for this policy change?
   (3) Do you see it as a policy rescue for exporters or a step back of exchange rate reform?

Z. Wang, *The International Political Economy of China's Exchange Rate Policy Making*, https://doi.org/10.1007/978-981-33-4578-2_1

4. The third group of questions is on the resumption of exchange rate reform after 19 June 2010.

    (1) What do you think is the most important factor that pushed the China's central government to re-initiate the second round of exchange rate reform?
    (2) What are the differences between the two rounds of exchange rate reforms?
    (3) What is your view on the relationship between the RMB internationalization and exchange rate reform?
    (4) What is your view on the current exchange rate regime and level?

Semi-structured Interview Questions—Officials of Local Government and Branches of MOFCOM

1. The RMB exchange rate began to appreciate against the dollar after 21 July 2005. How were the export-oriented industries or enterprises in Fujian province impacted?
2. After two years of gradual appreciation, the speed of RMB appreciation accelerated, especially in the first half of 2008. What were impacts of the rapid appreciation on the exporters in Fujian province?

    Two follow up questions require in-depth exploration.

    Follow up question (1): what were their attitude and responses towards the rapid appreciation?
    Follow up question (2): faced with pressures/voices from the local entrepreneurs and industry associations, what were your attitude and response?
    Follow up question (3): is there any way for you to influence the exchange rate policymaking of the central government?

3. The RMB exchange rate stopped appreciation and remained stable against the dollar from July 2008 to June 2010. What was its impact on the export-oriented industries or enterprises in Fujian province during the worst time of global financial crisis?
4. On 19 June 2010, the PBOC announced to further promote the RMB exchange rate reform.

    (1) How were exporters in Fujian province affected in the new period of gradual appreciation?
    (2) Any difference between the reforms of 21 July 2005 and 19 June 2010?
    (3) What is your view on the current exchange rate regime and level?

Semi-structured Interview Questions—Local Export Entrepreneurs

1. General questions:

   (1) What is your business?
   (2) How is your business affected by fluctuations (appreciations) of the RMB exchange rate?

2. The RMB exchange rate began to appreciate gradually against the dollar after 21 July 2005. How was your enterprise affected by the RMB appreciation in the following two years?
3. After two years of gradual appreciation, the speed of RMB appreciation accelerated, especially in the first half of 2008. What was the impact of rapid appreciation on your enterprise?

   Two follow up questions require in-depth exploration.

   Follow up question (1): did you have any way to alleviate the negative impact of rapid RMB appreciation on your business?
   Follow up question (2): is it possible to elaborate a bit more on your influence on the exchange rate policy? For example, to communicate with the local government or the industry association?

4. The RMB exchange rate stopped appreciation and remained stable against the dollar from July 2008 to June 2010. What was its impact on your enterprise during the global financial crisis?
5. On 19 June 2010, the PBOC announced to further promote the RMB exchange rate reform.

   (1) How was your enterprise affected in the second round of RMB appreciation?
   (2) What is your view on the current exchange rate regime and level?

Appendix E
The Development of RMB Internationalization—International Use of RMB in Trade and Investment, 2009–2013

8 April 2009

The State Council executive meeting decided to implement the pilot RMB cross-border trade settlement at Shanghai and four cities (Guangzhou, Shenzhen, Zhuhai and Dongguan) in Guangdong.

29 June 2009

PBOC and Hong Kong Monetary Authority signed a memorandum to promote RMB cross-border trade.

2 July 2009

PBOC, MOF, MOFCOM, General Administration of Customs, State Administration of Taxation, and China Banking Regulatory Commission jointly formulated and announced the "Regulations for pilot RMB cross-border trade settlement".

6 July 2009

Pilot RMB cross-border trade settlement was officially launched in Shanghai.

20 October 2009

The Chinese central government issued six billion RMB bonds in Hong Kong, which were three times oversubscribed.

22 June 2010

The State Council approved that the RMB cross-border trade settlement within the pilot areas expand to 20 provinces, and that the overseas coverage expands from Hong Kong, Macao and ASEAN to all countries and regions.

Z. Wang, *The International Political Economy of China's Exchange Rate Policy Making*, https://doi.org/10.1007/978-981-33-4578-2_1

19 July 2010

The PBOC signed "Agreement for Settlement of RMB Banking Business in Hong Kong" with Bank of China (Hong Kong) and a memorandum on expansion of RMB trade settlement with Hong Kong Monetary Authority.

17 August 2010

The PBOC announced the "Notice on Certain Issues Concerning the Pilot Programme on Three Types of Institution Including Overseas RMB Clearing Banks Making RMB Investment into the Inter-bank Bond Market". It allows foreign central banks or monetary authorities, RMB settlement banks in Hong Kong or Macau, and RMB cross-border trade settlement participating banks in Hong Kong or Macau to use RMB to invest in the Inter-bank Bond Market, provided that they have obtained approval from the PBOC.

29 October 2010

Pilot RMB cross-border trade and investment settlement was officially launched in Xinjiang. Xinjiang became China's first region to open RMB cross-border investment settlement.

22 November 2010

The MOF announced that the Chinese central government would issue eight billion RMB bonds in Hong Kong.

16 February 2011

SAFE announced the "Notice on Relevant Issues Concerning RMB-FX Currency Options", which approved the trading of RMB-FX currency options.

23 August 2011

PBOC, MOF, MOFCOM, General Administration of Customs, State Administration of Taxation, and China Banking Regulatory Commission jointly announced the "Notice on Expanding the RMB Cross-border Trade Settlement Areas", which approved that the RMB cross-border trade settlement be expanded to the whole country.

14 October 2011

The PBOC announced "Measures for the Administration on RMB Settlement in Foreign Direct Investment" to regulate foreign investors and banks to handle RMB settlement in foreign direct investment.

16 December 2011

Chinese government launched the RMB Qualified Foreign Institutional Investor (RQFII) Scheme, which allowed overseas investors to establish RMB-denominated funds in Hong Kong for investment in the mainland securities market.

19 April 2012

HSBC issued the RMB-denominated bond in London, the first issue of a RMB offshore bond outside Hong Kong.

29 May 2012

China Foreign Exchange Trade System announced to start the direct trading of RMB against the Japanese yen, which means China and Japan would directly convert each other's currencies rather than through the US dollar.

17 September 2012

HK Stock Exchange launched the USD/CNH futures, the world's first deliverable RMB currency futures product, to provide greater capital efficiency and flexibility for the offshore RMB market.

10 April 2013

China Foreign Exchange Trade System announced to start the direct trading of RMB against the Australian dollar, which means China and Australia would directly convert each other's currencies rather than through the US dollar.

Appendix F
The Development of RMB Internationalization—Bilateral Currency Swap Agreements Between the PBOC and Other Central Banks or Monetary Authorities, 2009–2013

	Central bank or monetary authority	Date	Value (RMB in billion)	Maturity (year)
1	Hong Kong	20 January 2009 22 November 2011 (renewal)	2000 4000 (renewal)	3
2	Malaysia	8 February 2009 8 February 2012 (renewal)	800 1800 (renewal)	3
3	Belorussia	11 March 2009 10 May 2010 (renewal)	200 70 (renewal)	3
4	Indonesia	23 March 2009 1 October 2013 (renewal)	1000 1000 (renewal)	3
5	Argentina	2 April 2009	700	3
6	South Korea	20 April 2009 26 October 2011 (renewal)	1800 3600 (renewal)	3
7	Iceland	9 June 2010 11 September 2013 (renewal)	35 35 (renewal)	3
8	Singapore	23 July 2010 7 March 2013 (renewal)	1500 3000 (renewal)	3
9	New Zealand	18 April 2011	250	3
10	Uzbekistan	19 April 2011	7	3
11	Mongolia	6 May 2011	50	3
12	Kazakhstan	13 June 2011	70	3

(continued)

Z. Wang, *The International Political Economy of China's Exchange Rate Policy Making*, https://doi.org/10.1007/978-981-33-4578-2_1

(continued)

	Central bank or monetary authority	Date	Value (RMB in billion)	Maturity (year)
13	Thailand	22 December 2011	700	3
14	Pakistan	23 December 2011	100	3
15	United Arab Emirates	17 January 2012	350	3
16	Turkey	21 February 2012	100	3
17	Australia	22 March 2012	2000	3
18	Ukraine	26 June 2012	150	3
19	Brazil	26 March 2013	1900	3
20	UK	22 June 2013	2000	3
21	Hungary	9 September 2013	100	3
22	Albania	12 September 2013	20	3
23	European Central Bank	8 October 2013	3500	3
Total sum			25502[a]	

Source Author-collected data from the official website of People's Bank of China
[a]For renewed agreement, the renewed amount has been calculated and the expired amount has been discarded

References

Alesina, A., & Wagner, A. F. (2006). Choosing (and reneging on) exchange rate regimes. *Journal of the European Economic Association, 4*(4), 770–799.

Anderlini, J. (2010). Beijing lays ground for renminbi shift: China could widen daily trading band for currency. *Financial Times*, 6 April 2010. https://next.ft.com/content/64c4bd04-4193-11df-865a-00144feabdc0.

Anderlini, J. (2015). Zhou Xiaochuan, Beijing's central radical banker. *Financial Times*, 14 August 2015. http://www.ft.com/cms/s/0/53ba324c-41cd-11e5-b98b-87c7270955cf.html#axzz3rkDOUOdG.

Anderson, J. (2005) The Complete RMB Handbook (Third Edition). *Asian Economic Perspectives*, 25 July 2005. http://www.econ.hku.hk/~xiaogeng/Teaching/Readings/The%20Complete%20RMB%20Handbook%203rd%20ed.pdf.

Andrew, B., & Jeffrey, C. (2014). *Process Tracing: From Metaphor to Analytic Tool*. Cambridge: Cambridge University Press.

Andrews, D. M. (Ed.). (2006). *International Monetary Power*. Ithaca: Cornell University Press.

Balassa, B. (1964). The purchasing-power parity doctrine: A reappraisal. *The Journal of Political Economy, 72*(6), 584–596.

Barber, L. (2009). Transcript: Wen Jiabao. *Financial Times*, 2 February 2009. http://www.ft.com/cms/s/0/795d2bca-f0fe-11dd-8790-0000779fd2ac.html#axzz4539B7huI.

Beach, D., & Pedersen, R. B. (2013). *Process-Tracing Methods: Foundations and Guidelines*. Ann Arbor: University of Michigan Press.

Bearce, D. H. (2003). Societal preferences, partisan agents, and monetary policy outcomes. *International Organization, 57*(2), 373–410.

Bell, S., & Feng, H. (2013). *The Rise of the People's Bank of China: The Politics of Institutional Change*. Cambridge: Harvard University Press.

Bergsten, C. F. (2010). Correcting the Chinese exchange rate: An action plan. Peterson Institute for International Economics, 24 March 2010. https://piie.com/commentary/testimonies/correcting-chinese-exchange-rate-action-plan.

Bernanke, B. S. (2009). Financial reform to address systemic risk. Council on Foreign Relations, 10 March 2009. https://www.federalreserve.gov/newsevents/speech/bernanke20090310a.htm.

Bernhard, W., & Leblang, D. (1999). Democratic institutions and exchange-rate commitments. *International Organization, 53*(1), 71–97.

Blackwill, R. D., & Campbell, K. M. (2016). Xi Jinping on the global stage: Chinese foreign policy under a powerful but exposed leader. Council on Foreign Relations Special Report No. 74. http://www.cfr.org/china/xi-jinping-global-stage/p37569.

Borio, C., & Disyatat, P. (2011). Global imbalances and the financial crisis: Link or no link? Bank for International Settlements Working Papers No. 346. http://www.bis.org/publ/work346.pdf.

Z. Wang, *The International Political Economy of China's Exchange Rate Policy Making*, https://doi.org/10.1007/978-981-33-4578-2_1

Bowles, P., & Wang, B. (2006). 'Flowers and criticism': The political economy of the renminbi debate. *Review of International Political Economy, 13*(2), 233–257.
Bowles, P., & Wang, B. (2008). The rocky road ahead: China, the US and the future of the dollar. *Review of International Political Economy, 15*(3), 335–353.
Bowles, P., & Wang, B. (2013). Renminbi internationalization: A journey to where? *Development and Change, 44*(6), 1363–1385.
Breslin, S. (1999). The politics of Chinese trade and the Asian financial crises: Questioning the wisdom of export-led growth. *Third World Quarterly, 20*(6), 1179–1199.
Breslin, S. (2003). Reforming China's embedded socialist compromise: China and the WTO. *Global Change, Peace & Security, 15*(3), 213–229.
Breslin, S. (2004). Capitalism with Chinese characteristics: The public, the private and the international. Murdoch University Asia Research Centre Working Paper No. 104. https://www.murdoch.edu.au/Research-capabilities/Asia-Research-Centre/_document/working-papers/wp104.pdf.
Breslin, S. (2007a). *China and the Global Political Economy*. Basingstoke: Palgrave Macmillan.
Breslin, S. (2007b). The political economy of development in China: Political agendas and economic realities. *Development, 50*(3), 3–10.
Breslin, S. (2010). China's emerging global role: Dissatisfied responsible great power. *Politics, 30*(1), 52–62.
Breslin, S. (2011a). China and the crisis: Global power, domestic caution and local initiative. *Contemporary Politics, 17*(2), 185–200.
Breslin, S. (2011b). The 'China model' and the global crisis: From Friedrich List to a Chinese mode of governance? *International Affairs, 87*(6), 1323–1343.
Breslin, S. (2012). China and the crisis: Global power, domestic caution and local initiative. In S. Breslin (Ed.), *East Asia and the Global Crisis* (pp.77–92). London: Routledge.
Breslin, S. (2013). China and the global order: Signalling threat or friendship? *International Affairs, 89*(3), 615–634.
Broome, A. (2010). *The Currency of Power*. Houndmills: Palgrave Macmillan.
Brown, K. (2009). *Friends and Enemies: The Past, Present and Future of the Communist Party of China*. London: Anthem Press.
Brown, K. (2012). *Hu Jintao: China's Silent Ruler*. Singapore: World Scientific.
Brown, K. (2013a). *Contemporary China*. Basingstoke: Palgrave Macmillan.
Brown, K. (2013b). The new leadership in Beijing: Political and economic implications. Chatham House, July 2013. https://www.chathamhouse.org/sites/default/files/public/Research/Asia/0713pmnt_brown.pdf.
Brown, K. (2013c). What did Hu Jintao and Wen Jiabao do for China? BBC News, 14 March 2013. http://www.bbc.co.uk/news/world-asia-china-21669780.
Brown, K. (2013d). Xi Jinping's new leadership and the challenge of modernising politics in China. *Analysis* No. 213, November 2013. http://www.ispionline.it/sites/default/files/pubblicazioni/analysis_213_2013.pdf.
Brown, K. (2015a). Will Xi's anti-corruption campaign become an outright purge? *The Diplomat*, 7 April 2015. http://thediplomat.com/2015/04/will-xis-anti-corruption-campaign-become-an-outright-purge.
Brown, K. (2015b). The role of leadership in political and economic transition in China. In E. Berman, M. Shamsul Haque (Ed.), *Asian Leadership in Policy and Governance* (pp. 213–231). Bingley: Emerald Group Publishing Limited.
Brown, K. (Ed.). (2011). *China 2020: The Next Decade for the People's Republic of China*. Oxford: Chandos Publishing.
Brown, K. (2016). A response to Francis Fukuyama's "reflections on Chinese governance". *Journal of Chinese Governance, 1*(3), 392-404.
Broz, J. L., & Frieden, J. A. (2001). The political economy of international monetary relations. *Annual Review of Political Science, 4*(1), 317–343.
Burnham, P., Lutz, K. G., Grant, W., & Layton-Henry, Z. (2008). *Research Methods in Politics*. Basingstoke: Palgrave Macmillan.

Campanella, M. (2014). The internationalization of the renminbi and the rise of a multipolar currency system. ECIPE Working Paper No. 1. https://ecipe.org/wp-content/uploads/2014/12/WP201201_1.pdf.

Carmignani, F., Colombo, E., & Tirelli, P. (2008). Exploring different views of exchange rate regime choice. *Journal of International Money and Finance, 27*(7), 1177–1197.

Chao, W., & Tung, C. (2013). Does China really say no? The impact of international political pressure on China's exchange rate policy. *Issues and Studies, 49*(2), 1–34.

Chaudoin, S., Milner, H. V., & Pang, X. (2015). International systems and domestic politics: Linking complex interactions with empirical models in international relations. *International Organization, 69*(2), 275–309.

Chen, G. J., Deng, W., & Kemme, K. (2008). Yuan real exchange rate undervaluation, 1997-2006: How much, how often? Not much, not often. William Davidson Institute Working Paper No. 934. https://deepblue.lib.umich.edu/bitstream/handle/2027.42/64348/wp934.pdf?sequence=1&isAllowed=y.

Chen, J. (2007). Behavior equilibrium exchange rate and misalignment of renminbi: a recent empirical study. DEGIT Conference Papers No. c012_013. http://degit.sam.sdu.dk/papers/degit_12/C012_013.pdf.

Cheung, Y., & Haan, J. (2012). *The Evolving Role of China in the Global Economy*. Cambridge: The MIT Press.

Cheung, Y., Chinn, M. D., & Fujii, E. (2005). Why the renminbi might be overvalued (but probably isn't). Federal Reserve Bank of San Franciso Conference on "External Imbalances and Adjustment in the Pacific Basin", 5 September 2005. http://www.frbsf.org/economic-research/files/paper-chinn.pdf.

Cheung, Y., Chinn, M. D., & Fujii, E. (2007). The overvaluation of renminbi undervaluation. *Journal of International Money and Finance, 26*(5), 762–785.

Cheung, Y., Chinn, M. D., & Fujii, E. (2009). Pitfalls in measuring exchange rate misalignment. *Open Economies Review, 20*(2), 183–206.

Cheung, Y., Chinn, M. D., & Fujii, E. (2010). China's current account and exchange rate. In R. C. Feenstra, & S. Wei (Ed.), *China's Growing Role in World Trade* (pp. 231–271). Chicago: University of Chicago Press.

Chin, G. (2014). China's rising monetary power. In E. Helleiner, & J. Kirshner (Ed.), *The Great Wall of Money: Power and Politics in China's International Monetary Relations* (pp. 184–212). Ithaca: Cornell University Press.

Clark, P. B., & MacDonald, R. (1998). Exchange rates and economic fundamentals: A methodological comparison of BEERs and FEERs. IMF Working Paper No. WP/98/67, May 1998. https://www.imf.org/external/pubs/ft/wp/wp9867.pdf.

Cline, W. R., & Williamson, J. (2007). Estimates of the equilibrium exchange rate of the renminbi: is there a consensus and, if not, why not? Conference on "China's Exchange Rate Policy" held by the Peterson Institute for International Economics, 12 October 2007. https://piie.com/publications/papers/cline-williamson1007.pdf.

Cline, W. R., & Williamson, J. (2008). Estimates of the equilibrium exchange rate of the renminbi: Is there a consensus and if not, why not? In M. Goldstein & N. Lardy (Eds.), *Debating China's Exchange Rate Policy* (pp. 131–154). Washington: Peterson Institute for International Economics.

Coase, R., & Wang, N. (2012). *How China Became Capitalist*. New York: Palgrave Macmillan.

Cohen, B. J. (1971). *The Future of Sterling as an International Currency*. London: Macmillan.

Cohen, B. J. (2008). *International Political Economy: An Intellectual History*. Princeton: Princeton University Press.

Cohen, B. J. (2010). *The Future of Global Currency: The Euro Versus the Dollar*. London: Routledge.

Cohen, B. J. (2015). *Currency Power: Understanding Monetary Rivalry*. Princeton: Princeton University Press.

Cohen, B. J., & Benney, T. M. (2014). What does the international currency system really look like? *Review of International Political Economy, 21*(5), 1017–1041.

Coudert, V., & Couharde, C. (2005). Real equilibrium exchange rate in China. CEPII Working Paper No. 2005-01. http://www.cepii.fr/PDF_PUB/wp/2005/wp2005-01.pdf.

Coudert, V., & Couharde, C. (2007). Real equilibrium exchange rate in China: Is the renminbi undervalued? *Journal of Asian Economics, 18*(4), 568–594.

Corden, W. M. (2009). China's exchange rate policy, its current account surplus and the global imbalances. *The Economic Journal, 119*(541), F430–F441.

Cowling, K., Dunn, S. P., & Tomlinson, P. R. (2011). Global imbalances and modern capitalism: A structural approach to understanding the present economic crisis. *Journal of Post Keynesian Economics, 33*(4), 575–596.

Cui, Y. (2013). How is the RMB exchange rate misaligned? A recent application of behavioral equilibrium exchange rate (BEER) to China. *Journal of East Asian Economic Integration, 17*(3), 281–310.

Cwik, P. F. (2011). The new neo-mercantilism: Currency manipulation as a form of protectionism. *Economic Affairs, 31*(3), 7–11.

Das, D. K. (2009). The evolution of renminbi yuan and the protracted debate on its undervaluation: An integrated review. *Journal of Asian Economics, 20*(5), 570–579.

Deng, G., & Kennedy, S. (2010). Big business and industry association lobbying in China: The paradox of contrasting styles. *The China Journal,* (63), 101–125.

Denscombe, M. (2003). *The Good Research Guide: For Small-Scale Social Research Projects.* London: Open University Press.

Di, D. (2013). The renminbi's rise and Chinese politics, In A. Wheatley (Ed.), *The Power of Currencies and Currencies of Power* (pp. 115–126). London: Routledge.

Dickie, M. (2005). Currency reform seen as question of sovereignty. *Financial Times*, 21 July 2005. http://www.ft.com/cms/s/0/e2f8d790-fa54-11d9-b092-00000e2511c8.html#axzz4BYuojsRh.

Dittmer, L. (1995). Chinese informal politics. *The China Journal,* (34), 1–34.

Dooley, M. P., Folkerts-Landau, D., & Garber, P. (2004). The revived Bretton Woods system. *International Journal of Finance & Economics, 9*(4), 307–313.

Dooley, M. P., Folkerts-Landau, D., & Garber, P. (2009). Bretton woods II still defines the international monetary system. *Pacific Economic Review, 14*(3), 297–311.

Downs, E. S. (2009). Business interest groups in Chinese politics: The case of the oil companies. In C. Li (Ed.), *China's Changing Political Landscape: Prospects for Democracy* (pp. 121–141). Washington: Brookings Institution Press.

Drazen, A. (2001). The political business cycle after 25 years, In B. Bernanke, & K. Rogoff (Ed.), *NBER Macroeconomics Annual 2000* (pp. 75–138). Cambridge: MIT Press.

Dunaway, S., & Li, X. (2005). Estimating China's "equilibrium" real exchange rate. IMF Working Paper WP/12/88. https://www.imf.org/external/pubs/ft/wp/2005/wp05202.pdf.

Edin, M. (2003a). Remaking the Communist party-state: The cadre responsibility system at the local level in China. *China: An International Journal, 1*(1), 1–15.

Edin, M. (2003b). State capacity and local agent control in China: CCP cadre management from a township perspective. *The China Quarterly,* (173), 35–52.

Edwards, S. (1996). The determinants of the choice between fixed and flexible exchange-rate regimes. National Bureau of Economic Research Working Paper No. 5756. http://www.nber.org/papers/w5756.pdf.

Eichengreen, B. J. (1998). *Globalizing Capital: A History of the International Monetary System.* Princeton: Princeton University Press.

Eichengreen, B. J. (2010). *Global Imbalances and the Lessons of Bretton Woods.* Cambridge: MIT Press.

Eichengreen, B. J. (2011). Exorbitant Privilege: *The Rise and Fall of the Dollar and the Future of the International Monetary System.* Oxford: Oxford University Press.

Eichengreen, B. J., & Razo-Garcia, R. (2006). The international monetary system in the last and next 20 years. *Economic Policy, 21*(47), 394–442.

Feigenbaum, E. A., & Ma, D. (2015). Lenin's Chinese heirs. Carnegie Endowment for International Peace, 14 October 2015. https://carnegieendowment.org/2015/10/14/lenin-s-chinese-heirs-pub-61628.

Ferdinand, P., & Wang, J. (2013). China and the IMF: From mimicry towards pragmatic international institutional pluralism. *International Affairs, 89*(4), 895–910.

Ferguson, Y. H. (2014). The renminbi-dollar relationship: Politics and economics of a diminishing issue. In T. Oatley & W. K. Winecoff (Ed.), *Handbook of the International Political Economy of Monetary Relations* (pp. 123–143). London: Edward Elgar Publishing.

Ferguson, N., & Schularick M. (2007). "Chimerica" and the global asset market boom. *International Finance, 10*(3), 215–239.

Fewsmith, J. (2001). The political and social implications of China's accession to the WTO. *The China Quarterly*, (167), 573–591.

Fewsmith, J. (2014). China's political ecology and the fight against corruption. China Leadership Monitor, No. 46. http://www.hoover.org/sites/default/files/research/docs/clm46jf.pdf.

Foot, R. (2006). Chinese strategies in a US-hegemonic global order: Accommodating and hedging. *International Affairs, 82*(1), 77–94.

Foot, R., & Walter, A. (2011). *China, the United States, and Global Order*. Cambridge: Cambridge University Press.

Foulon, M. (2015). Neoclassical realism: Challengers and bridging identities. *International Studies Review, 17*(4), 635–661.

Franzese, R. (2002). Electoral and partisan cycles in economic policies and outcomes. *Annual Review of Political Science, 5*, 369–421.

Freeman, C., & Yuan, W. J. (2011). China's exchange rate politics: Decoding the cleavage between the Chinese Ministry of Commerce and the People's Bank of China. Center for Strategic and International Studies, June 2011. https://csis-website-prod.s3.amazonaws.com/s3fs-public/legacy_files/files/publication/110615_Freeman_ChinaExchangeRatePolitics_Web.pdf.

Frieden, J. A. (1991). Invested interests: The politics of national economic policies in a world of global finance. *International Organization, 45*(4), 425–451.

Frieden, J. A. (1994). Exchange rate politics: Contemporary lessons from American history. *Review of International Political Economy, 1*(1), 81–103.

Frieden, J. A. (2014). *Currency Politics: The Political Economy of Exchange Rate Policy*. Princeton: Princeton University Press.

Frieden, J. A., & Rogowski, R. (1996). The impact of the international economy on national policies: An analytical overview. In R. Keohane & H. Milner (Eds.), *Internationalization and Domestic Politics* (pp. 25–47). Cambridge: Cambridge University Press.

Fung, H., Wu, J., & Yau, J. (2013). Recent policy changes toward the internationalization of the renminbi. *The Chinese Economy, 46*(4), 6–24.

Funke, M., & Rahn, J. (2005). Just how undervalued is the Chinese renminbi? *The World Economy, 28*(4), 465–489.

Galantucci, R. A. (2015). The repercussions of realignment: United States-China interdependence and exchange rate politics. *International Studies Quarterly, 59*(3), 423–435.

Gamble, A. (2009). *The Spectre at the Feast: Capitalist Crisis and the Politics of Recession*. Basingstoke: Palgrave Macmillan.

Garrett, G., & Lange, P. (1995). Internationalization, institutions, and political change. *International Organization, 49*(4), 627–655.

Ge, W. (1999). Special economic zones and the opening of the Chinese economy: Some lessons for economic liberalization. *World Development, 27*(7), 1267–1285.

Geithner, T. (2009). Statement by Treasury Secretary Timothy Geithner on Release of Semi-Annual Report to Congress on International Economic and Exchange Rate Policies. U.S. Department of the Treasury, 15 April 2009. https://www.treasury.gov/press-center/press-releases/Pages/tg90.aspx.

Gerring, J. (2004). What is a case study and what is it good for? *American Political Science Review, 98*(2), 341–354.

Gilbert, E., & Helleiner, E. (1999). *Nation-States and Money: The Past, Present and Future of National Currencies*. London: Routledge.
Gilpin, R. (1987). *The Political Economy of International Relations*. Princeton: Princeton University Press.
Gilpin, R. (2011). *Global Political Economy: Understanding the International Economic Order*. Princeton: Princeton University Press.
Gold, T., Guthrie, D., & Wank, D. (Eds.). (2002). *Social Connections in China: Institutions, Culture, and the Changing Nature of Guanxi*. Cambridge: Cambridge University Press.
Goldstein, M. (2004). Adjusting China's exchange rate policies. Peterson Institute for International Economics Working Paper No. 2004-1. https://www.piie.com/sites/default/files/publications/wp/wp04-1.pdf.
Goldstein, M., & Lardy, N. (2006). China's exchange rate dilemma. *American Economic Review, 96*(2), 422–426.
Goldstein, M., & Lardy, N. (2007). China's exchange rate policy: An overview of some key issues. Conference on "China's Exchange Rate Policy" held by the Peterson Institute for International Economics, 19 October 2007. https://www.piie.com/sites/default/files/publications/papers/goldstein-lardy1007.pdf.
Goldstein, M., & Lardy, N. R. (2009). *The Future of China's Exchange Rate Policy*. Washington: Peterson Institute for International Economics.
Gourevitch, P. (1978). The second image reversed: The international sources of domestic politics. *International Organization, 32*(4), 881–912.
Gruin, J. (2014). Asset or liability? The role of the financial system in the political economy of China's rebalancing. *Journal of Current Chinese Affairs, 42*(4), 73–104.
Guo, X. (2001). Dimensions of guanxi in Chinese elite politics. *The China Journal*, (46), 69–90.
Hall, P. A., & Taylor, R. C. R. (1996). Political science and the three new institutionalisms. *Political Studies, 44*(5), 936–957.
Hamrin, C. L. (1992). The Party leadership system. In K. Lieberthal, & D. Lampton (Ed.). *Bureaucracy, Politics, and Decision Making in Post-Mao China* (pp. 95–124). Berkeley: University of California Press.
Han, H. (2013). China's policymaking in transition: A hydropower development case. *The Journal of Environment & Development, 22*(3), 313–336.
He, B., & Thøgersen, S. (2010). Giving the people a voice? Experiments with consultative authoritarian institutions in China. *Journal of Contemporary China, 19*(66), 675–692.
Heilmann, S., & Stepan, M. (2016). China's core executive: Leadership styles, structures and processes under Xi Jinping. Mercator Institute for China Studies, No. 1, June 2016. https://merics.org/sites/default/files/2020-04/MPOC_ChinasCoreExecutive_web.pdf.
Helleiner, E. (2008). Political determinants of international currencies: What future for the US dollar? *Review of International Political Economy, 15*(3), 354–378.
Helleiner, E., & Kirshner, J. (Ed.). (2014). *The Great Wall of Money: Power and Politics in China's International Monetary Relations*. Ithaca: Cornell University Press.
Hentz, J. J. (2008). South Africa and the 'three level game': Globalisation, regionalism and domestic politics. *Commonwealth & Comparative Politics, 46*(4), 490–515.
Hu, Z., & Liu, S. (2013). Do external political pressures affect the RMB exchange rate against dollar?, *Monetary Theory and Practice*, (12), 26–34.
Huang, Y. (2008). *Capitalism with Chinese Characteristics: Entrepreneurship and the State*. Cambridge: Cambridge University Press.
Huang, Y. (2010). The RMB and Chinese exchange rate policy: Some misperceptions. *East Asia Forum*, 11 April 2010. http://www.eastasiaforum.org/2010/04/11/misperceptions-about-the-rmb-and-chinese-exchange-rate-policy.
Hudson, D. (2010). Financing for development and the post Keynesian case for a new global reserve currency. *Journal of International Development, 22*(6), 772–787.

Hufbauer, G., & Brunel, C. (2008). The US Congress and the Chinese renminbi. In M. Goldstein & N. Lardy (Eds.), *Debating China's Exchange Rate Policy* (pp. 219–238). Washington: Peterson Institute for International Economics.
Hufbauer, G. C., & Wong, Y. (2004). China bashing 2004. International Economics Policy Briefs No. PB04-5. http://www.iie.com/publications/pb/pb04-5.pdf.
Hung, H. (2008). Rise of China and the global overaccumulation crisis. *Review of International Political Economy, 15*(2), 149–179.
Hung, H. (2011). Global crisis, China, and the strange demise of the East Asian model. *Swiss Journal of Sociology, 37*(2), 305–320.
Hung, H. (2012). Is China saving global capitalism from the global crisis? *Protosociology: An International Journal of Interdisciplinary*, (29), 159–179.
Hung, H. (2015). *The China Boom: Why China Will Not Rule the World*. New York: Columbia University Press.
Ikenberry, J. (2008). The rise of China and the future of the West: Can the liberal system survive? *Foreign Affairs, 87*(1), 23–37.
International Monetary Fund. (2015). IMF survey: Chinese renminbi to be included in IMF's special drawing right basket. IMF, 1 December 2015. https://www.imf.org/en/News/Articles/2015/09/28/04/53/sonew120115a.
International Monetary Fund. Articles of Agreement of the International Monetary Fund. https://www.imf.org/external/pubs/ft/aa/.
International Monetary Fund. People's Republic of China: Article IV Consultation Reports. https://www.imf.org/external/country/CHN/index.htm?type=56.
Jiang, Y. (2013). *China's Policymaking for Regional Economic Cooperation*. London: Palgrave Macmillan.
Jiang, Y. (2015a). Vulgarisation of Keynesianism in China's response to the global financial crisis. *Review of International Political Economy, 22*(2), 360–390.
Jiang, Y. (2015b). This explains why China is taking so long to reform its economic system. *The Washington Post*, 21 September 2015. https://www.washingtonpost.com/blogs/monkey-cage/wp/2015/09/21/this-explains-why-china-is-taking-so-long-to-reform-its-economic-system.
Joseph, W. A. (Ed.). (2014). *Politics in China: An Introduction*. Oxford: Oxford University Press.
Ju, J., Lin, J. Y., & Liu, Q. (2011). Real exchange rates and current account imbalances in an economy with excess supply of labor. https://editorialexpress.com/cgi-bin/conference/download.cgi?db_name=FEMES11&paper_id=748.
Kaplan, S. B. (2006). The political obstacles to greater exchange rate flexibility in China. *World Development, 34*(7), 1182–1200.
Katzenstein, P. J. (1976). International relations and domestic structures: Foreign economic policies of advanced industrial states. *International Organization, 30*(1), 1–45.
Kennedy, S. (2009a). Comparing formal and informal lobbying practices in China: The capital's ambivalent embrace of capitalists. *China Information, 23*(2), 195–222.
Kennedy, S. (2009b). *The Business of Lobbying in China*. Cambridge: Harvard University Press.
Keohane, R. (1984). *After Hegemony: Cooperation and Discord in the World Political Economy*. Princeton: Princeton University Press.
Keohane, R., & Milner, H. (Eds.). (1996). *Internationalization and Domestic Politics*. Cambridge: Cambridge University Press.
Keohane, R., & Nye, J. (1977). *Power and Interdependence: World Politics in Transition*. Boston: Little, Brown.
Kirshner, J. (1997). *Currency and Coercion: The Political Economy of International Monetary Power*. Princeton: Princeton University Press.
Kirshner, J. (2000). The study of money. *World Politics, 52*(3), 407–436.
Kirshner, J. (2003). Money is politics. *Review of International Political Economy, 10*(4), 645–660.
Kirshner, J. (2012). The tragedy of offensive realism: Classical realism and the rise of China. *European Journal of International Relations, 18*(1), 53–75.

Kitchen, N. (2010). Systemic pressures and domestic ideas: A neoclassical realist model of grand strategy formation. *Review of International Studies, 36*(1), 117–143.

Korhonen, I., & Ritola, M. (2009). Renminbi misaligned–results from meta-regressions. BOFIT Discussion Paper No. 13/2009. http://papers.ssrn.com/sol3/papers.cfm?abstract_id=1471264.

Kroeber, A. (2011). The renminbi: The political economy of a currency. *Brookings*, 7 September 2011. http://www.brookings.edu/research/papers/2011/09/07-renminbi-kroeber.

Krugman, P. (2009). The Chinese disconnect. *New York Times*, 22 October 2009. http://www.nytimes.com/2009/10/23/opinion/23krugman.html?_r=0.

Krugman, P. (2010). Talking on China. *New York Times*, 14 March 2010. http://www.nytimes.com/2010/03/15/opinion/15krugman.html.

Kupchan, C. A. (2013). *No One's World: The West, the Rising Rest, and the Coming Global Turn*. Oxford: Oxford University Press.

Lai, H. (2010). *The Domestic Sources of China's Foreign Policy: Regimes, Leadership, Priorities and Process*. London: Routledge.

Lai, H., & Kang, S. (2014). Domestic bureaucratic politics and Chinese foreign policy. *Journal of Contemporary China, 23*(86), 294–313.

Lake, D. A. (2009). Open economy politics: A critical review. *The Review of International Organizations, 4*(3), 219–244.

Lam, W. (2006). *Chinese Politics in the Hu Jintao Era: New Leaders, New Challenges*. London: Routledge.

Lardy, N. R. (2012). *Sustaining China's Economic Growth After the Global Financial Crisis*. Washington: Peterson Institute for International Economics.

Larsén, M. F. (2007). Trade negotiations between the EU and South Africa: A three-level game. *JCMS: Journal of Common Market Studies, 45*(4), 857–881.

Leblang, D. A. (1999). Domestic political institutions and exchange rate commitments in the developing world. *International Studies Quarterly, 43*(4), 599–620.

Lee, G. C. (2014). *The Political Economy of the Sino-American Imbalance*, University of York PhD thesis. http://etheses.whiterose.ac.uk/7132/7/Gyu%20Cheol%20Lee%20-PhD.pdf.

Li, W. (2011) Political basis of currency rivalry–a research approach based on International Political Economy. *Foreign Affairs Review*, (3), 44–61.

Li, W., & Han, S. (2015). From a dependent to a reformer: China's changing role in the international monetary system. *Global Review, 7*(3), 44–66.

Li, Z. (2011). Politics and exchange rate: The political economy analysis of RMB appreciation. *World Economics and Politics*, (9), 136–155.

De Lichtervelde, I. (2012). Talking tough: Washington's evolving discourse on China's currency regime. *Asia Paper, 6*(1), 1–20.

Lieberthal, K., & Oksenberg, M. (1988). *Policy Making in China: Leaders, Structures, and Processes*. Princeton: Princeton University Press.

Liew, H. L., & Wu., H. X. (2007). *The Making of China's Exchange Rate Policy: From Plan to WTO Entry*. Cheltenham: Edward Elgar.

Liew, L. H. (2004). Policy elites in the political economy of China's exchange rate policymaking. *Journal of Contemporary China, 13*(38), 21–51.

Lin, Y. (2007). Thoughts and policy recommendations on the RMB exchange rate issue. *The Journal of World Economy*, (3), 3–12.

Liu, L., & Pauwels, L. L. (2012). Do external political pressures affect the renminbi exchange rate? *Journal of International Money and Finance, 31*(6), 1800–1818.

Liu, T., & Zhou, J. (2011). Do external pressures promote the RMB appreciation? An investigation based on the events of American pressure between 2005 and 2010. *Journal of Financial Research, 377*(11), 32–46.

Liu, X. (2013). Review of new political economy studies of exchange rate system choice. *The Journal of World Economy*, (2), 137–160.

Lobell, S., Ripsman, N., & Taliaferro, J. (Eds.). (2009). *Neoclassical Realism, the State, and Foreign Policy*. Cambridge: Cambridge University Press.

Lou, J. (Ed.). (1997). Macroeconomic reform in China: Laying the foundation for a socialist market economy. World Bank Discussion Paper No. 374. Washington: The World Bank.
Luo, Y. (1997). Guanxi and performance of foreign-invested enterprises in China: An empirical inquiry. *MIR: Management International Review, 37*(1), 51–70.
Ly, M. (2012). Special drawing rights, the dollar, and the institutionalist approach to reserve currency status. *Review of International Political Economy, 19*(2), 341–362.
Lynch, D. (2015). *China's Futures: PRC Elites Debate Economics, Politics, and Foreign Policy*. Stanford: Stanford University Press.
MacDonald, R., & Dias, P. (2007). Behavioural equilibrium exchange rate estimates and implied exchange rate adjustments for ten countries. Workshop on "Global Imbalances" held by the Peterson Institute of International Economics, February 2007. https://piie.com/publications/pb/pb07-4/macdonald.pdf.
Makin, A. J. (2009). Is China's exchange rate policy a form of trade protection? *Business Economics, 44*(2), 80–86.
McKinnon, R., & Schnabl, G. (2014). China's exchange rate and financial repression: The conflicted emergence of the RMB as an international currency. *China & World Economy, 22*(3), 1–35.
McNally, C. A. (2015). The political economic logic of RMB internationalization: A study in Sino-capitalism. *International Politics, 52*(6), 704–723.
Meijer, H. (2016). *Trading with the Enemy: The Making of US Export Control Policy toward the People's Republic of China*. Oxford: Oxford University Press.
Mertha, A. (2009). "Fragmented authoritarianism 2.0": Political pluralization in the Chinese policy process. *The China Quarterly*, (200), 995–1012.
Mesquita, B. B., Smith, A., Siverson, R. M., & Morrow, J. D. (2005). *The Logic of Political Survival*. Cambridge: The MIT Press.
Miller, A. (2008). Institutionalization and the changing dynamics of Chinese leadership politics. In C. Li (Ed.), *China's Changing Political Landscape: Prospects for Democracy*. Washington: Brookings Institution Press.
Miller, A. (2011). Dilemmas of globalization and governance. In R. MacFarquhar (Ed.), *The Politics of China: Sixty Years of the People's Republic of China* (pp. 528–599). Cambridge: Cambridge University Press.
Milner, H. (1997). *Interests, Institutions, and Information: Domestic Politics and International Relations*. Princeton: Princeton University Press.
Ministry of Commerce. (2003a). China to maintain stability of RMB yuan: Minister. MOFCOM, 25 July 2003. http://english.mofcom.gov.cn/aarticle/newsrelease/commonnews/200307/20030700112290.html.
Ministry of Commerce. (2003b). Observation: The experiences and lessons of the yen's appreciation for Chinese RMB. MOFCOM, 5 August 2003. http://sanfrancisco.mofcom.gov.cn/article/ztdy/200308/20030800114857.shtml.
Ministry of Commerce. (2003c). Lessons from yen appreciation. MOFCOM, 18 December 2003. http://www.mofcom.gov.cn/article/s/200312/20031200161190.shtml.
Ministry of Commerce. (2005a). Japanese multinational enterprises most worried that China would revalue the yuan. MOFCOM, 28 January 2005. http://www.mofcom.gov.cn/article/i/jyjl/j/200501/20050100340375.shtml.
Ministry of Commerce. (2005b). The US trade deficit will not decrease even if the RMB appreciates. MOFCOM, 25 April 2005. http://www.mofcom.gov.cn/article/i/jyjl/j/200504/20050400080169.shtml.
Ministry of Commerce. (2005c). RMB appreciation will not reduce the US trade deficit. MOFCOM, 11 May 2005. http://www.mofcom.gov.cn/article/i/jyjl/l/200505/20050500087898.shtml.
Ministry of Commerce. (2005d). Retail manufacturers moved to India under RMB appreciation pressure. MOFCOM, 24 May 2005. http://www.mofcom.gov.cn/article/i/jyjl/j/200505/20050500098484.shtml.

Ministry of Commerce. (2005e). Impact of renminbi appreciation on China's international trade. MOFCOM, 25 August 2006. http://www.mofcom.gov.cn/article/resume/n/200608/20060802972660.shtml.

Ministry of Commerce. (2005f). Different impacts of RMB exchange rate change on enterprises. MOFCOM, 2 December 2005. http://www.mofcom.gov.cn/article/resume/n/200512/20051200939621.shtml.

Ministry of Commerce. (2005g). Unfavourable situation for textile export. MOFCOM, 30 December 2005. http://pep.mofcom.gov.cn/article/guonyw/bt/200512/20051201239070.shtml.

Ministry of Commerce. (2007). How to deal with the challenge of RMB appreciation for foreign trade and economic development. MOFCOM, 3 March 2007. http://binchuan.mofcom.gov.cn/aarticle/xglj/200803/20080305408267.html.

Ministry of Commerce. (2008a). RMB appreciation and enterprise competitiveness: Empirical analysis of mechanical and electrical industries and textile and garment industries in Jiangsu. MOFCOM, 1 October 2008. http://kjxh.mofcom.gov.cn/article/r/200811/20081105883828.shtml.

Ministry of Commerce. (2008b). RMB appreciation and enterprise competitiveness: Empirical analysis of labour-intensive industries and processing trade industries in Guangdong. MOFOM, 1 October 2008. http://kjxh.mofcom.gov.cn/article/r/200811/20081105883925.shtml.

Ministry of Commerce. (2010). Chen Deming delivers a speech at the 2010 China Development Forum. MOFCOM, 21 March 2010. http://www.mofcom.gov.cn/aarticle/ae/ai/201003/20100306831415.html.

Ministry of Finance. (2005). End to tax on textile exports from next year. MOF, 14 December 2005. http://www.mof.gov.cn/zhengwuxinxi/caijingshidian/xinhuanet/200805/t20080519_22347.html.

Ministry of Finance. (2007). Ministry of Finance and State Administration of Taxation's announcement on lower export tax rebate rates of some commodities. MOF, 19 June 2007. http://www.chinatax.gov.cn/n810341/n810765/n812176/n812778/c1194297/content.html.

Ministry of Finance. (2008). Ministry of Finance and State Administration of Taxation's announcement on lower export tax rebate rates of some commodities. MOF, 30 July 2008. http://www.chinatax.gov.cn/n810341/n810765/n812171/n812700/c1191582/content.html.

Mundell, R. A. (1963). Capital mobility and stabilization policy under fixed and flexible exchange rates. *Canadian Journal of Economics and Political Science, 29*(4), 475–485.

Mussa, M. (2008). IMF surveillance over China's exchange rate policy. In M. Goldstein & N. Lardy (Eds.), *Debating China's Exchange Rate Policy* (pp. 279–335). Washington: Peterson Institute for International Economics.

Naughton, B. (2007). *The Chinese Economy: Transitions and Growth.* Cambridge: MIF Press.

Naughton, B. (2008). A political economy of China's economic transition. In L. Brandt, & T. G. Rawski (Ed.), *China's Great Economic Transformation* (pp. 91–135). Cambridge: Cambridge University Press.

Nishitateno, S. (1983). China's special economic zones: Experimental units for economic reform. *International and Comparative Law Quarterly, 32*(1), 175–185.

Niu, W. (2010). RMB appreciation as the biggest political issue in Europe and America. *Xinhua*, 28 September 2010. http://news.xinhuanet.com/fortune/2010-09/28/c_12614402.htm.

Nölke, A. (2015). Second image revisited: The domestic sources of China's foreign economic policies. *International Politics, 52*(6), 657–665.

Nordhaus, W. (1975). The political business cycle. *The Review of Economic Studies, 42*(2), 169–190.

Nye, J. S. (2010). American and Chinese power after the financial crisis. *The Washington Quarterly, 33*(4), 143–153.

Oatley, T. (1997). *Monetary Politics: Exchange Rate Cooperation in the European Union.* Michigan: University of Michigan Press.

Oatley, T. (1999). How constraining is capital mobility? The partisan hypothesis in an open economy. *American Journal of Political Science, 43*(4), 1003–1027.

Oatley, T. (2011). The reductionist gamble: Open economy politics in the global economy. *International Organization, 65*(2), 311–341.

Oatley, T. (2013). *International Political Economy*. London: Routledge.

Obstfeld, M., & Rogoff, K. S. (2009). *Global Imbalances and the Financial Crisis: Products of Common Causes*. London: Centre for Economic Policy Research.

Otero-Iglesias, M., & Vermeiren, M. (2015). China's state-permeated market economy and its constraints to the internationalization of the renminbi. *International Politics, 52*(6), 684–703.

Pak, C. (1997). *The Special Economic Zones of China and Their Impact on Its Economic Development*. London: Praeger Publishers.

Patterson, L. A. (1997). Agricultural policy reform in the European Community: A three-level game analysis. *International Organization, 51*(1), 135–165.

Paulson, H. M. (2007). Remarks by Treasury Secretary Henry M. Paulson, Jr. at the Heritage Foundation Lee Lecture: China and the Strategic Economic Dialogue. U.S. Department of the Treasury, 5 June 2007. https://www.treasury.gov/press-center/press-releases/Pages/hp439.aspx.

People's Bank of China. (2004). Personnel adjustment of PBOC Monetary Policy Department. PBOC, 3 September 2004. http://www.pbc.gov.cn/bangongting/135485/135491/135597/1002313/index.html.

People's Bank of China. (2005). Public announcement of the People's Bank of China on reforming the RMB exchange rate regime. PBOC, 21 July 2005. http://www.pbc.gov.cn/zhengcehuobisi/125207/125217/125922/125945/2816977/index.html.

People's Bank of China. (2007). Announcement of the People's Bank of China on expanding the floating range of RMB-dollar trading price in the inter-bank spot foreign exchange market. PBOC, 18 May 2007. http://www.pbc.gov.cn/bangongting/135485/135491/135597/999532/index.html.

People's Bank of China. (2010a). To further promote the reform of RMB exchange rate formation mechanism and enhance the RMB exchange rate flexibility. PBOC, 19 June 2010. http://www.pbc.gov.cn/bangongting/135485/135491/135597/1002571/index.html.

People's Bank of China. (2010b). The PBOC spokesman answers journalists' question on further promotion of the RMB exchange rate formation mechanism. PBOC, 20 June 2010. http://www.pbc.gov.cn/bangongting/135485/135491/135597/1002568/index.html.

People's Bank of China. (2012). People's Bank of China Public Announcement (2012) No. 4. PBOC, 14 April 2012. http://www.pbc.gov.cn/bangongting/135485/135495/135615/820559/index.html.

People's Bank of China. (2013). Financial term: Position for forex purchase. PBOC, 16 Sept 2013. http://wuhan.pbc.gov.cn/wuhan/123527/614607/index.html.

People's Bank of China. (2015). PBOC's announcement on improving the central parity quotes of RMB exchange rate against the US dollar. PBOC, 11 August 2015. http://www.pbc.gov.cn/goutongjiaoliu/113456/113469/2927054/index.html.

People's Bank of China. (2016). PBOC Monetary Policy Department Ordinance. http://www.pbc.gov.cn/huobizhengceersi/214481/214543/214782/2847827/index.html.

People's Bank of China. Monetary Policy Implementation Reports. http://www.pbc.gov.cn/zhengcehuobisi/125207/125227/125957/index.html.

Pettis, M. (2008). Chinese inflation: It's money, not pork. *Far Eastern Economic Review, 171*(3), 42–45.

Putnam, R. (1988). Diplomacy and domestic politics: The logic of two-level games. *International Organization, 42*(3), 427–460.

Putnam, R. D., Evans, P. B., & Jacobson, H. K. (1993). *Double-edged Diplomacy: International Bargaining and Domestic Politics*. Berkeley: University of California Press.

Rachman, G. (2008). China's economy hits the wall. *Financial Times*, 15 December 2008. http://www.ft.com/cms/s/0/a1ff5944-cac6-11dd-87d7-000077b07658.html#axzz3zs3Qxv4x.

Ramzy, A. (2010). Bo Xilai. *TIME*, 29 April 2010. http://content.time.com/time/specials/packages/article/0,28804,1984685_1984864_1985416,00.html.

Randall, H. C. (2006). The exchange-rate weapon and macroeconomic conflict. In D. M. Andrews (Ed.), *International Monetary Power* (pp. 117–138). Ithaca: Cornell University Press.
Rathbun, B. (2008). A rose by any other name: Neoclassical realism as the logical and necessary extension of structural realism. *Security Studies, 17*(2), 294–321.
Risse-Kappen, T. (1995). *Bringing Transnational Relations Back In: Non-state Actors, Domestic Structures and International Institutions*. Cambridge: Cambridge University Press.
Rodrik, D. (2013). The new mercantilist challenge. *Project Syndicate*, 9 January 2013. https://www.project-syndicate.org/commentary/the-return-of-mercantilism-by-dani-rodrik?barrier=accesspaylog.
Rose, G. (1998). Neoclassical realism and theories of foreign policy. *World Politics, 51*(1), 144–172.
Samuelson, P. A. (1964). Theoretical notes on trade problems. *The Review of Economics and Statistics, 46*(2), 145–154.
Schamis, H., & Way, C. (2003). Political cycles and exchange rate-based stabilization. *World Politics, 56*(1), 43–78.
Schweller, R. (2009). Neoclassical realism and state mobilization: Expansionist ideology in the age of mass politics. In S. Lobell, N. Ripsman, & J. Taliaferro (Eds.), *Neoclassical Realism, the State, and Foreign Policy*. Cambridge: Cambridge University Press.
Scott, R. E. (2010). Unfair China trade costs local jobs. Economic Policy Institute, 23 March 2010. http://www.epi.org/publication/bp260.
Scott, R. E. (2011). Growing US trade deficit with China cost 2.8 million jobs between 2001 and 2010. Economic Policy Institute, 20 September 2011. http://www.epi.org/publication/growing-trade-deficit-china-cost-2-8-million.
Scott, R. E. (2012). The China toll: growing US trade deficit with China cost more than 2.7 million jobs between 2001 and 2011, with job losses in every state. Economic Policy Institute, 23 August 2012. http://www.epi.org/publication/bp345-china-growing-trade-deficit-cost.
Seawright, J., & Gerring, J. (2008). Case selection techniques in case study research: A menu of qualitative and quantitative options. *Political Research Quarterly, 61*(2), 294–308.
Shambaugh, D. (2013). *China Goes Global: The Partial Power*. New York: Oxford University Press.
Sharma, S. D. (2010). China as the world's creditor and the United States as the world's debtor. *China Perspectives*, (4), 100–115.
Shen, D. (2014). With Xi's new power is collective leadership over? *East Asia Forum*, 19 October 2014. http://www.eastasiaforum.org/2014/10/19/with-xis-new-power-is-collective-leadership-over.
Shi, J., & Yu, H. (2005). Renminbi equilibrium exchange rate and China's exchange rate misalignment: 1991-2004. *Economic Research Journal*, (4), 34–45.
Shih, V. C. (2008). *Factions and finance in China: Elite Conflict and Inflation*. Cambridge: Cambridge University.
Snow, J. W. (2004). Statement by Treasury Secretary John W. Snow on US-China Trade Relationship. U.S. Department of the Treasury, 28 April 2004. http://www.treasury.gov/press-center/press-releases/Pages/js1483.aspx.
Snow, J. W. (2005). Statement of Secretary John W. Snow on the FOREX Report. U.S. Department of the Treasury, 17 May 2005. https://www.treasury.gov/press-center/press-releases/Pages/js2449.aspx.
Snow, J. W. (2006). Statement of Treasury Secretary John W. Snow before the Senate Committee on Banking, Housing, and Urban Affairs on International Economic and Exchange Rate Policies. U.S. Department of the Treasury, 18 May 2006. https://www.treasury.gov/press-center/press-releases/Pages/js4271.aspx.
Soros, G. (2010). China must fix the global currency crisis. *Financial Times*, 7 October 2010. https://next.ft.com/content/f4dd9122-d22a-11df-8fbe-00144feabdc0.
Steinberg, D. A. (2015). *Demanding Devaluation: Exchange Rate Politics in the Developing World*. Ithaca: Cornell University Press.

Steinberg, D. A. (2016). Developmental states and undervalued exchange rates in the developing world. *Review of International Political Economy, 23*(3), 1–32.

Steinberg, D. A., & Malhotra, K. (2014). The effect of authoritarian regime type on exchange rate policy. *World Politics, 66*(3), 491–529.

Steinberg, D. A., & Shih, V. (2012). Interest group influence in authoritarian states: The political determinants of Chinese exchange rate policy. *Comparative Political Studies, 45*(11), 1405–1434.

Steven, K. (2004). *The Political Economy of Exchange Rate Policy-Making: From the Gold Standard to the Euro*. Houndmills: Palgrave Macmillan.

Stone, D. (2002). Using knowledge: The dilemmas of 'bridging research and policy'. *Compare: A Journal of Comparative and International Education*, 32(3), 285–296.

Strange, S. (1970). International economics and international relations: A case of mutual neglect. *International Affairs, 46*(2), 304–315.

Strange, S. (1971). The politics of international currencies. *World Politics, 23*(2), 215–231.

Sun, S. (2010). The EU to follow the US to pressure on RMB. *Economic Information Daily*, 20 September 2010. http://dz.jjckb.cn/www/pages/webpage2009/html/2010-09/20/content_17388.htm?div=-1.

The Economist. (2004). Inviting China to dinner. *The Economist*, 4 October 2004. http://www.economist.com/node/3258391.

The Economist. (2008a). Earnings up, prices down: Risk aversion hits Chinese stocks. *The Economist*, 19 March 2008. http://www.economist.com/node/10881471.

The Economist. (2008b). Boom to bust: China's property bubble is about to burst. *The Economist*, 20 June 2008. http://www.economist.com/node/11605123.

The Economist. (2009). China's currency: a yuan-sided argument. *The Economist*, 18 November 2009. http://www.economist.com/node/14901104.

The Economist. (2010). Over to you, China. *The Economist*, 8 April 2010. http://www.economist.com/node/15868014.

The Economist. (2016). The Big Mac index. *The Economist*, 7 January 2016. http://www.economist.com/content/big-mac-index.

The Financial Times Chinese. (2009). Wen Jiabao defends the RMB exchange rate policy. *The Financial Times Chinese*, 30 January 2009. http://www.ftchinese.com/story/001024407?full=y. Accessed 30 Jan 2009.

The Wall Street Journal. (2010). The Yuan Scapegoat: The U.S. establishment flirts with a currency and trade war with China. The Wall Street Journal, 18 March 2010. http://www.wsj.com/articles/SB10001424052748704743404575127511778280940.

Thomas Library of Congress. US Congress bills and resolutions. http://thomas.loc.gov/home/bills_res.html.

Triffin, R. (1961). *Gold and the Dollar Crisis: The Future of Convertibility*. London: Yale University Press.

Tsang, S. (2009). Consultative Leninism: China's new political framework. *Journal of Contemporary China, 18*(62), 865–880.

Tsui, K., & Wang, Y. (2008). Decentralization with political trump: Vertical control, local accountability and regional disparities in China. *China Economic Review, 19*(1), 18–31.

Tufte, E. R. (1978). *Political Control of the Economy*. Princeton: Princeton University Press.

U.S. Department of the Treasury. Reports to Congress on International Economic and Exchange Rate Policies. https://www.treasury.gov/resource-center/international/exchange-rate-policies/Pages/index.aspx.

Waller, M. (1981). *Democratic Centralism: An Historical Commentary*. Manchester: Manchester University Press.

Walter, A. (2014). China's engagement with international macroeconomic policy surveillance. In E. Helleiner, & J. Kirshner (Ed.), *The Great Wall of Money: Power and Politics in China's International Monetary Relations* (pp. 127–155). Ithaca: Cornell University Press.

Walter, A., & Sen, G. (2008). *Analyzing the Global Political Economy*. Princeton: Princeton University Press.

Walter, S. (2014). Private actor exchange rate policy preferences. In T. Oatley & W. K. Winecoff (Ed.), *Handbook of the International Political Economy of Monetary Relations* (pp. 169–184). Cheltenham: Edward Elgar Publishing.

Waltz, K. (1979). *Theory of International Politics*. New York: McGraw-Hill.

Wan, M. (2014). *The China Model and Global Political Economy*. London: Routledge.

Wang, S. (2000). The social and political implications of China's WTO membership. *Journal of Contemporary China, 9*(25), 373–405.

Wang, T. (2004). Exchange rate dynamics. In E. Prasad (Ed.), *China's Growth and Integration into the World Economy: Prospects and Challenges* (pp. 21–28), IMF Occasional Paper No. 232. https://www.imf.org/external/pubs/ft/op/232/op232.pdf.

Wang, M. (2005). Political economy analysis of exchange rate system choice: A literature review. *Comparative Economic and Social Systems*, (3), 137–141.

Wang, J. (2014). Vertical power structure and social governance: An approach to the relationship of "government and society" in China. *Zhejiang Social Sciences*, (9), 128–139.

Wang, Z. (2017). China's exchange rate policy making: International pressures meet domestic politics. *Asian Studies Review, 41*(1), 20–39.

Wang, Z. (2017). The economic rise of China as rule-taker, rule-maker or rule-breaker? *Asian Survey*, 57(4), 595–617.

Wang, Y., Hui, X., & Soofi, A. (2007). Estimating renminbi (RMB) equilibrium exchange rate. *Journal of Policy Modeling, 29*(3), 417–429.

Wang, Z., & Zeng, J. (2016). Xi Jinping: The game changer of Chinese elite politics? *Contemporary Politics, 22*(4), 469–486.

Weiss, L. (2003). *States in the Global Economy: Bringing Domestic Institutions Back In*. Cambridge: Cambridge University Press.

Wen, J. (2004). Report on the Work of the Government. The Central People's Government of the People's Republic of China, 5 March 2004. http://www.gov.cn/test/2006-02/16/content_201193.htm.

Wen, J. (2005). Report on the Work of the Government. The Central People's Government of the People's Republic of China, 5 March 2005. http://www.gov.cn/gongbao/content/2005/content_158717.htm.

Williamson, J. (2010). FEERs update: China's persistently undervalued currency. Peterson Institute of International Economics, 29 January 2010. https://www.piie.com/experts/peterson-perspectives/feers-update-chinas-persistently-undervalued-currency.

Wolf, M. (2009). Why China's exchange rate policy concerns us. *Financial Times*, 8 December 2009. https://next.ft.com/content/afac7ada-e448-11de-bed0-00144feab49a.

Wolf, M. (2010). How to fight the currency wars with stubborn China. *Financial Times*, 5 October 2010. https://next.ft.com/content/52b8a8e4-d0b0-11df-8667-00144feabdc0.

Wong, E., & Landler, M. (2010). China rejects U.S. complaints on its currency. *New York Times*, 4 February 2010. http://www.nytimes.com/2010/02/05/world/asia/05diplo.html.

Wright, L. H. (2009). *The Elusive Price of Stability: Ideas and Interests in the Reform of China's Exchange Rate Regime*. George Washington University PhD Thesis. http://www.perpustakaan.kemenkeu.go.id/FOLDERJURNAL/The%20Elusive%20Price%20Of%20Stability.pdf.

Xiao, W., & Pan, J. (2013). The shocks and effects of external pressure on RMB appreciation: An investigation of American pressure. *Economic Theory and Economic Management*, (8), 101–111.

Xin, K. K., & Pearce, J. L. (1996). Guanxi: Connections as substitutes for formal institutional support. *Academy of Management Journal, 39*(6), 1641–1658.

Yan, I. K., & Kakkar, V. (2010). The equilibrium real exchange rate of China: A productivity approach. MPRA Paper No. 35229. http://mpra.ub.uni-muenchen.de/35229.

Yang, C. (2012). Research on China's coping strategy for pressure on the RMB. *Macroeconomics*, (2), 9–16.

Yang, J., Yin, H., & He, H. (2007). The Chinese currency: Background and the current debate. *International Journal of Public Administration, 30*(2), 117–135.

Yang, M. M. (1994). *Gifts, Favors, and Banquets: The Art of Social Relationships in China*. Ithaca: Cornell University Press.

Yi, G. (2009). Strictly control the money supply and optimize the credit structure. *Meditations on China's Financial Reform* (pp. 170–177). Beijing: The Commercial Press.

Yi, J. (2011). The political economy of China's exchange rate policymaking in the Hu-Wen era. *China: An International Journal*, *9*(1), 164–177.

Yu, Y. (2003). Elimination of renminbi appreciation phobia and the transition to balanced economic development. *International Economic Review*, (9), 5–11.

Yu, Y. (2004). China's macroeconomic situation since 2003. *China & World Economy*, *12*(4), 3–20.

Yu, Y. (2007). Global imbalances and China. *Australian Economic Review*, *40*(1), 3–23.

Yu, Y. (2010). Witness imbalances–twin surpluses, renminbi exchange rate and the dollar trap. *International Economic Review*, (3), 7–44.

Zeng, J. (2015). The Chinese Communist Party's Capacity to Rule: Ideology. Legitimacy and Party Cohesion. Houndsmills: Palgrave Macmillan.

Zhang, W. (2013). The impact of US political pressure on the RMB exchange rate. *LUX: A Journal of Transdisciplinary Writing and Research from Claremont Graduate University*, *3*(1), Article 21. http://scholarship.claremont.edu/lux/vol3/iss1/21.

Zhang, Y., & Zhang, J. (2005). The political economy of exchange rate: A study based on Sino-US exchange rate debates. *Journal of Contemporary Asia-Pacific Studies*, (9), 3–20.

Zheng, S. (1997). *Party vs. State in Post-1949 China: The Institutional Dilemma*. Cambridge: Cambridge University Press.

Zheng, S. (2005). The new era in Chinese elite politics. *Issues and Studies*, *41*(1), 190–203.

Zheng, Y., & Chen, G. (2015a). China's political outlook: Xi Jinping as a game changer. *East Asian Policy*, *7*(1), 5–15.

Zheng, Y., & Chen, G. (2015b). The Chinese Communist Party: An institutional perspective. In D. S. G. Goodman (Ed.), *Handbook of the Politics of China* (pp. 57–75). Cheltenham: Edward Elgar.

Zhou, X. (2009). Reflections on the reform of the international monetary system. People's Bank of China, 23 March 2009. http://www.pbc.gov.cn/hanglingdao/128697/128719/128772/825742/index.html.

Zhou, X. (2013). The main characteristics of China's monetary policy in the new millennium. *SINA Finance*, 18 January 2013. http://finance.sina.com.cn/money/bank/bank_yhfg/20130118/103214330306.shtml?wbf=more.

Zhu, M., Zhao, Q., & Wang, Y. (2015). Political incentives of the RMB exchange rate changes–based on the investigation of US political cycle spillover effects. *Management World*, (4), 38–51.

Zweig, D., & Chen, Z. (Ed.) (2007). *China's Reforms and International Political Economy*. London: Routledge.

Index

Z. Wang, *The International Political Economy of China's Exchange Rate Policy Making*, https://doi.org/10.1007/978-981-33-4578-2_1

S

U

W

The manufacturer's authorised representative in the EU is Springer
Nature Customer Service Centre GmbH, Europaplatz 3, 69115 Heidelberg,
Germany. If you have any concerns regarding our products, please
contact ProductSafety@springernature.com

Printed and bound by CPI Group (UK) Ltd, Croydon, CR0 4YY
30/09/2026
02225290-0005